WHERE RAILS MEET RIVERS

Where Rails Meet Rivers

THE STORY OF PORT COQUITLAM

Chuck Davis

HARBOUR PUBLISHING

Published by
HARBOUR PUBLISHING
P.O.Box 219
Madeira Park, BC V0N 2H0

Edited by Audrey McClellan
Cover design, page design and composition by Vancouver Desktop Publishing

Published with the assistance of the Canada Millennium Partnership Program

Colour photos on cover by Arthur Edwardson Photographers Ltd.

The publisher and the author wish to thank Arthur Edwardson Photographers Ltd. for the photos on pages 11, 13, 14, 15, 16, 17, 18 (centre), 19, 20 (top), 21, 22, 30, 46, 52, 80, 109, 130 (bottom), 131 (bottom left and right), 166 (top), 168 (bottom), 169, 171, 173, 175, 179, 182, 183, 184, 186, 187, 188, 189, 190, 191, 192, 193, 196, 197, 198, 199, 200, 201. Arthur Edwardson Photographers Ltd. is at 2270 Lougheed Highway, Port Coquitlam, BC, (604) 942-9644.

Thanks to the BC Archives and Records Service for the photos on pages 24 (C-09126), 28 (A-01724), 29 (B-05017), 32 (G-01256), 39 (B-06848), 43 (D-00707), 82 (B-08359), 83 (B-08381), 94 (upper F-01730, and lower A-09455), 104 (B-02573), and 132 (D-00706).

Thanks to the Vancouver Public Library, Special Collections, for photos on pages 95 (3836), 128 (79691), 135 (79375), and 136 (80048).

Thanks to the Terry Fox Foundation and Gail Harvey for the photo on page 162.

All other uncredited photos are from the Port Coquitlam Heritage and Cultural Society.

Harbour Publishing acknowledges the financial support of the Government of Canada through the Book Publishing Industry Development Program (BPIDP) and the Canada Council for the Arts, and the Province of British Columbia through the British Columbia Arts Council, for its publishing activities.

Printed in Canada

Canadian Cataloguing in Publication Data
Davis, Chuck, 1935-
   Where rails meet rivers

Includes index.
ISBN 1-55017-221-2

   1. Port Coquitlam (B.C.)—History. I. Title.
FC3849.P58D38 2000   971.1'33   C00-910307-4
F1089.5.P54D38 2000

THE CANADA COUNCIL | LE CONSEIL DES ARTS
FOR THE ARTS | DU CANADA
SINCE 1957 | DEPUIS 1957

Acknowledgements

I have first to thank the people of Port Coquitlam themselves. This was a genuine labour of love, one of the most enjoyable writing experiences of my career. I developed a real affection for PoCo and its people, made friendships that I know will endure, and grieved that I had to leave so much out of the book. I knew I'd been carried away by this project when, as the last few lines were being written, I came across my original agreement—which was to provide a 40,000-word book. At that point I had written more than 70,000. And could have hit 100,000 with no trouble.

Mayor Len Traboulay and every member of city council were receptive and helpful in many ways, opening doors that might have been harder to open on my own. Special thanks go to former councillor John Keryluk, who was council's liaison to the publisher and me when the book project began. John's long tenure at city hall was of real value to me in getting to know the city quickly. And an extra tip of the hat to Councillor Ron Talbot, who seems to know everybody in town and persuaded me that every one of them had a story to tell. He was right, too, but the book was already outsized! Many of the people cited in these pages are there because of Ron's thoughtfulness. Councillor Mike Gates drove me around town one long, sunny afternoon pointing out all sorts of interesting sights. What a treat that was! Scott Young introduced me to the Hyde Creek Streamkeepers, Michael Wright enlightened me on the city's library system (and Michael's wife Thelka—once a librarian—did volunteer research for me) and Jon Baillie had me falling off my chair laughing at his ironic description of his first triumphant entry into PoCo politics. He won by some minuscule amount—but he's been winning ever since. Council newcomer Darrell Penner, with his concern for the city's environment, will likely become an influential voice on council. It was a treat to meet all these gentlemen.

Most importantly, I have to thank Ernie Levesque, PoCo's Director of Development Services. It was Ernie who suggested I write the book. A December 1998 meeting with Ernie and Greg Moore of his staff helped shape the book, and both were unfailingly helpful during its writing, giving answers to questions, making suggestions for interview subjects, and providing liaison between me and PoCo people who had stories, pictures and information for me. It was Greg who came up with the book's title when he saw the phrase on an interpretive sign during a stroll along the PoCo Trail.

The administrative staff at city hall was terrific. Susan Rauh, Director of Corporate Services, and her staff, including Greg Beaumont, dug up musty old council minutes for me and answered a hundred questions on city minutiae; Janet Lee of Planning, Igor Zahynacz, the Director of Engineering, and Tony Chong, City Administrator, helped in dozens of ways. I also extend grateful thanks to Kathleen Vincent in the mayor's office; Barry Becker, Parks and Recreation Director; Cheryl Zipper, Manager of Projects and Planning; Susan Hull, Co-ordinator of Arts and Special Events; and all those other helpful folk in Parks and Recreation. Jim Maitland, City Treasurer and Deputy Administrator, sketched in the city's financial past and present.

Bill Herbst, the city's parks foreman, was an inspiration, as were landscape architect Judith Reeve, who designed City Hall Park, and architect Tom Annandale of the Toby Russell Buckwell firm, who oversaw renovations of city hall.

Thanks to fire chief Randy Shaw and his friendly staff for their co-operation. The staffs of the city's recreation centers were helpful, and I got a nice tour by Gabrielle Kosmider of the Hyde Creek Rec Centre. Ada Con, director of the Terry Fox Library, was ever helpful, and I must single out for special praise the library's Queenie Carr. Former councillors George Laking and Phil Ranger were fonts of information, and retired City Clerk Ron Freeman helped from the front of the book to the back.

Words cannot express my gratitude to Lois Milne, president of the Port Coquitlam Heritage and Cultural Society. Whew! She set a pace that had me puffing. Thanks, too, to the other members of the society, some of whom include Nancy Ogilvie, Louise Bailey, Morley Deans, Frances Fridge, Roy Yeo, Kay Grootendorst and Vi Holt.

Dave Matheson, principal of Terry Fox Secondary School, gave me an extensive and fascinating tour of the school as it was under construction. Teacher Bruce Kiloh at Riverside Secondary heard about this project and had me come in to talk to his social studies students. That was fun, and valuable, too: the kids had some good thoughts on the book and I took them away with me.

Larry Watkins and Dean McMillan of the Business Improvement Association were hugely helpful, and thanks to BIA president Sheila Retallick.

Old-timer John Galer, his sisters Mary and Ethel, and his son Joe were great fun to talk to, and had lots of good stories.

It was a genuine treat to make the Forrest family's acquaintance. The story of PoCo's waterfront has been undertold in the past, and the Forrests' stories go a little way toward redressing that. Nel's son, Mike, took me on a terrific tour of the Pitt and Fraser Rivers in one of his smaller boats so that I could get a water-level look at the area. I got to see a big group of grumpy sea lions up close, a sight I won't soon forget. Thanks, too, to Ray Forrest, Mike's brother, and their sister Joy.

I had lots of long conversations with Kate Poole of the *Tri-City News*, and she dug up tons of stuff for me. Photographer Craig Hodge was a genial source of information and advice, too, as was publisher Bryan McCristall. Thanks, too, to reporter Marci Good of *Coquitlam Now* (who came along with me on that Mike Forrest river trip).

To MLA Mike Farnworth, his office manager Gwen Ranger and his assistant John Rogers, many thanks. And the same for MP Lou Sekora, whose efforts helped in the financial backing for this project. Thanks to Judge Stu Leggatt and Dave Barrett. Fred Fox, Betty Fox and Rolly Fox of the Terry Fox Foundation are proud and tireless promoters of Terry's famous crusade and were great sources of information. Sharon Morton-Jones, Ingrid Hart and Tej Banns told me the history of the Carnoustie Golf, Racquet and Fitness Club. Thanks also to Steve Armstrong, administrator of the Kwayhquitlum First Nation; Dianne McConnell, president of the PoCo Ringette Association; Norm Loewen of Scouts Canada; Dr. James McFarlane of International Submarine Engineering; Valerie Patenaude, Wendy Sankey, Vic Coulter, Jim Jacobi, Ken Rempel, Michael Savvis, Bozena Lukomska-Khan, Zella Rieu, Joanne Hayward and Andrew and Judy Carroll for time, information and photographs. Thanks to photographers Arthur Edwardson and his son Brent. Their work is in evidence all though the book.

Only once in my life have I met someone who was the first person born in a place. In PoCo's case, the man was Jim David. He's in his late eighties now, alert and good humoured, and it was an honour to interview him.

One of the stories that, maddeningly, did not make it into the book was that of Ken Mackenzie and Harken Towing. I had scheduling difficulties and by the time I got to visit Ken and Dorothy Mackenzie and heard the great story of the rise of Harken Towing, it was too late to weave it into the book. We need another book!

This project leaned heavily on the 1988 book that marked PoCo's seventy-fifth birthday, and my gratitude goes to the compilers of *Port Coquitlam: City of Rivers and Mountains*, as well as to the late Edith Chambers, who in 1971 wrote *The History of Port Coquitlam*, a small and affectionate history that laid a lot of groundwork for the two succeeding books. Other books I drew on include the Akriggs' *British Columbia Chronicle, 1847-1871*; Norma K. Campbell's *Mountain Memories: A History of Burke Mountain*; R.E. Gosnell's *Year Book of British Columbia* from 1897; Rick Hansen's *Rick Hansen: Man in Motion*; Vicki Jensen's *Saltwater Women at Work*; Bev Le Francois and Helga Martens Enns's *Story of a Women's Centre*; H.A.J. Monk and John Stewart's *A History of Coquitlam and Fraser Mills, 1858-1958*; Margaret Ormsby's *British Columbia: A History*; the Pioneer Tales Book Committee's *Coquitlam, 100 Years: Reflections of the Past*; and Leslie Scrivener's *Terry Fox: His Story*.

Grateful thanks to Rob Craig and the senior staff at Stratford Internet Technologies, where I work, for abiding my occasional absences and distractions while I assembled the book at the same time I was writing copy for Stratford's growing family of web sites.

Teacher Bruce Moore was an early friend, and his words open the book's prologue.

Finally, to the project itself. Howard White and Audrey McClellan and Peter Robson treated this disorganized and ever-late contributor with unfailing kindness and concern, and added to my joy in doing the book. Patty Osborne of Vancouver Desktop Publishing put the book together with care and dispatch and now we release it to a waiting city.

Thanks, as always, to my long-suffering wife and daughter, Edna and Stephanie, for putting up with a messy house for yet another book. One of these days I'll build that gymnasium I keep whining about, the only room large enough to hold all my stuff.

I know I have missed names, and I apologize in advance for that. Port Coquitlam grabbed my heart while I worked on this book, and I'll be seeing her more often. I hope you enjoy reading about the city as much as I did writing about it.

—*Chuck Davis*

Contents

Prologue

There's a lot of good feeling here," a teacher shouts to a visitor over the roar of the crowd, "a lot of memories." It's February 12, 1999, and we're in the gym at the old Terry Fox Senior Secondary School in Port Coquitlam. The stands are jammed as the Ravens meet the visiting Pitt Meadows Marauders in a fine, fast-paced game, and the lead has changed yet again to the screaming of fans, the skreak of runners on the hardwood floor, the shouts of the coaches and players and the flash of the cheerleaders' new uniforms as the school's thunderous little jazz band belts out "In The Mood."

The Ravens really want this game. The winner will be Fraser Valley north zone champions. But there's another reason: this is the gym where Port Coquitlam's most famous citizen, Terry Fox, played basketball as a kid and this is the last league-level game to be played in the school named in his honour.

Virtually every Canadian remembers Terry Fox for his 1980 attempt to run across Canada to raise research money to finance the fight against cancer. The run was tragically halted partway across Canada when the cancer that had taken his leg spread to his lungs . . . but it was a blazing triumph nonetheless for the millions of dollars it raised and continues to raise today, mostly through the annual Terry Fox Run.

Some of the teachers here had Terry in their classes. And there are special guests, introduced before the game: Terry's mom and dad and others in the Fox family are here, and so is grad Bret Anderson. Bret, the first student at Simon Fraser University to win Most Valuable Player honours in both football and basketball, now plays for the BC Lions football team. He recalled his days at Fox ("I think one of the reasons we did so well was that the lighting in the gym was really tough on our opponents") and introduced teacher Terry Fleming, Terry Fox's high-school basketball coach.

Teacher Don van Os spoke to the crowd before the game. "We're very proud of our namesake, very proud of what he stood for. Each student at this school takes that challenge. Everyone here wants to emulate Terry." And Betty Fox spoke gently about her son. "All four of our children went to school

Terry Fox on his Marathon of Hope in 1980. (Photo courtesy Terry Fox Foundation and Gail Harvey)

here, and all graduated. This is a sad night, walking in and seeing Terry's memorabilia. I really hope his spirit carries on in the new school. God bless all of you." The crowd rose to its feet in a roaring, spontaneous standing ovation as Betty and the others in the Fox family stood smiling in mid-gym.

The old school, a PoCo landmark for forty years, will be empty when you read this. Students and teachers opened the 1999–2000 season at a new school—also named for Terry—where the gym is twice as big.

The last league-level game played here would have made Terry proud. After a shaky beginning, with the Ravens nine points down very early in the game, the team came back to tie, dropped back again, tied again, dropped back, tied, went ahead, tied, dropped back . . . until the final minutes of the game when they surged ahead and won.

It was a little bit like the story of the town itself.

The closing of the old school and the opening of the new signify tradition and change. As you'll see in this book, the vigorous little city of Port Coquitlam has generous portions of both.

ONE

PoCo Now

B y Commerce and Industry We Prosper

City hall is a good place to begin. It's the administrative centre of town, a big, handsome building right on Shaughnessy, the main street, but it's something else, too: it's evidence of the superheated enthusiasm that attended the birth of Port Coquitlam.

Back in 1914, when the original hall (the older, northern half of the building) was built, the population of PoCo—one year old—was about 1,300. But look at the size of that original building! Its three storeys of solid brick and concrete were built for a city expecting a lot more than 1,300 people. This was built by eager pioneers who anticipated mighty things. At Port Coquitlam's 1913 inauguration ceremonies, the first mayor predicted the new city would reach a population of ten thousand in three years.

In fact, it took more than fifty. City hall sat virtually empty for decades. We'll find out why in later pages, where we'll also discover why Port Coquitlam is now one of the five fastest-growing cities in Canada. (The population today is just over fifty thousand.)

So we start at city hall, at the southeast corner of Shaughnessy and McAllister. A building that was sturdy, but somewhat stolid, was transformed in 1988 into a handsome blend of stone, brick and glass, a fitting celebration of the city's seventy-fifth anniversary. "It's the jewel in our crown," says Mayor Len Traboulay. (The next time you're in city hall, have a look on the third floor for a thin vertical line on the wall near the council chambers. It shows the division between the building's two halves.)

City hall sits within a small, pleasant and carefully tended park, surrounded by blossoming cherry trees, dogwoods, magnolias and a spectacular tulip tree, and holding neat beds of rhododendrons, tulips, azaleas and a

City hall before its expansion, with the entrance on McAllister Street.

A Colourful Career

Bill Herbst and his flowers.

Bill Herbst's year is full of colour and life. Port Coquitlam's parks foreman and his full-time three-person crew keep the city's parks alive and fresh with new plantings and careful tending of the thousands of trees, shrubs, flowers and other flora under their care.

It is a joy to be shown around PoCo's City Hall Park by this man, so obviously in love with his work. Everywhere one looks are new, sometimes unfamiliar, flowers and shrubs, some brought back from his journeys to other countries. When we spoke he was looking forward to the May flowering of a Chilean fire bush, a spectacular and exotic burst of blazing orange against the west wall of city hall. (On a later visit it proved to be every bit as striking as he'd predicted.) A gigantic tulip tree looms over people walking through the park, while just east of the McAllister gateway to the park is a lofty and eye-popping magnolia—a Yulan magnolia, to be exact (also called the tulip tree). The *Magnolia denudata* had yet to bloom.

Herbst's use of Latin terminology for the multitude of plants around this splendid park is as casual as conversation. The *Helleborus orientalis* is, a visitor learns, the lenten rose; an unusual specimen of *Nandina domestica* may be known to the layman as heavenly or false bamboo. Its beautiful red berries are prominent in the fall. Also prominent is the paperbark maple (*Acer griseum*), with its peeling cinnamon-brown bark and its green trifoliate leaves that blaze into colour in autumn.

It didn't take long for Herbst to get into his chosen field: fresh out of high school he worked for the Vancouver Parks Board "pulling weeds." By 1982 he was ready for four years of apprenticeship, and by 1991 he was Port Coquitlam's head gardener. He became a certified arborist in 1993.

That's his job. His hobby is fun, too: he carries around a metal detector and sometimes makes fascinating discoveries. Like the time he was poking around the grounds of the New View Society on Mary Hill Road and discovered, deep within the earth, a beautifully preserved "Inauguration" medallion, the very prize handed out to local children by Port Coquitlam's first mayor, James Mars, more than eighty years before to mark the city's birth. The date of incorporation, March 7, 1913, was still visible on the sterling silver medallion. (In the same expedition Herbst also found a metal token for a now-vanished product, Cascorets, with a proud claim: Best For The Bowels.)

If you haven't taken the opportunity yet, stroll through little City Hall Park, crowded with a world's worth of interesting and beautiful plants and flowers: Japanese cherry trees, Barrett Browning daffodils, Himalayan blue poppy, Virginia creeper, Acanthus (or "Bear's Britches"), many species of rhododendron and azalea, Chinese witch hazel, white and purple hyacinth . . . and try to get Bill Herbst to come with you. Wandering through the garden with this expert by your side increases your enjoyment tenfold.

rich mix of other flowers. Attractive tiled walks lead the stroller from point to point. The park pivots around a central point, a simple cenotaph bearing the names of Port Coquitlam's war dead of two world wars and a plaque commemorating the Korean War. Behind and to the right of city hall is Leigh Square, named for Roy Leigh, a man you'll meet later, who figures largely in PoCo's early history. A major upgrading of Leigh Square is in the offing, which may include a bandshell.

Speaking of upgrading, PoCo entered the twenty-first century with a major beautification of Shaughnessy Street. The entrance to the city via Shaughnessy is now more spacious, colourful

Shaughnessy Street today with Burke Mountain in the background.

and modern. Broad and attractive sidewalks, new plantings, improved lighting . . . the change is dramatic. (For newcomers, that peak you see looking directly north on Shaughnessy is 1,097-metre-high [3,600-foot] Burke Mountain.)

At the southern portal is Granny Smith Park, a neat little pocket park named in tribute to the late Dorothy Smith, affectionately called Granny. She was a bit dotty, lived near the corner where the park is, pushed a shopping cart around and occasionally went into Vancouver and preached to people on the street. Locals liked her. It's splendid that she's remembered in this way. Former Councillor John Keryluk tells a charming story about Granny Smith: "She used to carry around in her hand tiny little representations of the bluebird of happiness. If she liked you, she would very discreetly press one into your hands. I have one in my home."

When the conversion of city hall took place in 1988, the orientation of the building changed: it used to face McAllister Street. The 1988 architects did more than just double (and then some) the floor space of city hall; they moved the entrance around to the Shaughnessy Street side so that visitors to the hall now approach the building through that lovely little park. But take a look at the original entrance on McAllister. Above the cornice over the unused entrance steps is PoCo's original emblem—two beavers sculpted in concrete—symbolic of the city's motto: By Commerce and Industry We Prosper.

The Commerce and Industry citation is appropriate: this is a city that owed its existence to commerce and industry, and a lot of the street names reflect that. McAllister, for example, was an early realtor, and Shaughnessy was the president of the Canadian Pacific Railway (CPR) when Port Coquitlam was born. The CPR's rail yards are a powerful—some say intrusive—presence to this day, cutting a broad diagonal east-west path right through the heart of the city, just as they have since the beginning. One result: tension in the past between the two halves of Port Coquitlam, with the north side (lacking the city hall-centred "downtown") sometimes feeling underserved. That's no longer true, with city council painstakingly ensuring both halves of PoCo get equal treatment, but there's a more lasting result of the railway cleaving the town: the most direct route between the city's two parts is through an underpass beneath the rails, a short, dark and noisy stretch of Shaughnessy that nobody likes . . . especially at rush hour. "The best thing that could happen for Port Coquitlam," said Mayor Len Traboulay at a 1999 meeting of the city's Business Improvement Association, "is for the CPR to uproot and move to Regina. We'd have 440 acres [178 hectares] and a road connecting the south and north parts of the city!" Considering the huge chunk of PoCo occupied by the railway, it's astonishing that there is, to quote a senior city staffer, "virtually nonexistent contact with the CPR." This appears to be changing, however. Mayor Traboulay says the railway now is being more co-operative and helpful.

More than thirty thousand vehicles use that downtown stretch of Shaughnessy every working day. Ask PoCo residents what the city's biggest problem is, and the answer you hear most often is "traffic." (An all-candidates meeting just before the November 20, 1999, civic election underscored the point: every candidate talked about the city's transportation problems.)

Ask locals what the city's biggest *attraction* is, and you may be told "parks." Port Coquitlam is rich with them. One of the best is Lions Park. The Lions Club of Port Coquitlam, which marked its fiftieth anniversary in 1999, has made a lot of contributions to the city's life, but none of its gifts is more popular than this beau-

One of PoCo's murals adds a colourful backdrop to the street scene.

tiful park. On fine days it's filled with PoCo people, especially parents and their kids. A big mural on Lions Way marks the entrance. Designed by Tammy Pilon and painted by volunteers, the mural shows that before it was a park, the area was used as a source of timber.

On your first visit Lions Park will surprise you with its size; it is much bigger than it appears from Shaughnessy. It broadens to a wide and beautiful green expanse with lots of tall trees providing shade. A colourful adventure playground is there for the kids, and springing up from it—right up through the middle of a tiny playhouse—is a towering evergreen. The PoCo Trail runs along the western edge of the park, which has an unusual origin: it is made up of a big block of 10-metre (33-foot) lots that reverted to the city for nonpayment of taxes.

The PoCo Trail is another of Port Coquitlam's great attractions. Mostly built atop level dikes, the trail completely encircles the town, with ever-changing views of city, river, farm, slough, residential developments, waterfront industry, railway workings, a golf course, parks . . . it's wonderful. But one of the funnier facts of PoCo life is that nobody seems sure exactly how long this unique trail is. Ask a dozen locals and you'll get a dozen different answers. The official version: 25 kilometres or 15.6 miles. (Extended study of the trail's users by the writer—over the course of an afternoon—indicates that virtually all of them walk, jog or cycle the trail in a clockwise direction. Another observation: the trail is a great place to see charming little black-capped chickadees, one of PoCo's more common birds.)

Another pleasant city park, and one of the largest, is Reeve Park, slightly downstream from Lions Park on the Coquitlam River. Much of it was created from what used to be Marshall Island, named for pioneer Matt Marshall, an early Presbyterian Church supporter, a fine football player and one of the victims of the murderous 1918 influenza epidemic. The "island" is now part of the mainland.

PoCo's Elks Park, just south of downtown, is notable as the site of one of the more sociable spots in town: the city's community garden. There are over forty individual plots set out

PoCo Trail runs through vastly different surroundings, from Lions Park—with its playground, green space and treehouse (above)—to the office buildings and warehouses of Meridian Industrial Park (below).

by people who have no growing room at home. (Elks Park is bisected by long, tree-shaded Donald Park, a pleasant linear stroll.)

PoCo has more parkland acreage per capita than any city in the Lower Mainland; it's no wonder one of the city's informal titles is City Within a Park.

Several historic murals splash colour and images of the past around PoCo's streets. The first one created, on the south side of Elgin near Shaughnessy, is a tribute to the railway that made the city possible and to Engine 371, the first locomotive to reach Port Coquitlam. That was in 1885, and the location was just west of the railway bridge over the Coquitlam River. It was here that the CPR's main line threw out a spur, a line running south to New Westminster. This point is the famous Westminster Junction, PoCo's original, if informal, name. Port Coquitlam began at this very spot.

The Lougheed Highway, paralleling the tracks of the CPR through the heart of the city, also played a major role in Port Coquitlam's growth. The population was virtually static for several decades before the Lougheed went through in 1951.

Near the highway as it runs through town is Agricultural Park. "Aggie Park" was the site of another key event in PoCo's history in April 1913, when Mayor James Mars and the entire town happily celebrated the "Inauguration" of Port Coquitlam and planted four commemorative maple trees. (Not far away is Kwayhquitlum Middle School, a reminder of the First Nation after which the lake, the river and the two cities have been named. Of all the spellings, Kwayhquitlum is the most complicated!)

Farther north, near the border that separates PoCo from Coquitlam, is the city's cemetery. Many names mentioned in this book will be found on the grave markers in that broad green swath of land. Terry Fox's gravesite is here, modest but impressive, like the man himself.

One of the Lower Mainland's oldest streets is not far from here. The colourfully named Coast Meridian Road, originally pushed through in 1859, served as an early marker for Royal Engineer surveyors.

On Coast Meridian Road, the city's first Community Police Station handles local crime reports and serves as a headquarters for volunteer neighbourhood patrols. The RCMP and a corps of volunteers staff this station and a second one that opened on Mary Hill Road on the south side in 1999. Just as there are two police stations, there are also two fire halls, unusual for a city of this size. But it makes a lot of sense: trying to get through the Shaughnessy Street underpass in heavy traffic, or going the long way round to the east, would be a nightmare. So you'll find Fire Hall #2 on Toronto Street, half a block south of Prairie. (Fire Hall #1 is on Broadway in the city's major industrial area.)

Narrow and about 13 kilometres (8 miles) long, Hyde Creek—flowing down from the forested southwest flank of Burke Mountain—makes an abrupt left turn shortly after it enters PoCo, flows under Coast Meridian Road and continues through the northern part of the city, on to DeBoville Slough and the Pitt River beyond. Over the years the level of the creek has been dropping, and it occasionally dries up during hot summers—fatal for the salmon and trout that live in it. A rescue effort is underway, with a small but valuable hatchery located on the river (see the sidebar in this chapter). The man who tends the hatchery (it's in his backyard) is Ken Rempel, and he's seen the creek drop 12 to 15 centimetres (5 to 6 inches) just in the last decade or so.

Downstream, the city-owned-and-operated Hyde Creek Recreation Centre is one of the busier spots on the north side. A big part of the attraction is a 25-metre-long swimming pool. Sports and recreation play a major role in the lives of PoCo's people. They're particularly fond, as you'll discover, of box lacrosse. People have been playing the game here as long as the city has existed, and there are many active lacrosse boxes in town. One of the city's councillors, Mike Gates, is a member of the Canadian Lacrosse Hall of Fame. Thanks to Gates, the lacrosse box at the new Terry Fox school on the north side was named for Gordon Stidolph, who coached kids' lacrosse for thirty years and was a former teammate of Gates.

Today's favoured mode of transportation is parked in front of a mural commemorating the railway that made the city possible (above). A tiny city began to cluster around Westminster Junction (below, as it looks today), the point where the CPR built a spur line south to New Westminster.

Otto Jacobi with his infant son Jim and daughter Vivian at the entrance to the Blakeburn Ranch. (Photo courtesy Jim Jacobi)

The clubhouse at Carnoustie golf course.

Pat Burns Meat Market in PoCo's early days.

A major topographical feature of Port Coquitlam is the Blakeburn Lagoons, a marshy expanse near the city's northeastern corner that's slated to become parkland, complete with an artificial lake and a walk that would go completely around the park. The name commemorates the long-vanished Blakeburn Ranch that thrived here in the 1920s. The "Burn" element of the name came from Pat Burns, the meat packer whose Burns Meats was a Canadian institution for many years; the "Blake" from Blake Wilson. (The same two men were partners in the Blakeburn coal mine at Princeton, BC, which was active from 1918 to 1940.) There was a time when hundreds of cattle were kept at the ranch, which covered more than 324 hectares (800 acres), before their final journey into Vancouver and the Burns slaughterhouse. From a plane you can just make out the old railway right-of-way along which those doomed cattle travelled. The western boundary of the ranch was at Fremont, the eastern at the Pitt River by Dominion Avenue. Later the property was named the Minnekhada Ranch.

PoCo's only golf course is nearby. Carnoustie opened in 1974 as the PoCo Valley Golf and Country Club. The club, named after the famous one in Scotland, has eighteen holes.

Northeast of Carnoustie is the last remaining area of agricultural land in the city, with small-scale operations. Beyond, and actually in Coquitlam, is the beautiful DeBoville Slough (view it from the PoCo Trail and you'll see that the word "beautiful" is not misused) and the Pitt River Boat Club, near the eastern end of Lincoln Avenue.

South of Carnoustie, a developing light industrial area, the "Dominion Triangle," is taking shape. Named for Dominion Street, the Triangle has lots of room for growth.

Nearby, what is likely Port Coquitlam's most well-known landmark, the Tudor-styled Wild Duck Inn, has been sitting by the Lougheed Highway, right beside the Pitt River, for nearly ninety years. The Pitt River is PoCo's eastern boundary. Across the bridge is Pitt Meadows.

Back downtown, one of the more distinctive new structures in Port Coquitlam is the provincial courthouse at the eastern end of McAllister. It was built in 1993 and serves Port Coquitlam, Coquitlam, Port Moody and the villages of Anmore and Belcarra. PoCo encourages heritage themes in new construction, and the courthouse follows that guideline: undeniably modern, it was nonetheless inspired by medieval building forms, right down to the clock in the tower. It's a delight to the eye.

Across the street from the courthouse is the city's second community police station. Like its sister station on the north side, it is staffed by volunteers and RCMP officers. A bicycle patrol squad works out of the little building. Right next door is the Port Coquitlam Heritage and Cultural Society display centre. Pop in to see the (admittedly modest) display of artifacts and memorabilia. This is the embryonic form of a Port Coquitlam Museum.

A few steps south, at the corner of Mary Hill and Wilson, is the Terry Fox Library, opened in 1983. A statue of Terry, caught in mid-stride by sculptor George Pratt, stands dramatically at the corner.

Just down the street is Michael's on Wilson, a well-known restaurant singled out here because of the inexhaustible community spirit of its owner, Michael Savvis, who is heavily involved in many community events: Canada Day, May Day and—a tradition he began—Greek Days.

Not too far from Michael's is one of the city's busiest places. You may have been around on November 6, 1999, (a lot of people were!) when the greatly enlarged Port Coquitlam Recreation Centre (now renamed Port Coquitlam Wilson Centre–Recreation Complex) re-opened on Wilson Street, serving the south side as the Hyde Creek Rec Centre does the north. Immediately adjacent, to the west, is Wilson Centre, a seniors' activity complex and one of the busiest places in town.

Now let's turn north again and move back to the past. It was the railway that made Port Coquitlam possible. Stand by the station of the West Coast Express commuter line at Kingsway just north of Wilson, and as the trains pull in and leave you'll get a sense of the excitement generated decades ago by the arrival and departure—on these same rails—of the CPR's now-vanished passenger trains. Commuters by the hundreds swarm on or off the trains, grateful for the convenience and quiet of a direct and unimpeded thirty-six-minute journey between Port Coquitlam and Vancouver, with connections to a number of local bus lines.

Reminders of the city's not-too-distant agricultural past are numerous. At 2235 Hawthorne, for example, is the Swire home. Mr. Swire was a carpenter at Essondale Hospital and built this home in 1913. There was a time when a cow barn stood behind this house, and Mr. Swire sold the milk the cows produced to his neighbours.

In world terms, this is a very young city, born in the twentieth century, a fact underlined by the presence of the house at the southeast corner

DeBoville Slough, with the Coast Mountains in the background.

A farm scene on Prairie Road.

Wild Duck Inn on the Pitt River..

The West Coast Express arrives at Port Coquitlam Station.

of Mary Hill Road and Pitt River Road. Its inhabitants believe it to be the oldest house in the city, about 100 years old.

Much of PoCo's industrial heart is found along Kingsway. Esco Ltd. is here, as it has been for more than forty years. So are Recochem Inc. and many other companies, including one of the most interesting in all Canada: International Submarine Engineering (see chapter 8). In this same region you will find Fire Hall #1, a modern and quirky five-bay building (think lots of galvanized metal), and the city's works yard. The road ends at Kebet Way, where Meridian Industrial Park stretches for several blocks alongside the Pitt River. This 36-hectare (90-acre) park of mainly light industrial, manufacturing and distribution centres was established in 1987 by Keith and Betty Beedie (hence "Kebet" Way). It

PoCo's Oldest House

At the northeast corner of Pitt River Road and Mary Hill Road in Port Coquitlam stands what is likely the oldest house in the city, older than the city itself. It's occupied today by Wendy Sankey, David Shewchuk and their daughter Meghan. The house is at least a hundred years old: Wendy and David have a hand-drawn map dated 1900 that shows the house and a now-vanished stable and barn.

The house was built and lived in by George Black, the gentleman gambler who was one of the earliest residents of the area. It originally stood on 68 hectares (167 acres), which Black bought in 1879 for $167. Over the years the two-storey home has been occupied by a variety of families: the Matt Marshalls, the Mansells, the Munros, the Campbells, the Joneses. In 1947 the Munro family added a sick room for their son, Morris, who had rheumatic fever. The house didn't have a bathroom until 1938, so a little outhouse stood outside for the first four decades.

Wendy and David moved in in July 1997, attracted by the age of the house and by its features, which included knotless fir floors and nine-foot ceilings. "We spent four days gutting the house," Wendy says, "pulling out the old carpeting, the old linoleum, the blinds and the panelling, and we moved in on the fifth day."

Wendy is an interior decorator and David works all over the Lower Mainland as a restoration specialist, so they know what they're

The Sankey-Shewchuk house in 1995.

about. "The bathroom was in awful shape," says Wendy. "There was water and ant damage. This fall while I was gutting the master bedroom we discovered that the back of the house used to have a gable roofline over the kitchen. The flashing and clapboard siding are intact in the attic crawl space. The foundation is in relatively good shape, but the post-and-beam support structure was rotten from water damage. We gutted it down to the studs. Oh, and there were rats in the basement." They've added French doors they got from another old house and a ceiling light fixture from yet another.

The restoration work is slow and painstaking, but Wendy and David are patient. They expect to spend *fifteen years* getting it just right.

also features an attractive park, walkways and river access. Some major tenants at Meridian include Yamaha, Old Dutch (makers of those famous potato chips), Met-Tec, Web Press Graphics and Apex Express. Not far away is Mary Hill Industrial Park, 262 hectares (648 acres) easily accessible from Highways 1 and 7 and close to the CP rail yards. Some major tenants here are Lilydale Poultry, Kennametal, Konings Wholesale (one of the bigger food distributors in BC) and CP Transport. The riverside is home, too, to Forrest Marine and Harken Towing, two long-time PoCo firms on the city's often forgotten working waterfront. Look south and you'll see nearby Douglas Island, in mid-Fraser, the newest addition to PoCo's real estate. The city annexed the island in 1991.

And now, towering 122 metres (400 feet) above the waterfront, comes Mary Hill. In a sense, the city's history began here. When Colonel Richard Moody and his Royal Engineers saw this lofty prominence in 1858, they realized it was an ideal point from which to survey and defend the young colony. The hill, in fact, came within a whisker of being the site of the colony's capital city. Today it's a busy warren of residential development, parks and schools. The Genstar Corporation, which developed much of the area, named it Citadel Heights, a graceful nod to its past. Citadel Middle School is up here, and so is Hazel Trembath Elementary, named for a famed local teacher and situated right beside one of the city's most dramatic sites, Settler's Park. The hill's Castle Park, with broad views of the surrounding country, has become a traditional place for Port Coquitlam's Canada Day celebrations.

Stand on the southern slopes of Mary Hill and look out over the Fraser. Behind you is a thriving city of fifty thousand people—a city some say will one day be home to eighty thousand. Below you is the broad river that made the creation of that city possible. Let's now turn back to the past to follow the line of events that led to the Port Coquitlam of the twenty-first century. We'll start our journey to the past at the same place we have ended our present-day tour: at the river.

Port Coquitlam's Fire Hall #1.

Konings is one of the largest food distributors in the Lower Mainland.

The view from Mary Hill Elementary School.

Hyde Creek Fish Hatchery

In early May every year the "population" of PoCo's Hyde Creek rises by many thousands. Working mostly at night, Ken Rempel takes pail after pail of chum and coho salmon fry that he has carefully raised in the Hyde Creek Hatchery and gently pours the pails into the burbling creek, which runs right through his backyard. The hatchery is in his backyard, too, and for twelve years Ken and his volunteer helpers, mostly from the Hyde Creek Streamkeepers, have been tending their yearly crop of thousands of baby chum and coho and some cutthroat trout, working to get the creek back to its old self when it teemed with fish. (Streamkeepers are active at other creeks, and they also run the program that sees yellow fish forms painted at points where polluting products are prohibited.)

There are few kids in this part of PoCo who haven't shared in the excitement of stocking Hyde Creek with the tiny fish … and who haven't winced watching Ken cut open a female salmon to extract her eggs. During one late spring visit in 1999 we learned that Ken had himself taken some 45,000 chum fry out of the hatchery within the last two weeks and put them into the creek. "I usually put them in at night. These fry are 3 1/2 months old; they know that night is safer for them and they start heading downstream. In the daytime their instinct is to go 'home,' and they head upstream." At peak, about 100,000 chum are in various stages of development, with from 15,000 to 20,000 coho.

While Ken talks, two-year-old Josh Brietzke, carefully watched by his mom Anna and dad Paul, toddles down to the banks of the creek and pours in a couple of tiny pailfuls of fish. He watches in quiet delight as the fry squiggle away. From here, they will go down the creek into DeBoville Slough, from there into the Pitt, from the Pitt into the Fraser and from the Fraser down to the ocean.

The hatchery is a modest operation, fitting into one corner of Ken's property on Charleton Court. But in its tanks and racks are the eggs and the infant fish that will bring Hyde Creek back. The water running through the tanks is brought up by pumps and pipes from the creek itself, a few metres away, but filtered to remove any impurities. The water is kept in constant motion, and the tiny fish—bunched by the thousands in doughnut-shaped masses in the centre of the tanks—constantly swim "upstream." That builds their strength and gets them acclimatized to the water: after thirty days swimming in it, the fry "recognize"

Streamkeepers at Hyde Creek Hatchery.

the creek's water and will return to this creek during their lifetimes. If, that is, they make it back. The vast majority are lost to predators, including other fish, but that happens in unassisted nature, too.

The Streamkeepers, with some technical assistance from the federal department of fisheries and oceans (DFO), are planning to drill a well along the creek to put more water into it, to make it, in the words of the experts, "wet." Sometimes the creek runs dry. That's disastrous for the fry. It seems that stretches of the creek that lack a clay bed also lie within an area of tidal water table. In 1998 water levels dropped within the span of an hour and the fry had no chance to move into other parts of the creek. When the word went out, volunteers and City of Port Coquitlam workers spent hours rescuing stranded fry. "It was a tremendous effort," says Darrell Penner, Streamkeepers' president. "The City was great, sent about a dozen workers to the job." The Streamkeepers hope the new well will keep Hyde Creek "wet," just as a similar 1997 project did for PoCo's Maple Creek.

Another of DFO's contributions is a clever fish-feeding gizmo. Ken Rempel keeps it well stocked: a small conveyor belt is covered with fish food (looking not unlike instant coffee: tiny, granular, dark brown, containing chicken, fish, vitamins, etc.) and moves along very slowly, almost imperceptibly, impelled by a small clock mechanism. As the belt advances, the food drops off the end into the holding tank and the little fry gobble it up. "They go," says Ken, "to the point where the food drops down because they expect food to hit the water above them."

Learning about the salmon's life cycle isn't confined to the creek. Irvine Elementary School, for example, has two salmonid enhancement programs, one in English, one in French. It's a great way to plug the kids into yet another part of the natural world around them.

TWO

The Settlers

A small station was built at the point where the tracks diverged.

I n the winter of 1824, the Hudson's Bay Company (HBC) began establishing a network of fur-trading posts on the Pacific slope. This set in motion the development of what we know today as Greater Vancouver, and Port Coquitlam would be right in the heart of it.

A party of men led by HBC Chief Factor James McMillan reached what is now the Langley area on December 16, 1824. They approached from the west, entering the Nicomekl River from its mouth on Boundary Bay, paddling through what is now Surrey, then portaging to the Salmon River. The men encountered the Fraser River about 50 kilometres (31 miles) from its mouth and carried on north into the Interior. But McMillan noted the location and, to remind himself of it, singled out a prominent tree, which he nicknamed the Hudson's Bay Tree. Two and a half years later he was back by the tree aboard the *Cadboro* with twenty-five men and supplies and with instructions from his employers to build a trading fort in the area. Construction of Fort Langley began July 27, 1827. That's as good a date as any to mark the birth of Greater Vancouver.

There were Native people living along and near the lower Fraser, and they began to bring furs to Fort Langley. The Kwantlens' winter site in the early 1800s (before the fort was built) was near what is now New Westminster, the Katzies' on lower Pitt Lake and the Kwikwitlems' probably on the upper Coquitlam River. The city owes its name to that latter group, but there is still some confusion about the location and even the names of the various tribes.

By 1832 Fort Langley was shipping out more than two thousand beaver pelts annually. Then salted salmon (with Native women employed to cure and pack it) became a major industry. The HBC abandoned the original fort in 1839 and built a new one 35 kilometres (22 miles) upstream, at the present site. By the late 1840s the fort was the largest fish exporter on the Pacific Coast, with Hawaii a major market. In the new location, farming also became an important source of income. Thirty years after its establishment, Fort Langley was thriving. That encouraged further settlement.

It began to get busy downriver. In 1853 the first white people settled in what is now Port Coquitlam when the Alexander McLean family arrived aboard the two-masted schooner *Rob Roy*. The same ship had originally brought the family up from Bellingham Bay in Washington to Delta. Their prosperous 285-hectare (700-acre)

Fort Langley in the 1870s.

dairy farm at Ladner's Landing in Delta had been flooded out (by a tidal wave!) after they had lived there just a month. It must have been hugely frustrating for McLean to be forced to move yet again, and so soon after arriving. He had to pull his cattle aboard the *Rob Roy* by their horns.

"Leaving the vessel anchored," the *Coquitlam Star* relates, "McLean hired an Indian to row [sic] him up the Fraser River in a canoe, and then heard from the Indian for the first time about Pitt Meadows. Pitt Meadows then was full of Indian villages and wigwams [sic] and the Indians, as they moved among the camp fires, from which the smoke curled up, regarded the white man with curious and hostile looks. Avoiding their wigwams as much as possible, he walked over the prairie, and as he looked about him he thought out just what quantity of stock he would require to go in for stock-raising. He then went back to his ship, hauled up anchor and sailed with his family for Pitt Meadows." (The meadows extended along both banks of the Pitt, and the McLeans were heading for the west bank: that's in PoCo today.)

McLean, his wife and their two small boys, Alexander Jr. and Donald, arrived with fifty milk cows. At first the Native people living in the area refused to let them ashore. But after they handed over provisions and blankets as payment, the family was allowed to land. They immediately began clearing and fencing the land, and built a log home. The McLean boys became friends with and played with the local Native boys.

Pioneer Otis Munday recalled that his grandfather often visited the McLeans, and he places their property between what is now the CPR railway bridge and Pitt River Road. The family's 220 hectares (540 acres) were unsurveyed, which means they got them free. Later, after surveyors moved in, the price of land in the Port Coquitlam area would be set at ten shillings an acre.

PoCo's first settlers are commemorated by McLean Avenue, a short stretch between Pitt River Road and Kingsway.

It was some time before the second pioneer family came. In February 1860, seven years after the arrival of the McLeans, the Atkins family arrived from County Kerry in Ireland and, according to a later retrospective in the *Coquitlam Star*, came up the Coquitlam River in a boat they had built themselves, dubbed the *Shannon Cop*. (*Cop* is an Old English term for a summit.) The boat was heavily loaded with tents, blankets, guns, lumber, a stove and provisions. They landed at Marshall's Island, not far from what would become Westminster Junction, and pitched their tents in the brush, building a house in a week. (Local historian Lois Milne places that location as just behind Riverside Secondary.) Another source says the family "took 160 acres [65 hectares] east of Mary Hill near the foot of Pitt River Road."

All but one member of the Atkins family left for Hawaii in 1868—son Edmund Arthur Atkins (more commonly known as Ned) had married a local Native woman named Susan and decided to stay. Edith Chambers, in her history of Port Coquitlam, writes that the couple "adopted" two Native boys. Ned told the *Star* that the local Natives had been peaceful,

An Early Catastrophe

*O*ne of the most dramatic, yet little-known stories of the Port Coquitlam area came to light as a result of a major archaeological excavation carried out in the late 1970s at the mouth of the Pitt River. The dig was conducted by Val Patenaude, who today is the curator at the Maple Ridge Museum in Haney. Many local students were lucky enough to be on hand while Ms. Patenaude and local First Nations people worked at the site. Ms. Patenaude wrote this account of her discoveries especially for this book.

Centred on the foot of Pitt River Road, the prehistoric site spanned nearly a kilometre in length. The impending construction of the Mary Hill Bypass was to destroy much of the site and so excavations were conducted to preserve as much information from the site as possible.

The earliest dates established for use of the site were nearly 4,500 years ago (around 2500 BC). These dates were associated with a hunting, fishing and gathering culture that occupied what were two small islands with sloughs between them and behind them. Over time the sloughs silted in and more and more of the site became dry land. For three thousand years the artifact evidence indicates seasonal use for fishing and plant gathering. The tools recovered were made of chipped and ground stone and included many exotic types of materials brought in by the Native occupants. In addition to tools were decorative items, particularly beads.

About fifteen hundred years ago a local environmental catastrophe struck Mary Hill. It was most likely a forest fire, which stripped the tree cover off the hill, exposing the sand deposits there to erosion. Over a very few years, ton upon ton of sand washed down the slope, forming a large sand fan around the mouth of Baker Creek. This entirely changed the landscape and the use to which the site was put.

For the following 1,250 years, the sand deposits were used to form earth ovens for the baking of plant foods. Sand holds its heat well and there were indications that cedar boughs were placed over hot coals and that the food itself was wrapped in skunk cabbage leaves—Native wax paper—to slowly steam and bake.

About 250 years ago, catastrophe struck again, but this time of a

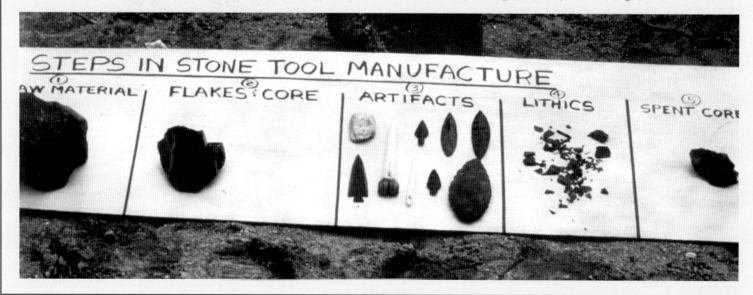

STEPS IN STONE TOOL MANUFACTURE
RAW MATERIAL | FLAKES & CORE | ARTIFACTS | LITHICS | SPENT CORE

different sort. The last apparent use of the site was in the mid-1750s when there was a mass cremation. While bone didn't preserve well at the site, many personal ornaments of a type usually passed on to descendants rather than left with the dead were recovered, all with fire damage. This almost certainly represents the first wave of small-pox to hit the south coast—after travelling up the Columbia River, it reached the Fraser at the height of the summer salmon fishing season, well in advance of any European settlers. With losses of 70 to 90 percent of the population, we get a tragic picture of people burning their dead and then leaving, never to return.

At the time the excavations were conducted, neither the Coquitlam nor the adjacent Katzie people specifically claimed this site, even though it is located on the boundary of both territories. While it is possible that Halkomelem relatives from Vancouver Island owned this particular village site on the Fraser, it is also possible that the memory of the tragedy at that site kept people from returning there for so long that its ownership and use went out of memory.

The photos on this page and the previous show some of the students and volunteers who participated in the Pitt River dig in the late 1970s. The chart at the far left shows artifacts found at the site and their significance. (Photo courtesy Val Patenaude)

Ned Atkins, one of the early pioneers in the Coquitlam–Port Coquitlam area.

and even the bears, wolves and wildcats in the surrounding forest were no problem. There was plenty of game, and it was easy to shoot: they took geese, ducks and deer. The larder was always full. Ned Atkins recalled that James Douglas, governor of the colonies of British Columbia and Vancouver Island, visited his place in 1861 and that Douglas planted an apple tree to commemorate the visit. In 1892 Ned sold his farm to John Smith, Coquitlam's municipal clerk, and bought 8 hectares (20 acres) near Westminster Junction.

Ned Atkins got work driving stagecoaches between New Westminster and Hastings Townsite. He later became a member of Coquitlam's first municipal council and was reeve (mayor) for five years, from 1897 to 1904. Susan died in 1907 and Ned said he "missed her all my life" until he himself died in November 1924.

The Atkins are also remembered in a PoCo street name: Atkins Avenue runs off Shaughnessy a block south of Granny Smith Park.

In 1858 a dramatic change occurred in BC. Gold was discovered March 23 near Yale on the Fraser River. The news travelled quickly south to California and almost overnight, prospectors began to arrive, first in trickles, then a flood. Within weeks more than twenty thousand American prospectors had swarmed in, prompting an alarmed Governor Douglas—acting on his own authority—to declare the mainland a British colony, too. That proclamation was made at Fort Langley on November 19, 1858.

Douglas needed to ensure British control of the new colony and discourage any thoughts of American expansion. (The threat of American encroachment was not imaginary: not long before, in a dispute south of the forty-ninth parallel, Americans had briefly seized Hudson's Bay Company boats, one of them the aforementioned *Cadboro.*) Douglas wrote urgently to London asking for a detachment of Royal Engineers to underline the British presence. The Engineers would show the flag—and build the new colony's roads and bridges. The first twenty-five "sappers" arrived from England on November 25, 1858, under the command of Colonel Richard Moody. (The Engineers get their nickname from an old word, *sap*, which refers to a spade used in digging trenches.) By April 1859 the last of the 165 men had arrived. Their settlement, Sapperton, is now a New Westminster neighbourhood.

Richard Moody is the first important figure in the Lower Mainland's earliest history. He and his officers selected the routes for its first roads and the sites for the first military reserves and the colony's first capital.

Colonel Richard Moody of the Royal Engineers helped open up mainland British Columbia for settlement and development.

Moody began scouting for a location on which to build a capital city as soon as he arrived in the new colony. He was appalled by Fort Langley's strategically poor location on the south side of the river, with its "back" to the Americans. Governor Douglas had chosen the fort's site because of its accessibility by water and the availability of good arable land, but Moody was a professional soldier and he wanted a location easier to defend against an American invasion if one ever came. That meant somewhere on the north bank, putting the river between himself and any invaders. He found a place, as historians G.P.V. and Helen B.

Akrigg relate, "close to the river's mouth." The sloping ground chosen by Moody was the spot where the federal penitentiary stood for years, just east of the present New Westminster downtown. "Nearby was Mary Hill," write the Akriggs, "ideal for a citadel whose guns would guard the capital and keep the Americans from crossing the Fraser."

Moody's first choice for the location of the capital had been Mary Hill itself. But, as made clear in this account from R.E. Gosnell's *British Columbia Year Book* (1897), that plan changed quickly. "[Moody] ordered his senior captain, Captain Jack Grant, as he was familiarly termed, now General Grant, R.E., to take the axe and make the first cut at one of the trees nearest the river. He was in the act of swinging the axe to deliver the blow, when he was so much impressed with the mistake they were making that he said, 'Colonel, with much submission I will ask not to do it. Will you yourself be pleased to take the responsibility of making the first cut?'"

A group of Royal Engineers gathered for a reunion in New Westminster in 1910. Premier Richard McBride (back row at left) welcomed them to the city.

Grant then explained why he thought the location was not the best that could be chosen, that one farther downriver was better, and gave his reasons. "These were of so cogent a nature," Gosnell's account continues, "one being that the lower site being at the head of tide water, big ships could come up the Fraser to it and that it was easily defensible by a *tête du pont* [bridgehead] on the opposite side of the river, and similar reasons, that the colonel was convinced, rowed down the river and ordered the first cut to be delivered on one of the huge cedars with which the hill was covered, and named the town Queensborough." (After a brief period as Queensborough, the town was renamed—at Queen Victoria's command—New Westminster.)

So Port Coquitlam makes an early entry into British Columbia's European-era history thanks to Mary Hill, where a citadel was established to guard the new colony's capital city. In 1866, when the two colonies were united as British Columbia, New Westminster became capital of both until the capital was moved to Victoria in 1868.

Mary Hill, 122 metres (400 feet) above the Fraser, may have been named for Colonel Moody's wife, but there is evidence it has also been called St. Mary's Heights. It is shown as "Mary Hill" on an 1859 Admiralty survey chart made by Captain George Richards of HMS *Plumper*. The hill's history is reflected in the names of some of its streets and parks: Citadel Drive, Palisade Crescent, Garrison Court, Fortress Park and the like.

In the spring of 1860 the McLean family was startled by a visit from the peripatetic Governor James Douglas. He was en route to Pitt Lake (called Bedford Lake at the time,

---

HISTORICAL FOOTNOTE

Alexander McLean's milk cows were the first brought up the Fraser River, so Port Coquitlam was the pioneer in the Fraser Valley's thriving dairy industry.

Chief Marvin Joe stands in the regalia of his Kwayhquitlum Nation. As 2000 began, Chief Joe's people were pondering development of their 205-acre Indian Reserve #2. (The band's reserve #1 is on the Coquitlam side of the Coquitlam River.) Just three families reside on IR#2, so the potential is great.

after C.N.J. Bedford, magistrate at Langley) and dropped in briefly to look over the McLean dairy farm. Douglas left a description of the area: "The banks of the Pitt River are exceedingly beautiful; extensive meadows sweep gracefully from the very edge of the river towards the distant line of forest and mountain. The rich alluvial soil produces a thick growth of grass, interspersed with the Michaelmas daisy, the wild rose, and scattered groups of willows."

Thanks to the Royal Engineers, this "exceedingly beautiful" area began to open up to the outside world. North Road, which connects New Westminster to Burrard Inlet, was built in 1859 and still exists as the border between Coquitlam and Burnaby. The Coast Meridian Road was also built that year and is now an important arterial route within Port Coquitlam. When the Engineers began surveying virgin land in the Fraser Valley, they started from the "Coast Meridian"—a base line that ran due north from the first survey post east of Boundary Bay on the forty-ninth parallel.

Another important PoCo thoroughfare, Pitt River Road, was constructed in 1862 by a private firm contracted by the Engineers. It connected the Engineers' camp at New Westminster with the Pitt River. One of the major reasons for this road's construction apparently was to facilitate trade between the local Native people and white urban settlers to the west. A bridge taking the road across the Coquitlam River was the first built in this area. It was swept away by flood waters, and its replacement has long since vanished. Over the years, portions of the road have been renamed. Today, only the section from the Lougheed Highway to the Mary Hill Bypass remains Pitt River Road.

Floods were a common occurrence on all the local rivers. Donald McLean recalled having to take two lengths of pipe out of the stove in order to raise it on blocks when they were going to bake bread and were up to their knees in Pitt River water. The organ—a mainstay of family entertainment—also had to be raised on blocks to let the water run underneath it.

The weather was an important variable in early settlers' lives. Winters really *were* colder back then, before urbanization tempered the climate. From January 1 to March 13, 1862, the Fraser was frozen over and people could walk from shore to shore. (In the winter of 1858–59 the Fraser froze over for several months!)

As settlement expanded, the original inhabitants of the land began to be squeezed out. Governor Douglas issued a proclamation that all land in the Lower Mainland was Crown property and therefore Native people would not be entitled to sell it. They were moved onto small reserves. Later, the right to pre-empt land was also denied to Native people. Douglas wrote to Colonel Moody about this time, saying, "I hear very general complaints of the smallness of the areas set aside . . ." and adding that the Coquitlam Natives had complained their reserve on the river was altogether insufficient to raise vegetables enough for their own use. (The arrival of Europeans brought more woe to local Native people than the loss of their lands. In 1862 they began to die from smallpox. The disease tore through Native bands all through the colony. There were an estimated sixty thousand Native people in BC at the beginning of 1862. By the end of that year twenty thousand of them had died. The scourge would come again.)

A group of Chinese workers pause in their labours for a photograph on the CPR line in British Columbia.

Their work largely done, and with the threat of an American invasion now deemed unlikely, the Royal Engineers left for England on November 11, 1863. Many sappers stayed behind as settlers (each was given 60 hectares [150 acres] of land), but some sappers and all the officers left, never to return. In 1860 Colonel Moody's influence on BC's early history was commemorated when Captain Richards named the eastern end of Burrard Inlet Port Moody.

So far the population of what was to become Port Coquitlam was sparse: by 1864 the McLeans, the Atkinses and a "gentleman gambler" named George Black (who later became a well-known meat merchant in Gastown) were the only people actually living in the area, although other land was owned by speculators. The "gambler" tag may have been inspired by Black's raising of horses, which he then entered in races held down New Westminster's main street, Columbia.

Assured that a transcontinental railway would be built by Canada—a country that existed only from Ontario east and that was just four years old at the time—British Columbia joined Confederation in 1871. From now on British Columbians would also be Canadians.

If they had known the railway wouldn't reach them for another fifteen years, they might not have been so willing to sign on. It took eight years just to get tracks to the BC–Alberta border.

But the railway, when it finally came, was the dominant factor in Port Coquitlam's early history. The city was created and, briefly, thrived because of it.

In an article in *The Greater Vancouver Book* on the history of railways in the Lower Mainland, David Mitchell writes:

One of the most significant debates of this era revolved around the difficult question of where the railroad company—the Canadian Pacific Railway—would locate its western terminus. As the rail line moved toward completion during the 1880s, this controversy fuelled hopes, dreams and rampant real estate speculation.

Victoria and New Westminster were the only communities of any significance in British Columbia at the time. However, neither of them was deemed suitable for the CPR terminus. Several different locations along the Pacific Coast were considered before it was generally agreed that the railway would end at Burrard Inlet.

The location of the terminus had a direct bearing on the creation of Port Coquitlam.

The first location for rail-end announced by the CPR was Port Moody, but plans changed and the railway located the terminus farther west along the Inlet at Granville Township, later to become the City of Vancouver. On July 4, 1886, the first passenger train to reach Burrard Inlet pulled into Port Moody—fated now to be merely another stop en route to Vancouver. The celebration of the train's arrival was somewhat muted, as resentment still simmered in the minds of men who had invested in land in the neighbourhood in hopes of profiting. (Lots purchased for $15 early in 1885 sold just weeks later for $1,000. When the CPR bypassed Port Moody, those lots sat empty.)

New Westminster was no happier. The new line ran several kilometres to the north of the city, largest on the mainland at the time with a population of four thousand. Something had to be done. According to historians Archie and Dale Miller, who researched the issue specifically for this book:

> In order to build the 8.4-mile [13.5-kilometre] branch line to New Westminster, the CPR demanded a cash subsidy of $75,000, with right-of-way and station grounds. The land required for railway purposes cost about $35,000, making the total expense of securing the branch line about $110,000. The provincial government agreed to furnish one half the cash bonus, leaving $72,500 as New Westminster's share.

There was little doubt in anyone's mind that even without the bonus, the CPR would have put in the line within a couple of years since it could not afford to leave the Royal City without a railroad connection when it had "such splendid facilities for doing business over the Northern Pacific." The purpose of the bonusing was to hasten

The first transcontinental train, pulled by Locomotive 371, steamed into Port Moody on July 4, 1886.

the railroad's arrival and to ensure that the branch line opened at the same time as the main line into Port Moody. However, because of numerous delays, the first regular CPR train did not arrive in New Westminster until November 1, 1886.

This caused great consternation among the citizens of New Westminster, and on April 8, 1886, three members of the provincial parliament for New Westminster, John Robson, James Cunningham and James Orr, were burned in effigy for allowing the $75,000 subsidy. The three all owned property in the Coal Harbour area as well as in New Westminster and were accused of favouring Vancouver over New Westminster. The public was appeased, however, by the sod-turning ceremony at Sapperton a couple of weeks later. The rail line continued smoothly, albeit much more slowly than anticipated.

"Giving a substantial bonus to a new company to entice them to open in a new city," the Millers conclude, "was not unusual. In 1888 New Westminster agreed to grant to the Southern Railway Company a bonus of $100,000, right-of-way, land and water lots and exemption from taxation for five years in order to encourage them to construct a rail line from the city to the American border."

Construction of the CPR's spur line south to New Westminster began, as mentioned, in late April 1886. A small station was built at the point where the tracks diverged.

On August 28, 1886, the *Mainland Guardian* reported that "the whistle of the locomotive has at last been heard . . . The long line of Chinamen occupied in grading, the white men laying rails, and the locomotive Kamloops, with the train of section cars, had a great attraction for our citizens and large numbers collected to witness the novel scene." That casually racist reference to "Chinamen" is a reminder that the provincial government had originally pledged to pay for part of the rail work only if no Chinese were employed. That proved to be impractical and the proviso was withdrawn.

The name chosen for the place where the tracks diverged, 27 kilometres (17 miles) east of Vancouver, was New Westminster Junction. Locals shortened the name to Westminster Junction, or

The station at Westminster Junction was called Coquitlam Station, even after it became part of Port Coquitlam. (Photo courtesy Lyle LeGrove)

Until the traffic bridge was built, this ferry carried passengers to Pitt Meadows. The CPR bridge is in the background.

sometimes just "The Junction." Stand on Kingsway a little west of the railway bridge in downtown PoCo and you're there. A triangular building, occupied until recently by Pine Lighting, and by Pop Ticehurst's Pop's Cafe years before that, is the very spot where Port Coquitlam was born. Nothing marks the spot as special—no plaque or monument—but city historian Lois Milne is working to change that.

It has to be said that the creation of a place called Westminster Junction was not uppermost in the minds of those New Westminsterites: what they wanted was rail access to Burrard Inlet. Daily passenger service between Port Moody and the Junction began November 3. The first CPR passenger train arrived in Vancouver in May 1887. According to a 1912 interview with pioneer Ned Atkins, the arrival of the railway "raised prices and increased the demand for produce of all kinds."

The Coquitlam Water Works Company was also formed in 1887. Up to now, locals had fetched water for household use in buckets from nearby streams. H.A.J. Monk and John Stewart, who wrote a history of Coquitlam and Fraser Mills, say, "At first there was a goodly supply of clean, cold water from the spring-fed creeks, but as the area became more developed and the loggers cut down the trees to supply the sawmills, the abundant supply of clean water became less certain, and people could see the necessity of a water system . . ." Even before construction began, however, Coquitlam Water Works (which had secured rights to a water supply from Coquitlam Lake) sold out to the City of New Westminster on March 18,

By 1890 there was a schoolhouse and regular classes at Westminster Junction.

1889. The following year New Westminster installed a water pipeline from Coquitlam Lake, down the Coquitlam River and along the north side of the Fraser to the city. Locals around the Junction could tap this line for their water.

Slowly, steadily, commerce was gaining a foothold in the area. In 1889 A. Mouldey, in partnership with William Richardson, built a boat and scow to carry loads of sturgeon from the head of Pitt Lake to New Westminster. Mouldey also established a ferry service, carrying passengers across the Pitt River in the days before the traffic bridge went in.

With the arrival of the CPR the population of the Lower Mainland began to grow. According to the 1881 census, five years before the railway's arrival the entire population of Greater Vancouver was less than 3,000. The 1891 census, five years *after* the railway, showed a population of just under 22,000.

On one of those trains passing through was an Englishman named William Towler, who with his young son had left Peterborough, England, aboard the SS *Circassian* on February 27, 1889. Towler wrote a short series of reports titled "Letters From an Emigrant" for a Peterborough newspaper. By March 9, he informed his readers, he and the boy (unnamed) were aboard a CPR train heading for the Pacific coast. A week later they were in the Rockies, which impressed him mightily. "I have read somewhere," Towler wrote about these fabled mountains, "that when the Creator had finished forming the world, He threw the remnants into British Columbia." From his March 17 instalment: "They say it always rains in British

Early settlers brought a variety of religious faiths to what is now Port Coquitlam. The Methodist Mission (above) and St. Andrew's Presbyterian (below) were just two of the early churches built in the area.

Columbia. By 9:45 we had reached New Westminster junction, where the rain had ceased . . . Many of our passengers got off here for Victoria and other parts of Vancouver Island, to where they proceed by boat to-morrow. The balance of our 6,000 miles was now reduced to a dozen, and about that number of passengers remained aboard our cars, who had left Liverpool with us. One by one, and sometimes a half score or more at a station they were now scattered, never more to meet; all of us filled with the desire to better our circumstances, all full of sorrow at leaving the old land, all full of hope on reaching a new one."

Promise and hope were everywhere in the air, much of it inspired by the magnificent and seemingly endless tracts of giant trees. In 1887 (some accounts say 1889), two men, Frank Ross and James McLaren, erected a big sawmill at a location called Millside, in what would become the southwestern corner of Coquitlam. In time the mill became the largest in the British Empire. In 1913, a couple of weeks after Port Coquitlam's incorporation, the little corner—all 390 acres of it—broke away from Coquitlam to become a small incorporated community on its own, Fraser Mills. It would be welcomed back into the Coquitlam fold in 1971.

Settlement began to cluster around the meeting of rails called Westminster Junction. A schoolhouse was built there in 1890, a tiny one-room green-painted

Trinity United Church

Trinity United Church was established in the early 1900s as St. Andrew's Presbyterian Church, which held its services in the old community hall at Burleigh and Dewdney Trunk Road (the latter now Kingsway). One of the parishioners, pioneer Donald McLean, donated land at Dewdney and Shaughnessy (very near where the Legion Hall is today) to the church. The first service in the new St. Andrew's on that site was held May 21, 1911. The name of the church was changed to Trinity United in 1925 when union of the Presbyterian, Methodist and Congregational churches took place all across Canada.

A church hall went up in the 1930s to accommodate a growing number of community events and youth groups, and in 1947 the church building itself was picked up and gently transported to the corner of Whyte and Shaughnessy in "downtown" Port Coquitlam. The congregation held Sunday School in the basement, and by the late 1950s enrolment had reached an astonishing three hundred children.

A few years later a developer made an offer to buy the church's property. A sale was agreed upon after many months' deliberation, and a new site was purchased at the northwest corner of Shaughnessy and Prairie. (At the time, that stretch of Shaughnessy was called Chester Street.)

The present church was dedicated in 1966 and has been there since. The congregation grew so much that an extension had to be built in 1982. Happily, there was land available at the back of the church property for the construction of housing, and the church built Stewart House, an affordable housing complex. "In 1996," says a church history, "we launched a renovation program that gave us a new entrance, a new kitchen, a new Thrift, new administration offices, a custom-built facility for preschool and a comprehensive sprinkler system throughout the church."

In the spirit of ecumenism, in early 2000 Trinity was also being used by local Anglicans while their own church was rebuilt.

Trinity United Church today.

A choir concert fills the interior of Trinity United with a joyful noise.

box in which Miss Dixon taught twelve students of assorted grades. It was on what was then called Schoolhouse Road (now Mary Hill Road), at the location occupied today by the Mary Hill–Wilson Avenue lacrosse box.

One of the students was six-year-old Alice Ross, who would have an extraordinarily long life in PoCo. Her 1884 birthplace was the family home at the south foot of the Pitt River Road. She liked to say she had been born "on the banks of the Fraser." Alice's mother, Sarah, had been the first white baby born at Fort Langley, and her Welsh-born father, John Ross, was the man employed to open the CPR's wooden swing bridge over the Pitt River. There was a lot of river traffic in those days, and he was kept busy . . . and strong: the bridge had to be opened by hand.

In 1977, at the age of ninety-three, Alice—by then, having married twice, she was Alice Ross Carriere Heckbert, but known to all as "Nanny"—moved to Port Coquitlam's Hawthorne Lodge. "When she turned one hundred," her daughter Wanda Frey recalled, "she received a telegram from the Queen, silver coffee spoons from city hall and a lapel pin from Mayor Traboulay." Nanny Heckbert died at Hawthorne Lodge on September 1, 1988. She was 104 years old.

In the early 1900s, Anglican parishioners used Alice's little school for services while the city's first Anglican church was being built on the Dewdney Trunk Road, west of the bridge over the Coquitlam River. It opened in 1910. Church services were held in a variety of places back then: also in the early 1900s the Baptists built a church at the corner of Flint and Prairie. Presbyterians gathered at the old community hall at Burleigh and Kingsway. In 1911 they built St. Andrew's Church on land donated by Donald McLean on the Dewdney Trunk east of the Coquitlam River. Early Methodists met in the Methodist Mission, a humble building that would serve for nearly thirty years. In 1913 they built a church on Salisbury, where the pulpit was handmade by the appropriately named Fred Handy. Local Catholic families held services at parishioners' homes or travelled to Maillardville or New Westminster. Edith Chambers says Catholics also held occasional services in the first Agricultural Hall, with a Father Kientz on hand. In 1904 the first meeting of the Congregational Church was held, with the Reverend J.J. Fernie presiding. Twenty families attended and it is said that each brought $5 every Sunday, though that seems high for the time.

The map of Greater Vancouver was beginning to fill in. New Westminster had been incorporated in 1860; the Township of Langley in 1873; Maple Ridge the following year (with a 405-hectare [1,000-acre] chunk of it still on the west side of the Pitt River); Surrey, Richmond and Delta all on one day in 1879; Vancouver in 1886; and the District of North Vancouver on August 10, 1891. Twelve days later it was Coquitlam's turn.

On August 22, 1891, a huge expanse of land 16,576 hectares (64 square miles) in area was incorporated as the District Municipality of Coquitlam. The spelling of the name Coquitlam was, happily, a simplified form of the name of the Native people in the area, a name sometimes spelled Kwikwitlem and sometimes Kwayhquitlum.

THREE

Port Coquitlam Starts Here

BUILDING A PACIFIC PORT AND THE FOUNDATIONS
- OF AN -
INDUSTRIAL CITY

What Pittsburgh is to
the United States,
so will Coquitlam
be to Canada.

—*Coquitlam Star*

For twenty-two years after Coquitlam's 1891 creation, that city's story is also the story of Port Coquitlam, or at least that portion of PoCo clustered around the Junction. In all the broad expanse of the new municipality there were about two hundred people, most of them near the train station. All the commercial activity was centred around Westminster Junction. On November 11, 1893, the land west of the Pitt River that had been part of Maple Ridge was transferred to Coquitlam. Land could be bought in this area for $20 to $25 an acre.

The district's first council meeting was held August 22, 1891, at Kelly's Hall, a homely two-storey wooden building on the Dewdney Trunk Road, then the Junction's main street. The hall had been built by Robert Brenton Kelly, the new municipality's first reeve (mayor).

R.B. Kelly was the owner of the thirty-four-room Junction Hotel, PoCo's first. He and his father-in-law, Colonel A. Scott, built the hotel. (Scott's son, Loftus, and Loftus's son, Bruce, would later be involved in PoCo politics.) Kelly, a man of many parts, was also Coquitlam's postmaster. The post office was in his hotel's lobby until 1909, when it moved to the train station.

Kelly's Hall in 1913 with the famous bell tower.

A photograph of Kelly's Hall, taken in 1913 when it was being used as Port Coquitlam's city hall, shows it had a little bell tower. That came in handy when the building was later converted to the town's fire hall.

One of the first bylaws passed by the new council set bounty payments ranging from $2.50 for a bear and $2.00 for a wildcat down to 25 cents for a skunk. There was a lot of uncleared land in Coquitlam back then, and that meant a lot of wildlife: bears, raccoons, skunks, deer, mink and wildcats.

It was still a wild area, where nature had more sway over day-to-day life. In early February 1893 a train leaving New Westminster for the Junction took two hours to go the first 90 metres (295 feet), thanks to a 30-centimetre (12-inch) fall of snow the night before. That winter the Fraser River froze to a depth of 15 centimetres (6 inches). People crossed from Surrey to New Westminster by sled. Impromptu hockey games—the first recorded in BC—were organized on the river's frozen surface. (The same thing happened in the 1920s and 1930s when the Pitt River froze over several times, once to a depth of 25 centimetres [10 inches]. A charming photograph of the time shows the Wally Stewart family warmly clad and ready to skate.)

The rivers that so neatly delineate Port Coquitlam's

boundaries have also caused many of its woes. Flooding on the Pitt, the Coquitlam and the Fraser has time and again caused damage to the town, and as recently as the summer of 1999 there were fears the Fraser and the Pitt might top the city's dikes and inundate its streets. The Fraser flood of 1894 was an early indication the city would often be at the river's mercy. That flood was easily the greatest in the river's recorded history, even surpassing the later disaster of 1948. (In 1894 the Mission gauge read 25.8 feet [7.9 metres] at its peak, compared to 24.6 [7.5 metres] in 1948.) Property damage in the latter flood was much higher because there was more property to be damaged, but the earlier flood covered far more land. Handmade dikes did nothing to stop the river's invasion. It washed out a traffic bridge over the Coquitlam River—not the last time that happened. *The Vancouver Daily World* of June 6, 1894, tells the story:

> To get a proper idea of the extent of the inundations now spreading misery and loss throughout the Fraser River valley, one has to study the map of that part of the country. The immense acreage then found to be under water is appalling. The Pitt meadows, the plains in and about Harrison lake district, Matsqui prairie, part of Langley district, the greater part of Chilliwack, as well as all the islands in the upper part of the river are now under water . . . municipalities and the Government have lost heavily through the sweeping away of bridges and added to this is the tremendous loss of the Canadian Pacific railway and that of store-keepers in flooded villages.

Brothers Arthur Mars (left) and James Mars were both mayors of Port Coquitlam.

Augustus R. (Gus) Millard came to the area to log, but became a successful merchant.

Some Coquitlam people, flooded out, left for good. The Mounces, for example, who had been farming in the area for ten years, left for New Westminster. The Richardson family, living next to Ned Atkins in his old log house on Pitt River Road, also left.

But there was also gain: construction was started on an extensive system of dikes, completed in 1896 (though now and again the work would be found wanting).

And over the next few years the Junction gained a number of people important in its history, like the Jacob Rowland family, which arrived in 1894. Jake Rowland had been appointed the CPR agent and eventually succeeded R.B. Kelly as postmaster. He later became part owner of the Junction Hotel and was a co-builder of one of the city's major commercial buildings. Jake's sister Hanna followed him as postmaster, and his sons were genuine stars in a game—lacrosse—that PoCo has fervently embraced over the years.

Another group that thrived was the Tom Mars family, which came from Scotland via Tacoma, Washington, in 1896. One of the boys, James, twenty-five when he arrived, was later elected mayor of Coquitlam—and was the first mayor of Port Coquitlam. Tom's younger son, Arthur, also became a PoCo mayor, and he married May McLean, daughter of the area's earliest pioneer, Alexander McLean.

Seventeen-year-old Wilfred David came to Coquitlam in 1896. He later courted Elizabeth Mars, Tom's daughter, and after their marriage their first-born, James, was the first baby born in Port Coquitlam following incorporation. As the twenty-first century begins, Jim David is alive and well at eighty-seven.

There's no doubt what the major industry in the Lower Mainland was in the 1890s: logging. The big first-growth trees are gone now, but there was a time they soared above the land to astonishing heights. Trees 91 metres (300 feet) high were not unknown, and the quality of the wood in them was unmatched anywhere in the world. Knot-free beams from southwestern BC are part of the ceilings in the Imperial Palace in Beijing, China.

A California-born man named Augustus R. Millard was among the first to concentrate on the trees in this area. Around the turn of the century he logged extensively along the Coquitlam and Pitt Rivers and on Burke Mountain, and he thrived. Gus Millard went on to become a Port Coquitlam merchant, running a general store, a hardware store and the liquor store. He served on the first PoCo council, was chairman of the fire committee and was a school trustee for one term. Oddly, no street is named for him, even though he was one of the most prominent of PoCo's earliest citizens. Gus was married to Mary, nee David, who was Wilfred David's sister.

Another man active in logging at this time was Michigan-born Dennis Welcher, who worked the forests for seven or eight years, then bought a farm and invested in real estate. Welcher settled in Coquitlam in 1897 and went on to serve as a councillor and then reeve of the municipality. When Port Coquitlam was incorporated, Welcher served a term there as an alderman and chairman of the Board of Works. He was president of the Coquitlam Agricultural Society for ten years. (He gets a commemorative street: Welcher runs off Shaughnessy, across from Elks Park.)

The Scott family, shown here (left) at an outdoor gathering, were long-time residents of the area, while Jim David (right) was the first person born in Port Coquitlam following incorporation. (Photo at left courtesy Margaret Jackson)

The 1903 class stands outside Junction School.

Early 1900s logging in the District of Coquitlam.

An interesting map made around this time, about 1900, shows that fewer than twenty-five people owned all the land that today makes up the city. Many of them may have been absentee owners: their names (e.g., Keary, Pickering, Townley, etc.) do not appear in city histories . . . although Keary's name is familiar in Coquitlam's and New Westminster's past, and Townley's in Vancouver's. There are six, however, that do appear: G. Black, D. McLean, J. Morrison, E.A. Atkins, J. Flint and J.A. Fox.

PoCo's city hall sits today on land that once belonged to "gentleman gambler" George Black. The first school was on property donated by Black. The first football game (what we'd call soccer today) in the Fraser Valley region was played on Labour Day, 1902, on Black's Ranch, near the Red Bridge.

"D. McLean" would be Donald McLean, son of the earliest settler, Alexander McLean. If you live in the area where Cedar Drive begins to curve to the northeast, just past Chelsea, you're on or near what was once McLean property. (Edith Chambers' 1973 history of Port Coquitlam notes that Donald McLean eloped in 1881 with Annie Mundy of Sapperton.)

Joe Morrison went into partnership with a Mr. Rodgers in a locally famous grocery store on the east side of Shaughnessy at Dewdney Trunk.

Another prominent pioneer in both the city and the local Presbyterian Church, R.W. Hawthorne arrived in 1902 at age thirty-three. He served on council from 1914 to 1918. Hawthorne Street is a well-known PoCo thoroughfare and gives its name to Hawthorne Lodge.

One Chinese name appears as a property owner on the map—Flint Road runs diagonally through the land owned by Lam Tung—but we know nothing more about him.

On December 31, 1901, the District Municipality of Coquitlam totted up its assets. They consisted of $901 in cash, $1,000 in buildings and furniture "and $11.56 in other assets." Coquitlam also noted that it had 147 ratepayers, 120 of whom lived elsewhere. Those outsiders were speculating, hoping their land purchases would pay off as population increased and land values rose. Until their lands were easier to get to, however, they would have to be patient.

A network of roads and streets was beginning to develop all through Vancouver's suburbs, but they were mostly intended for horse-drawn rigs and short journeys. The Dewdney Trunk had been completed, although not paved, by 1900 and in some cases provided the only means of communication between neighbours. Just as the Lougheed does today, the Dewdney ran through the heart of Port Coquitlam. (In some stretches—like that in front of Essondale/Riverview—the Lougheed is the Dewdney renamed.) It wasn't

A worker spreads gravel on Flint Street to maintain the road surface and make it better to travel on.

until the 1920s that cars were important and popular enough to warrant major road and street improvement projects.

More jobs became available for locals when the Buntzen hydroelectric project was put in service by the Vancouver Power Company to provide the first hydroelectric power to the city of Vancouver. Up to that time Vancouver had had to depend on a steam plant for its power supply. Work on the project began in 1903 and involved building a dam on Coquitlam Lake and excavating a tunnel 3.6 kilometres (2.2 miles) long to carry water from Coquitlam Lake to Buntzen Lake. (That body of water, which had been called Beautiful Lake, was renamed for Johannes Buntzen, first president of BC Electric.) The tunnel ran under Eagle Mountain and emptied into the north end of Buntzen Lake. Then the water from that lake flowed through penstocks down the steep mountain slope to a power plant, Buntzen Powerhouse No. 1, on Indian Arm. The plant has been supplying power to the Lower Mainland for nearly a hundred years.

In 1909 the BC Electric Company received permission to start selling electrical power in Coquitlam. The Junction's power came from a dam on Stave Lake in Maple Ridge operated by the Stave Lake Power Company.

When Thomas Routley (born 1869 in Ashburn, Ontario) moved from Vancouver to Coquitlam with his family in 1906, he had a contract to transport supplies to BC Electric's

The Wild Duck Inn

The Wild Duck Inn is always associated with William Routley, but it had existed for more than a decade before he obtained it. It was called the Minnekhada Hotel when it was built in 1912 by the Minnekhada Land Company as a two-storey bunkhouse for CPR workers. At the time it was located on the Dewdney Trunk Road, on a stretch of the road that is now part of the Lougheed Highway. Besides providing temporary housing for the CPR, the Minnekhada was also an inn for travellers on the Dewdney. It was briefly known as the Meadow Brook, and later it was a hunting lodge, a stopping place for hunters who came from throughout the Lower Mainland to shoot waterfowl found in the Pitt Polder area. Hence its third and likely final name.

In the mid-1920s, along with just about everyone else, the Inn's owners defaulted on their taxes, and William Routley was able to buy it from the city at a very good price. He got a team of horses, moved the building from the ferry landing to its present location and decorated it as an English country manor house. Then he began to take in boarders. The business did well and in 1931 he got a beer licence and opened a hundred-seat pub. He also added a third storey.

William sent for his nephew Harold and Harold's wife, Mary. They'd been living on the Prairies where, Hazel Postma wrote later in *Coquitlam Now*, Harold had been recuperating from the effects of a mustard-gas attack in World War I. Harold and Mary became partners in the enterprise.

"Uncle Will ran a very strict bar," Mary Routley told Postma, "no women allowed. I worked as cook and had eight girls helping, one just as a runner, standing by ready to fetch things as I never moved from the cookstove." Once in the late 1930s, dog trials were held in the area and the staff had to feed three hundred people in two hours. Her youngest daughter waited tables and was stunned—and delighted—when she began picking up twenty- and fifty-dollar tips from American millionaires attending the trials. Around the same time Mary recalls a large group of men staying at the Inn while they drilled for oil in the vicinity.

The Wild Duck Inn on the Lougheed Highway.

"The Routleys," Postma continues, "lived in a cottage behind the Inn and raised two daughters, after losing a third at the age of five in a boating accident on the Pitt River. 'The boat capsized and threw eight of us in,' Mary Routley says. 'I couldn't swim, but I tried to save her. Three men and my daughter lost their lives'."

Mrs. Routley said the Inn provided a good living. "When Uncle Will sold out in 1943, one of the customers said he didn't think Uncle Will would live long after selling the place. He died six weeks later."

The Wild Duck Inn is likely PoCo's most well-known landmark outside of the downtown, as thousands drive by it daily. Incidentally, the Inn used to sponsor a team in football—what we'd call soccer today—and one year in the 1920s they won the provincial championship. "You wouldn't believe the enthusiasm for football in those days," says current city councillor Ron Talbot. "They used to have excursion trains coming out from Vancouver full of people to see the games." Today, the Inn still rents rooms and still provides food in the restaurant and drinks in the bar. The entertainment has changed, however, with naked dancing ladies the featured attraction.

Thomas John Routley and his son, Harold Thomas John Routley, in front of T. Routley's fish market.

A view of Coquitlam Dam in August 1913.

Coquitlam Lake dam site. The Routley's home was on the north side of Wilson Avenue not far from Shaughnessy, just about where the restaurant Michael's on Wilson sits today. By 1912 Thomas Routley was also a PoCo fish merchant. William Routley, Thomas's brother, and his wife Ida came to Coquitlam about 1908, and the name Routley appears throughout PoCo's history, particularly in connection with the Wild Duck Inn, the Music Festival and the PoCo Trail.

By 1903, logging had taken second place to farming in the Junction's economy. (A few folks engaged in both trades.) Local farmers took their produce to New Westminster, either travelling on the Pitt River Road or on a river scow that ran a regular service from the mouth of the Pitt River. Japanese labourers who toiled on the farms earned a dollar a day. To further the aims of the farmers, the Coquitlam Agricultural Society was formed in 1903, and its seventeen members, paying two dollars a year, included many names now familiar in local history: Donald McLean,

Pioneer Matt Marshall standing in his oatfield.

HISTORICAL FOOTNOTE

Here's a bit of local history you may not believe: Mary Salanger, who married Harold Routley in 1921, remembered that in 1905 Coquitlam there were slot machines on the sidewalks of the main street!

Ned Atkins, James Fox, Jacob Rowland and a man named T.W. Quilty, then the proprietor of the Junction Hotel.

Coquitlam was becoming thoroughly involved in the economic life of BC's Lower Mainland. The next time you go through New Westminster, have a look at the low-level railway bridge just east of the Pattullo Bridge. It's been there since 1904. Rock from Coquitlam Mountain provided much of the foundation for that bridge. Contractors Gilley Brothers of New Westminster had a rock quarry by the Pitt River and hauled out tons for this major project, the first crossing of the lower Fraser River. The Gilley quarry supplied a great deal of rock for projects all around the Lower Mainland, including some of the fill for Vancouver's False Creek. One pioneer said it well: "There's a little bit of Coquitlam Mountain in a lot of places!"

An employer's name that pops up again and again in early PoCo history is Essondale, the mental hospital. The official name was the Coquitlam Hospital for the Insane, but everyone called it Essondale, after Dr. Esson Young, the provincial secretary at the time, whose responsibility it was. The hospital is called Riverview today and sits on the Coquitlam side of the Coquitlam River—with the exception of the Forensic Psychiatric Unit, which is in Port Coquitlam.

A lot of PoCo residents have Essondale connections; either they worked there or their fathers or mothers did. Wilfred David worked at Essondale cutting wood. Ken Mackenzie of Harken Towing recalls his dad working there. Annie Osborne started at the hospital in 1949 as a nurse's aide (a "glorified Pinky," she laughs), and Rose Phillips (who was then Rosa Maria Chine) was there for more than thirty years, latterly as a senior nurse. Harry Mounce was there for thirty-one years and married a nurse he worked with. PoCo Councillor Ron Talbot was born in New Westminster but grew up right on the Essondale grounds, where both his parents, Arthur and Evelyn, worked. "My father," says Ron, "helped to build West Lawn, the first building at the hospital." Former mayor George Laking's father worked there, and so did George's future bride. So did Alderman Rosina Morrill. So did a great many other PoCo people!

The Essondale story begins in 1904 when the provincial government acquired 405 hectares (1,000 acres) of land at the junction of the Coquitlam and Fraser Rivers, on the west bank of the Coquitlam and extending up it for about two miles. "About half of the area," writes

David J. Davies, in his paper *A History of the Mental Health Services of British Columbia 1850–1925*, "was composed of rich alluvial soil, and being level and not too difficult to clear would require only drainage for it to be used as a Colony Farm." (A word of explanation about that name: one dictionary definition of "colony" is "a group of people forced to live isolated from society, as because of disease or criminal behavior." This, presumably, is the sense used in this case.) Davies' paper is an excellent overview of its subject, with much detail on the treatment methods of the time.

The head of the Public Hospital for the Insane in New Westminster in 1904, Dr. G.H. Manchester, commented: "I am convinced that in view of the antiquated nature of the present institution, and the great need for considerable extension to meet future requirements as to accommodation, it would be a wise policy for the Government to lay out plans for the erection of a complete modern hospital for the insane upon that property . . . The uses to which the Farm Colony shall be put at once are the production of all necessary vegetables for the Hospital, fodder for the horses and hogs, all dairy products by the maintenance of a large dairy herd and the supply of fuel for the bakery and for the boilers in summer."

On July 10, 1905, a start was made in clearing land (patients did the clearing work under

Essondale Branch Hospital, later known as West Lawn, was the first building at the Coquitlam Hospital for the Insane.

An office at Essondale (above) and the pharmacy (below).

an attendant) and erecting temporary buildings at the Colony Farm site. The farm eventually covered 182 hectares (450 acres) of the site's lower land, and before long it was famous throughout Canada for the quality of its produce and livestock. (Today the larger portion of Colony Farm is on PoCo's side of the river. See the sidebar later in this chapter for more on the farm and its future.)

Around the same time a recommendation was made that the asylum planned for the site should be able to accommodate 1,500 patients. In 1908 a road was built to connect the asylum site to the Dewdney Trunk Road. (Colony Farm Road is still there.) An architectural competition attracted the interest of many BC firms, and by 1909 construction had started on the institution's first building. It began as the Essondale Branch Hospital, but later became known as West Lawn. Not until February 25, 1911, would the lieutenant governor lay the foundation stone for the main building. The first 500 patients moved in in the summer of 1912.

Around the same time construction on Essondale got underway, the Women's Institute was founded. It continues to be a force in PoCo's social life more than ninety years later. In the beginning, members would meet to talk and hear lectures on home nursing, domestic work, recipes, methods of home preserving and the like. But then they began to broaden their scope. Ninety-five-year-old Annie Osborne ticks off the list of good works: they were responsible for the town library in the early years; helped families in need; did valuable local work during both world wars; volunteered their services during every flood that hit PoCo, housing, feeding and clothing refugees when need be; worked with the Red Cross; decorated May Day floats and won prizes for many of them; organized an annual Flower Show (a favourite activity for Annie); baked, sewed and knitted (afghans, sweaters, pyjamas, dresses); helped during the annual Elks' Day; even staged Christmas events—Annie played Santa Claus one year!

And there was action in the commercial realm, too. James and Arthur Mars, who would come to figure so prominently in PoCo's history, went into business in March 1909 as Mars Brothers General Merchants on Schoolhouse Road (now Mary Hill Road.)

Another merchant, Jacob Rowland, strengthened his role in town in partnership with Augustus Millard. They built a solid, stubby little office building, which everyone called the "Cement Block," to house the Coquitlam Real Estate Company, the Bank of Vancouver (which had come to Coquitlam in 1901) and a general store run by Millard. The Cement Block was on the Dewdney Trunk Road, which at the time was the town's main street. Later that particular stretch of the Dewdney would be renamed Kingsway.

Meanwhile, Fraser Mills—never a part of Port Coquitlam, but an employer of many people from the city—was having trouble finding enough experienced local men to work in its rapidly expanding operation. One of the staff, Quebec-born Jean-Baptiste Dicaire, went back to Quebec and started recruiting workers. On September 22, 1909, Dicaire left Montreal with thirty families, 110

A group of women gather at Aggie Hall for "Baby Day," held at the District of Coquitlam's annual Fall Fair.

The Women's Institute has been a vital force in the community from the time of its formation until today, more than ninety years.

Colony Farm: "An oasis of meadow and forest"

In 1904 the provincial government bought a thousand fertile acres (405 hectares) where the Coquitlam and Fraser Rivers meet, to be used as a farm to provide both food and an opportunity for rehabilitative labour for patients of a mental health facility to be built on the adjacent uplands. The hospital, first called Essondale (for Dr. Esson Young, the provincial secretary and minister of education), was formally dedicated in 1911. Its agricultural component was called Colony Farm. The hospital is known today as Riverview.

The nearest sizeable town was New Westminster, 8 kilometres (5 miles) to the west, and many members of the hospital and farm staff lived right on the site. (PoCo councillor Ron Talbot, for example, whose parents worked at Essondale, grew up on the hospital grounds.) The rich flood-plain soil was ideal for crops, and soon the little Essondale community became virtually self-sufficient. "The fertile fields," says a 1995 report written by Michael McPhee, "produced vegetables, meat and dairy products as well as hay for the Clydesdale horses used to till the fields. Colony Farm became one of British Columbia's earliest, and most outstanding, agricultural successes." In 1910, with a few locally purchased cows, the farm began a dairy operation. Holstein cows were imported from New York state and from Carnation Farms of Seattle to upgrade the herd. At its peak, there were 250 cows in the dairy.

"By 1911," says the book *Coquitlam: 100 Years*, "the farm was considered the best in the west, yielding 700 tons of crops and 20,000 gallons of milk." Its barns, stables, dairy equipment and yards were termed the best in Canada, maybe on the continent. Colony Farm regularly won

Patients plowing at Colony Farm in 1913.

top prizes at the annual Pacific National Exhibition, and its dairy herd provided foundation stock for most of the province's dairy farms. It did so well, in fact, that it was able to ship surplus foods and dairy products to other provincial government institutions.

"Colony Farm," said Jenny Gardner Lenihan, who grew up there, "was absolutely gorgeous. The cattle were knee-deep in straw, the barns were immaculately kept, all the timbers and buildings were painted white, and you could walk in your white shoes and not get dirty ... It was the province's showpiece."

Fires and the 1948 flood dealt severe blows to the farm, but it came through and survived until 1983, when the economic restraint policies of the provincial government of the time forced its closure

people in all. They arrived September 27. A second contingent arrived May 28, 1910, and more came later. They established a little colony of their own just north of the mill and, in honour of their local oblate, Father Edmond Maillard, called it Maillardville. For the first two weeks, until the company built them modest homes, the newcomers lived in railway baggage cars. Their wages were $2.50 for a ten-hour day, and they worked six days a week. (Some PoCo people also worked at the mill, so this information gives an indication of what working conditions were like in the area.) The new arrivals were also given, for $150 repayable at $5 a month, an acre of land and the lumber to build a home. They settled in after more than seventy years of productive life. The equipment and the famed herds were sold off.

But the land, more than 235 hectares (580 acres), remained.

Some 101 hectares (250 acres) of the farm are on the Coquitlam side of the river, with 134 hectares (330 acres) on the PoCo side. The government tried to sell it, but BC was going through a recession in the 1980s and no buyers were found, especially since the farm was in the Agricultural Land Reserve and was unavailable for industrial or commercial development. Still, that land was a tempting target, with highways and residential development pressing in from all sides. Stand in Colony Farm today and look up to the hills: once thickly covered with forest, now they're just as thick with houses.

In December 1993 the British Columbia Buildings Corporation, which administers the land, set up a committee to do a land-use study for Colony Farm. Among the committee members were Port Coquitlam's chief planner at the time, Carlos Felip, Paul Dutton of PoCo Citizens for Colony Farm and Elaine Golds of the Burke Mountain Naturalists. Michael McPhee of Quadra Planning Consultants co-ordinated the study, which involved a series of public workshops, presentations by interested parties and a public open house that was attended by two hundred people. In February 1995 another open house was held at Wilson Centre, but this time there was a draft land-use plan to study and discuss, and more than three hundred people attended.

The Burke Mountain group began to sponsor an annual walkabout at the farm to increase public awareness of its natural history. Nature helped, too: with the land now free of farm workers and livestock (except for some sheep and cattle grazing, mostly on the Coquitlam side), animals and birds displaced by the surrounding development moved in.

"Small mammals—rodents, raccoons, mink and muskrats—moved into the long grasses," says the 1995 report. "Beaver took up residence along the river banks. Song birds nested in the trees and waterfowl frequented the Coquitlam River." This rich infusion of new life began to attract predatory owls, hawks and coyotes. Nature was reclaiming Colony Farm.

And that's pretty much the way it's going to stay. Large tracts of the farm's land have been set aside and will be protected so that wildlife can continue to flourish there. The river has been recognized as an important habitat for salmon, trout and other fish species. The mouth of the river is now an official wildlife management area, with an established colony of great blue herons. Bald eagles and wood ducks are seen, too. More than 150 species of birds have been identified as living on the farm's lands or migrating through. It's a birdwatcher's delight. Says the McPhee report, "Several species considered sensitive or vulnerable are found at Colony Farm. These include the Green Heron, Bald Eagle, Barn Owl and Short Eared Owl. The Farm is the only known breeding site for Western Kingbirds, Eastern Kingbirds and Least Flycatchers within the Lower Mainland . . . The increasing use of Colony Farm by regionally uncommon species of birds is indicative of how critical the Farm has become in providing habitat types being lost elsewhere in the Lower Mainland."

Colony Farm is now a regional park of the Greater Vancouver Regional District, which is developing places to stroll, birdwatch, cycle, jog, walk dogs, fish, canoe and take pictures. Port Coquitlam has inherited a priceless legacy.

nicely and, over time, became a familiar part of local life. Old-timer Morley Deans tells a funny story about being part of a PoCo baseball team playing one day against a team of Maillardville kids who openly discussed their game strategy—in French. "It didn't work," says Morley, grinning. "I spoke French, too."

Sport was hugely popular in Coquitlam. The town's football team (soccer, remember) was champion of the Lower Mainland in 1910, the baseball team seemed to win every game it played, the 1912 lacrosse team won the Malkin Cup . . . wrestling, women's grass hockey, tennis, cricket, all were played and played well.

The city's prominent role in sport was very nearly matched by a role in education: for a brief, heady moment in 1910, Mary Hill was seriously considered as a site for the proposed University of British Columbia. In retrospect it seems a good idea: a dramatic, high and central location. But Point Grey won the nod.

By this time, Colony Farm was beginning to show the results that eventually made it famous. "They exceeded," writes David Davies, "even the most sanguine expectations. The crop included 230 tons of hay, 130 tons of potatoes, 130 tons of barley and wheat, 250 tons of mixed root vegetables and 600 cords of firewood. Dairy and meat produce consisted of almost 20,000 gallons of milk, 24 calves and eight colts. The farm buildings were completed and the farm was already conceded to be the best in Western Canada." In competition at the Dominion Fair held in Regina early in July 1911, Colony Farm livestock entries won more than twenty prizes, including five championships and three grand championships. It did even better at the Dominion Fair in Ottawa, winning thirteen championships out of a possible fourteen.

In September 1911 a new shoe shop opened in Coquitlam. This was an event slightly more portentous than it seemed. The fellow who ran it, a young man named R.C. Galer (the initials stood for Roger Charles, but everyone called him "Harry"), would become in later years a very prominent PoCo citizen, businessman and politician.

Coquitlam's 1910 champion football club with trophies. Members are (front row, left to right): F. Watson, W. Wilson, J. Black, R.A. Perkins, A. Millard, A. MacKenzie, (back row) R.C. Welch (president) C. Davies, G. Doyle, A. Jackson, M. Marshall, J. Stewart, W. Pringle

Harry Galer was born in Wangford, Suffolk, England, on December 17, 1874, the very same day, the family likes to tell you, as Canadian prime minister Mackenzie King. (His son John laughingly theorizes, "Maybe that's why he was a dyed-in-the-wool Liberal.") Harry's first wife died in childbirth in England in 1901. He came to Canada in 1907 at age thirty-three to make a new life and went first to Moose Jaw, Saskatchewan, to work as a bricklayer. Later he prospected for a while around Yale. By 1910 Harry Galer was in Coquitlam, and he married Christina Marshall there on June 1, 1910. The Galers soon were active members of the community. Harry was a natural leader: just a few months after his arrival he became president of the Coquitlam board of trade, and when PoCo was incorporated, he was a member of the first city council. Harry went on to become the city's longest-serving mayor (though Len Traboulay will likely capture that title in 2002).

Now the seminal event in the creation of Port Coquitlam occurred. The CPR—which had been buying land and waterfrontage in the area since 1910 and would end by spending more than $1 million—proposed a major expansion of its modest operations at Westminster Junction. It involved nothing less than moving the railway's freight yards and engine facility out of Vancouver and onto the broad, flat land surrounding the Junction. (Two major reasons were behind the move: the railway's twenty-five-year tax exemption in Vancouver was about to expire, and the company believed the opening of the Panama Canal would bring much new business.) More than 243 hectares (600 acres) of land cutting diagonally through Coquitlam would be needed to hold 290 kilometres (180 miles) of track, roundhouses, "coal docks," repair shops, etc. The railway's proposal included a forty-eight-stall roundhouse, and a shipyard at the mouth of the Pitt River. Work started in November 1911.

Protests by local farmers were drowned out by the clamour of excitement over the huge new development. In fact, the *Weekly Globe and Canada Farmer* was moved to write: "The natural geographic position is the most desirable for an industrial site and a port. Level land in a 'Sea of Mountains' is more valuable than in any part of the Dominion. Considering there are 6,000 acres [2,430 hectares] of level territory, with more than six miles [9.5 kilometres] of frontage on Pitt River, the possibilities are unlimited. In her capacity as a Port, however, Coquitlam will achieve her greatness. The CPR Co. has noted that by its interest."

There was an explosion of land speculation, new people began arriving and lots changed hands. A new newspaper, the *Coquitlam Star*, was founded. (The paper's address was on Fleet Lane, wherever that was.) The *Star*'s inaugural issue on September 8, 1911, featured a map of the area and a blaring headline: WHAT PITTSBURGH IS TO THE UNITED STATES, SO WILL COQUITLAM BE TO CANADA. Suddenly Vancouver's daily newspapers were carrying real estate advertisements for land in the area—more advertising, in fact, than for any other municipality in the Lower Mainland.

On the strength of the railway's announcement, Coquitlam's reeve, James Mars, and council passed huge borrowing bylaws: $150,000 for road improvement; $50,000 for water mains;

Everyone piled aboard for a photo to celebrate the arrival of the district's first fire truck in 1912.

$75,000 for sidewalks (another source says $50,000); $25,000 for a new city hall (another source says $20,000); $25,000 for Central and James Park schools; and $15,000 for a fire truck and a hall to keep it in. Some 40 kilometres (25 miles) of sidewalks were built in 1912–13. "The roads, wooden sidewalks and water mains extended in a grid through the bush in all directions," wrote the *Star*. The district council held a plebiscite on the loans and they were approved. That gigantic loan—$340,000 for an area whose population was only about 1,500—was understandable, given the confirmation of the railway's expansion. No one could have predicted what lay ahead.

Just eight months after its first issue, on May 8, 1912, the *Star* published an excellent "Progress" edition, packed with information about the city (all of it aggressively favourable), pictures of its pioneers and its civic leaders, and a dynamic full-colour cover featuring drawings of industrial works, farming, shipping and an aerial view of the city. The drawing of that view features a curiosity: an electric railway is shown running parallel to the CPR from Vancouver into the Fraser Valley and passing right through the heart of Port Coquitlam. A story inside relates that the "Burrard, Westminster and Boundary Railway and Navigation

The forty-six-room Commercial Hotel was a grand edifice in the small town. The bar from the now-vanished hotel will be a feature in a new pub at this same location.

Company is also building an electrical road from Vancouver to Mission, with branch lines to Westminster and Port Moody." That "electrical road," impressive as it sounds, was never built.

An advertisement in the special issue concluded, "COQUITLAM WILL PULL YOU IF YOU HITCH YOURSELF UP TO IT."

The board of trade became involved, along with the Coquitlam council and the Ratepayers Association, in pushing for a fire department. In May 1912 a meeting of the three groups decided that Kelly's Hall, which had been the Coquitlam municipal hall, would become the area's first fire station. It opened as such in 1914. Police headquarters were in the rear of the building. This was also the year the department bought its first fire truck, a brand new LaFrance. T.B. Thomas was appointed both police chief and fire chief. He had an assistant chief, Tom McIlveen; a deputy assistant, W. Wilson; and two firefighters, N.J. Hunter and H. Hull. Fires in the first few years were mostly in the forests of Burke Mountain (which was then, by the way, called Dollarton Mountain).

Most of the activity in the big municipality that was Coquitlam was concentrated around

Roy Greer (left) and his sisters Lillian and Edith. Their parents, Tom and Emma, were among the first ten settlers in the Port Coquitlam area. (Photo courtesy Norma Warren).

the Junction. Why, Junction leaders began to ask, should the people clustered there subsidize the construction of roads and such for the vast empty areas that lay beyond? Support for a separate city, one centring on the Junction, began to build. On October 17, 1912, a petition to create the City of Port Coquitlam was sent off to Victoria. To get an idea of the size and shape of the new city, Coquitlam's municipal clerk, John Smith, conducted his own census. It showed there would be 1,342 people there and that 438 of them were "male British subjects of the full age of twenty-one years" (i.e., eligible voters).

One issue of the *Star* announced a contest to choose a new name for the proposed city. The Vancouver-based Coquitlam Terminal Company, which was promoting the Junction as a site for major industries, sponsored the contest. We haven't discovered the name of the winner, but we do know the name that won the prize: Port Coquitlam.

It seemed as if the new city, when it was incorporated, would be off to a thriving start. New buildings were popping up everywhere. A contractor named Charles Davies, who had gone into business the year before (and who would later become one of PoCo's more popular mayors), built the Commercial Hotel, which opened January 18, 1913, and stood for decades at the northeast corner of Flint Street and the Lougheed Highway. The hotel was an ambitious one for a small town: it had forty-six bedrooms, eight bathrooms, a bar, dining room, reception area, ladies rooms and two stores on the ground floor. "The hotel," said an advertisement, "will be furnished in modern style and in every room there will be hot and cold water, each room being heated by hot water radiators and lighted with electricity." (Renamed Frisco's Inn, the old hotel was finally torn down in February 1998 after eighty-five years of use, but a memory will remain: the bar from the Commercial Hotel is planned to go into a pub in the residential/commercial development replacing the Commercial.)

There were predictions of "great elevators" along the local riverfront to hold prairie grain destined for export. In fact, plans to build a grain elevator on the Pitt River were announced in June 1913 but not carried through.

The Coquitlam Terminal Company wrote to council asking it to build more roads and ditches, saying the company itself had spent $17,000 in 1912 on public sidewalks, streets and bridges. "The major portion of this sum," the company wrote, "represents a permanent improvement of which the Municipality has the benefit." The letter was signed by Theo. M.

Knappen. The company was spending a lot of money on advertising, too: a full-page ad placed by the Coquitlam Terminal Company, Limited/Coquitlam Townsite Company, Limited, was aimed directly at CPR employees. It says in part, "The question of money need not bother you if you are a C.P.R. employee. We will sell you a lot and build you a house on it, or on one of our own on terms that you can meet readily . . ."

Activity was now feverish. The Greer Block, another sturdy office building, went up in 1912 at the corner of what is now Kingsway and Mary Hill. Perhaps it was erected by the brand new Coquitlam Construction Company, which had started April 1.

It was around this time that the little Coquitlam Theatre was built, with 135 individual wooden chairs in neat rows, and locals began going to see Chester Conklin and Fatty Arbuckle, Norma Desmond and the Keystone Kops. A 1912 advertisement for the theatre noted the "programme changed three times weekly." There were live concerts there, too. A photograph of the building indicates it was rather a ramshackle affair. Long-time resident Annie Osborne remembers sitting in the theatre watching movies and on rainy days having to hold an umbrella over her head to shield herself from the leaking roof. Today, there is no movie house within PoCo's borders.

By May, seven hundred men were building the railway's yards, which opened for business May 31. In early August the CPR called for tenders to build a new steel bridge over the Coquitlam River. In late August 1912 a switch was thrown and, lo!, the Junction had street lighting.

The pace began to quicken even more. On September 11 the Coquitlam Shipbuilding and Marine Railway Company decided to locate at the foot of Pitt River Road with a capital of half a million dollars, the same day the $2 million contract for the CPR's bridge was let. The next day, September 12, BC Premier Richard McBride visited the Junction to open a brand new Agricultural Hall. This "Aggie Hall" replaced an earlier, smaller building that stood where Earl's Restaurant is today. Work on the shipbuilding plant started in early October, and on October 9 Coquitlam council began the process to incorporate Port Coquitlam as a city. The CPR's double track system was in place by year's end.

By the end of 1912 there were five schools in Coquitlam (Millside, Blue Mountain, East Coquitlam on Victoria Street, Westminster Junction and James Park) and four churches, not counting a small Catholic church on the No. 1 Indian Reserve. And 1912 was the year the Wild Duck Inn was born, in a slightly different location than the current version; one description puts it on the east side of the Pitt River.

The state of the Coquitlam River was an issue that year. The *Coquitlam Star* reported that the stream was carrying a heavy load of sediment caused by sluicing operations of the BC Electric Company. The condition had existed "for some months past," and as a result "the temper of local officials is becoming somewhat riled. They propose to see that the contamination of the river is stopped, or according to [Coquitlam Councillor Ernest] Morgan they

G. Roy Leigh steered the little city through perilous times.

The Coquitlam City, *shown here under construction about 1913, was the first vessel built in Port Coquitlam.*

will take other steps with that end in view in the near future." The BCE told council the sluicing operations were about completed and that what bars had been formed would probably be washed away at the first freshet. (Nearly ninety years later, the health of the Coquitlam River is still a local concern. In 1985 Alderman George Laking, referring to pollution problems with the river, said "We need a forever-and-ever committee, because we're dealing with a forever-and-ever river.")

The year 1912 was memorable for another reason: G. Roy Leigh began working for Coquitlam. He was just twenty-five, not long out of Northamptonshire, England, where he had taught school. Leigh had come to Canada to teach at Chesterfield School in North Vancouver, but was there for just a year. An opportunity to become Coquitlam's collector and assessor opened, and Leigh took it. Portly, maybe even a little stuffy (one newspaper story admiringly referred to him as "this man who wears his dignity as a garment"), Leigh was a charter member of the Port Coquitlam civic staff when the city came into being. He quickly proved to be the perfect man for the job. (A bit of trivia: Leigh had one of the largest stamp collections in the province.)

Roy Leigh had a lot on his plate. The city's commercial and industrial base was growing rapidly. A hydrographic survey of the Pitt River was conducted by the Coquitlam Terminal Company in January 1913, and the Pacific Dredging Company bought a site on the river the following month for a plant. On March 10 the Hynes Stone and Staff Company started up out on Dominion Avenue, nine days later the R.B. Johnson Boot and Shoe Factory—late of Vancouver—began operation, and something called the Call Switch Company was just about ready to start. The Johnson shoe factory, by the way, had been persuaded to move to PoCo by shoe merchant Harry Galer. In March or April—accounts differ—the keel of the first vessel built at the shipyards was laid.

This blizzard of plant openings and construction would be exceptional in a city of half a million; in Port Coquitlam, with 1,500 people, it was intoxicating. And it wasn't over yet.

In twenty-two months, a hundred boarding houses, hotels and business blocks had been built. So had three hundred houses—a new house every two days for the better part of two years. Permanent employees of the CPR poured into town.

With all this frenetic urban activity going on, it's important to note agriculture was still a major economic factor locally: according to the *Star* the two largest ranches in BC, the Minnekhada and the Coquitlam, each of 810 hectares (2,000 acres), were in the municipality. Local farming families had been

The Agricultural Society (below) built Aggie Hall (above) for its meetings and social events.

The house at Minnekhada Ranch, which was owned by Eric Hamber, later BC's lieutenant governor.

behind the push to form an Agricultural Society and to build the new hall in which to hold its meetings. "Aggie Hall," said PoCo pioneer Archie Johnson, "was a real community centre," and it was a PoCo landmark for years—its clandestine, early-dawn destruction in the 1970s would be bitterly criticized by many old-timers. (The Kinsmen Centre at 2175 Coquitlam is where the Hall used to be.)

Prospects seemed golden for the new city. Its location on two navigable rivers and the CPR's plans for the shipbuilding plant had prompted Junction residents to choose the name Port Coquitlam. As soon as people heard that name, they knew the city was on navigable water. The soon-to-be-opened Panama Canal promised a great increase in trade with Europe, and the city's waterfront would surely be a great benefit. In fact, "Panama fever" proved so virulent it resurrected a wildly ambitious scheme for a canal of PoCo's own.

The canal idea had been bouncing around for a couple of decades already, apparently originally hatched in the mind of Vancouver businessman David Oppenheimer (who was the bigger city's second mayor, from 1888 to 1891). In 1891 Oppenheimer sent engineers to survey the route to see if it was feasible. They reported it was. One local source says Coquitlam's municipal engineer John Kilmer had plans drawn up for the $5 million project. They showed a new waterway going from Port Moody, at the head of Burrard Inlet, to the Pitt River, allowing ocean-going ships to get to the Pitt River faster than by going up the Fraser. The plan included a dam to be built across the Second Narrows. (Another of the touted benefits: the fresh water of the Pitt River flowing into Burrard Inlet would rid the ships anchored there of barnacles.) Needless to say, the canal didn't happen.

Adding to the optimism was word that China was interested in greatly increasing its trade with Canada. The new city would be nicely situated to share in that bounty.

FOUR

Brave Beginnings

To celebrate the town's creation, they held a parade . . . with virtually no spectators. Everyone was in the parade!

On March 7, 1913, the separation became official. Port Coquitlam was incorporated and was now its own city. The western boundary of the new town was the Coquitlam River—except for a small triangle west of the river with Lincoln Avenue at the top. The Fraser River was the southern boundary, the Pitt River was the eastern. A chunk of land fifteen or so blocks wide and half a dozen blocks deep jutted up north of Lincoln on the east side of the Coquitlam River, and that was part of PoCo, too . . . including a quiet, sloping, green swath of land that today holds the town cemetery.

Port Coquitlam assumed five-eighths of Coquitlam's municipal debt, which at the time was $225,000 (in 1913 dollars). The new city got Junction School, the District Hall, all the district's horses and road machinery, fire brigade equipment, office equipment and so on. It also got as mayor Coquitlam's reeve of three years, James Mars, who didn't even have to move his office. Overnight, Kelly's Hall had ceased being Coquitlam's municipal hall and had become Port Coquitlam's city hall.

The new council—which was elected by acclamation on March 22 and met for the first time April 2, 1913—had a mayor and, oddly, five aldermen. The usual practice is to have an even number of aldermen so that in the event of a tied vote the mayor can cast the deciding vote. We don't know why this practice wasn't followed in Port Coquitlam.

Across the top of the minutes for that first meeting, the words CITY OF PORT COQUITLAM are writ large. And down the page, the clerk begins to write "Councillors" or "Council Members," but crosses it out and writes "Aldermen" instead, then lists the first five aldermen:

Port Coquitlam's first council. Left to right, R.C. "Harry" Galer, Dennis Welcher, John Langan, Mayor James Mars, Ernest Morgan, City Clerk John Smith, Augustus Millard.

John Langan, Roger (Harry) Galer, Ernest Morgan, Dennis Welcher and Augustus Millard.

More than 150 people had signed the original petition for incorporation, and James Mars and his brother Arthur, both Junction merchants, were among them. So were many familiar names: Greer, McLean, Rowland, Lee. Some fifty-three of the petitioners lived in Vancouver. Five were from New Westminster, and two weren't even in the Lower Mainland. As property owners, or representatives of property-owning companies, however, all were eligible.

On Port Coquitlam's Inauguration Day, April 18, 1913, a little over a month after incorporation, there was a parade (briefly delayed by a passing train), the city band played, there was a rugby game, the children took part in races and Mayor Mars made a bold prediction. He told the throng of celebrants on the grounds of the Agricultural Hall that the little city—population somewhere between 1,500 and 2,000—would be home to ten thousand people within three years. Then, as the crowd applauded, four commemorative maple trees were planted in front of Aggie Hall: Mayor Mars planted the Civic Tree; the Girls' Tree was planted by Olga Smith, May Hawthorne and Marguerite Siggelks; the Boys' Tree by Harry Mounce, Harry Mouldey and Cecil Rowland; and the Women's Tree by Mrs. Campbell, president of the Women's Institute.

Dr. Esson Young, the provincial secretary and minister of education, presided over the ceremony and accepted as a keepsake from the citizens the silver trowel used to open the soil. Dr. Young told PoCo's children the maple trees symbolized Canada, "the land of equal rights, liberty and education—everything, in fact, that meant good citizenship."

There were people attending the ceremony, as PoCo historian Edith Chambers has written, "who could remember the area when the Indians far outnumbered the first white settlers." And on the subject of longevity, one of the children at that tree planting,

It seemed like all the town's residents gathered outside Aggie Hall for Inauguration Day (above). The Coquitlam City Band (below) provided musical entertainment for the festivities. Band members included Jack Conway, Pat Fiorie, Bud Fisher, Arthur Johnson, Bert Johnson, Bert Jolly, Reg Marshall, Mr. Shoemaker, and Joe Young.

The Mayor, Aldermen and Incorporation Committee of the City of Port Coquitlam,

have the honour to request the company of

at a Banquet to celebrate the

Incorporation

of the City of Port Coquitlam,

to be held at the Commercial Hotel, Port Coquitlam, Friday Evening, 18th of April, 1913, at 7 o'clock.

John F. Langan *James Mars,*
Chairman Incorporation *Mayor.*
Committee. *P. J. McIntyre,*
R.S.V.P. *Secretary.*

An invitation to a banquet celebrating Port Coquitlam's incorporation.

HISTORICAL FOOTNOTE

The first couple to be married in St. Catherine's Anglican Church after PoCo's incorporation were G. Roy Leigh and Alice Seabrook, on July 28, 1913. They lived just about where Shaughnessy Mall is today.

Harry Mounce, was around long enough to be given a surprise birthday party in August 1996 when he turned ninety-nine. Harry was one of that long line of PoCo people who worked at Essondale. He was there as a psychiatric nurse from 1931 to his retirement in 1963. He and his wife Merle bought a house on Fraser Street in 1937 for $900. Merle died in 1960. Harry Mounce died at age ninety-nine, having lived in Port Coquitlam all his life.

The city's inauguration was a heady and wonderfully encouraging day, and to mark it forever in the minds of the youngsters, Mayor Mars presented each of them with a small silver medallion, a replica of the city's emblem with its motto: By Commerce and Industry We Prosper.

Port Coquitlam was off to a dazzling start.

The mayor's optimism about the growth of the new city was justified: the entire Lower Mainland of British Columbia was experiencing an astonishing burst of growth, a growth that looked as if it might go on for a long time, and Port Coquitlam was right in the heart of it.

There were all sorts of indications the little city had a brilliant and busy future. It had recently been hooked up to an assured source of power from the BC Electric dam on Stave Lake. The CPR had moved its huge marshalling yards right into the centre of town. The new hospital at Essondale, just across the Lougheed Highway in Coquitlam, had opened on April 1, 1913, with plenty of jobs for locals. The city got twenty-four-hour telephone service on May 28, 1913, the same day the shingle mill on Pitt River Road began manufacturing. The Coquitlam Terminal Company announced plans to build a first-class hotel that would cost $45,000 (in 1913 dollars), and the city had a new water system installed by July 9, the same day on which the secretary of the school board reported an increase of 30 percent in school attendance over three months. And, reported the *Province* on April 10, 1913, "Dr. Hall of New Westminster had promised to donate a two-acre site on Mary's Hill for the erection of a hospital for Port Coquitlam city." The paper went on to say that the council thanked Dr. Hall, and appointed a committee to investigate the possibility of buying a further adjacent 3 acres (1.2 hectares) from him. Port Coquitlam Hospital opened July 16 at 25 Pitt River Road. A factory building cabinets started operations July 30, a $12,000 contract to build James Park School was let . . . and the Panama Canal was soon to open. What wonders the new canal would do for British Columbia's economy was anyone's guess, but PoCo's access to the deep waters of the Fraser River held great promise.

Port Coquitlam's first city clerk and police magistrate and tax collector—posts like these were often combined in small towns—was John Smith, a serious man, a devout Anglican and as plain as his name. Smith served the city steadily and competently for twenty-four years. (Incidentally, his salary when he began was $150 a month.) Smith and his wife Frances had been major financial forces behind the 1910 construction of the area's first Anglican church, St. Catherine's. Mrs. Smith was the first president of the church's Ladies Auxiliary, and it was under her auspices that the sale of needlework paid for the church organ. That first St. Catherine's was on the Dewdney Trunk Road (now Kingsway) just west of the railway bridge.

Considering the importance of the Dewdney Trunk, it's puzzling that finding detailed information on its history is extraordinarily difficult, but one telling item from a February 11, 1913, meeting of Coquitlam council (in which the main subject was the upcoming creation of Port Coquitlam) reads: "The Reeve reported verbally that he had gone to Victoria and interviewed the Government regarding completing the Dewdney Trunk Road and that he received assurances that the road from the Junction to

Harry Mounce at his ninety-ninth birthday party in 1996 (above), and his family's home nearly ninety years earlier (left). Could the small boy be Harry?

Vancouver would be completed early this year." By April 8 the mayor, engineer and Alderman Langan were named to a committee to "get other municipalities' support for the paving of Dewdney Trunk Road from the Pitt River to Vancouver."

Sometimes these council minutes are maddeningly incomplete, as in this item from February 26, 1913: "The report of Chief of Police Rounds as to the accidental shooting of Constable Marshall was received and ordered placed on file." There is a later reference to the location of the wound (Constable Marshall's leg), but no other information is forthcoming. Who shot the constable and what were the circumstances? A March 11, 1913, entry reads: "The action of the clerk in paying the account of the Coquitlam Transfer Co. for 7 tons of hay was endorsed." The hay was likely for the horses used by the city to carry out various public works, but the phrasing of that entry hints at a bit of contention. One longs to know!

First police chief was T.B. Thomas, and the first city engineer was the estimable John Kilmer. The latter had been born in Workworth, Ontario, in 1861, came to BC in 1898, and had been Vancouver's assistant engineer from 1900 to 1906. He and Mrs. Kilmer, the former Amy Root, had three children: Jane, Anna and Edward. Edward's daughter Cate (Mrs. M.C. Nicholson), who came to Port Coquitlam from Kamloops in 1929 at age six months, was the source for a good deal of information on the Kilmer family. Her grandfather's salary as chief engineer was $300 a month, a goodly sum for the time, underscored by this item from the May 14, 1913, *Star*: "The foundations have now been completed for City Engineer Kilmer's

Port Coquitlam residents gathered for social events like this church picnic at St. Andrew's Presbyterian in the city's early years.

residence at the corner of Knappen and Pooley Streets. It will be a modern eleven-roomed house." The house, a big beauty that John Kilmer built himself and which is now a day-care centre, is still standing . . . and nearby are Kilmer Elementary School (named for his daughter Jane) and Kilmer Park. "There used to be quite a big log cabin on his property," Cate Nicholson says, "and it was the oldest building in Port Coquitlam. The fellow who bought it took it apart very carefully and numbered all the logs and offered them to the city. I don't know what ever happened to those logs."

A note on salaries: a *Province* story dated March 29, 1913, reported from Ottawa that the income of the average Canadian family was estimated at $800 a year. The weekly expenditure "of a typical family of five on staple goods, fuel, lighting and rentals" in 1912 was $13.63 a week. So the Kilmer family could be described as comfortable. The four lots he bought cost $900.

An early PoCo council minute (April 22, 1913) noted that it had been resolved to "pay the Scavenger $100 per month, from May 1st, he to feed his own horse." The scavenger was employed to keep the streets clean, pick up refuse and so on. A week later, more expense was incurred: twenty-five chairs were purchased for city hall at $1.25 each.

A new city needed a new city hall, however. Kelly's Hall wasn't grand enough for the prosperous Pittsburgh of Canada that would soon be rising on the banks of the Fraser and the Pitt. A few days after incorporation, some members of council began visiting other city halls in the Lower Mainland (among them North Vancouver and Point Grey, then a municipality of its own) looking for inspiration and advice. There had been a plebiscite to approve the spending of funds to build the new hall, and a substantial three-storey structure was commissioned. Embarrassingly, someone forgot to include a provision for the cost of the land it would sit on. It took the better part of a year to work that out. Finally a portion of George Black's property at the corner of Shaughnessy and McAllister was chosen. (McAllister Street had been

John Kilmer, Port Coquitlam's first city engineer, with his granddaughter Cate Nicholson in June 1930. (Photo courtesy Cate Nicholson)

Aggie Hall was the scene of many community events, including this 1914 flower show.

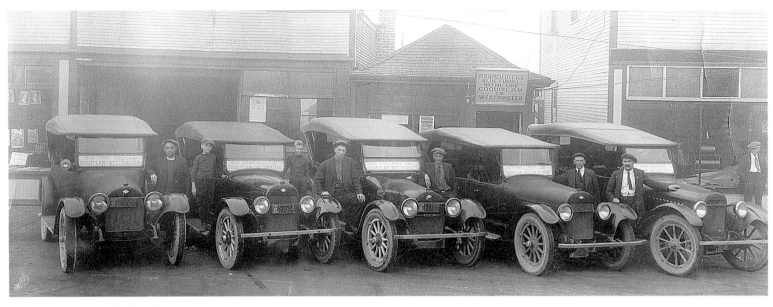

Arthur R. Smith's Blue Funnel jitneys carried passengers from PoCo to other Lower Mainland towns. The drivers were, left to right, unknown, Douglas R. Smith, Bruce McArthur, Arthur Smith, Dick Irvine, and William Pringle. (Photo courtesy Douglas R. Smith)

HISTORICAL FOOTNOTE

A nice historical coincidence: The first time the Fraser River name was used was on an informal 1813 map of Western Canada prepared by David Thompson, exactly one hundred years before PoCo's incorporation. Thompson's sketch of the river, which he named the Fraser, also showed the as-yet-unnamed Pitt and Coquitlam Rivers.

named for R.H. McAllister, a realtor working out of the Vancouver office of F.N. Trites & Company. "Values are Bound to Double in a Short While," he advertised.) Two lots adjacent to the Black property were purchased at $2,000 each, that money to be raised from general revenue.

A Masonic Lodge was established in 1913. That was the same year a new highway—which had been known as the Vancouver Road—was paved and re-opened as Kingsway between Vancouver and New Westminster. It increased and improved traffic flow in the area and, among other things, provided a convenient route for Tom Coldicutt's Blue Funnel bus line. By 1920 Blue Funnel jitneys (maximum number of passengers: seven) were serving PoCo, among other Lower Mainland towns. Annie Osborne—here since 1923 with her husband Lint—remembers those jitneys, which took about thirty-five minutes to transport you to New Westminster.

With all these transportation improvements, the city approached the CPR and asked the railway to build a new train station for PoCo, one more fitting the city's expected prosperity. But the railway refused. Then in October 1913, city residents voted 178 to 70 to move the station to the north end of Schoolhouse Road, now Mary Hill Road. The railway refused to do that, too, and that old Westminster Junction station at the old Kingsway Avenue location was used for nearly fifty more years until it was torn down in the 1960s. (It was replaced by Shaughnessy Station.) The CPR did build a new bridge in 1913 to replace its original wooden swing span, and it's there to this day.

Relations between the railway and the town have often been prickly, sometimes downright angry. One councillor recalled a time when the railway was going to spray some herbicide. The city put in an application to the railway to have the spraying delayed while they studied it. "They finished their spraying, *then* they dealt with the application."

For all its aloofness toward the city, the railway occasionally shows its less corporate side: starting in 1984 it donated $8,000 a year for three years to the library to pay for a microfilm reader that served into the 1990s. And the CPR, of course, made PoCo possible. The city's Business Improvement Association has mulled the possibility of emphasizing the city's railway past (and present) to increase its attractiveness as a tourist destination.

Essondale, which would also provide many jobs for locals, opened officially in 1913 as a branch of the main asylum in New Westminster. It was built to accommodate 650 patients, and the man in charge was a Dr. Freeze. Some 340 "chronic" male patients transferred from New Westminster, and by the end of 1913 there were 453 patients at Essondale and 466 at New Westminster. Three years later there were more patients in Essondale (687) than at the main asylum (518). Centre Lawn opened (as the Acute Building) on November 1, 1924. There were more than fifty buildings on the site during its mid-'50s peak, with a staff of 2,000, and by 1956 there were 4,306 patients.

Port Coquitlam held its first real election on January 15, 1914. (The first council had run unopposed.) James Mars's cachet as first mayor proved insufficient: he was defeated 203 to 174 by John R. MacKenzie, who would serve four one-year terms. MacKenzie was good friends with the Harry Galer family, and Harry named his son after his friend. (James

The CPR built a new railway bridge (above) in 1913.

A few years later it was patrolled by the military during World War I.

John R. MacKenzie, Port Coquitlam's second mayor, lived in this house, which still retained a rural aura.

HISTORICAL FOOTNOTE

Scattered evidences of the city's railway past pop up now and again. In 1999 city historian Lois Milne was approached by a woman who had just bought a piece of property in town and had found some burned bricks and a kiln on her land. Was it possible there was some historical significance to the find? Lois did some research and discovered the property in question had once been used by Chinese railway workers to make charcoal from local maple trees.

Mars returned as an alderman in 1920 and '21 when his brother Arthur was mayor.)

According to the May 9, 1914, *Star*, the "new $50,000 two-storey Terminal Hotel on Busteed Avenue will be completed early next week." The twenty-room inn came complete with a small cafe. Busteed Avenue, named for F.F. Busteed, who was the CPR's general superintendent in Vancouver at the time, is now Tyner Street.

A week later the *Star* published plans for the new city hall. The architects were G.P. Bowie and C.H. Flow. One feature: a jail in the basement. A 1914 report by the Board of Works, echoing the optimism of the previous year's Inauguration Day, stated: "During the year the City Hall has been built. This is a substantial structure of brick and stone, total cost being about $19,000. Ample room has been provided for a staff necessary for a city of 25,000 people."

However, a cataclysmic event half a world away had an effect on the little city's future. On June 28, 1914, Austrian Archduke Ferdinand was assassinated by a Serbian nationalist in Sarajevo in Bosnia. The outcome: Europe and then much of the rest of the world stumbled into war. Britain's turn to declare war on what came to be called the Central Powers came August 4, following the German invasion of Belgium. Britain's involvement automatically meant Canada would be drawn in, and the very next day Ottawa ordered the enlistment and mobilization of a Canadian army division of 21,000 men. Many more than that volunteered.

In PoCo, most men enlisted in the Royal Westminster Regiment, a recruitment regiment for the 47th and 131st battalions. Many men served in the army's Railway Construction Corps. The first troop train left Vancouver on August 21, 1914, and the first Canadian contingent sailed from Quebec on October 3 in some thirty merchant ships packed with troops, weapons, vehicles and horses. More than thirty thousand men were aboard, and it's certain PoCo men were among them.

In the midst of all this, the Panama Canal opened for business on August 15, 1914, and PoCo's new city hall opened Tuesday, October 27, with a public celebration for which the Women's Institute provided tea and refreshments. Total cost for the building: $19,180, under budget by $820. The hall wasn't fully furnished—and it wouldn't need to be for many years! The Hynes Cement Company designed an unofficial coat of arms for the new city, a concrete crest showing two beavers. They were symbolic of the city's motto, and city fathers—who approved the design in May 1913—happily mounted the crest above the McAllister Avenue entrance where it may be seen to this day. When the new building opened, Kelly's Hall became the city's fire hall.

As a result of the world war, PoCo's Pacific Construction Company became one of the Lower Mainland's largest shipyards. It had started in 1905 as the Standard Construction Company, which in 1914 expanded to take over the yards of the Coquitlam Shipbuilding and Marine Railway Company.

This latter company operated at the foot of Pitt River Road, where the CPR had planned to build a shipyard. It is not clear why the railroad did not go ahead with that particular project, but a December 4, 1965, retrospective in the *Columbian* does report that in 1913 a Nova Scotia shipbuilder named Shaftner set up the Coquitlam Shipbuilding and Marine Railway Company just at the mouth of the Pitt River. Shaftner hired a great number of local men, and with some experienced supervisors set to work to build a four-masted sailing vessel. Sometime during 1914 the *Coquitlam City* went down the ways to the cheers of hundreds of well-wishers. The ship, sadly, came to a bad end. Heavy with a load of lumber, it ran aground on a tropical reef on its maiden voyage to Australia and sank. (An excellent model of that ship, built by the art department at Terry Fox Senior Secondary, can be seen on the second floor of city hall.) Shaftner, it's said, lost the $85,000 profit he'd made

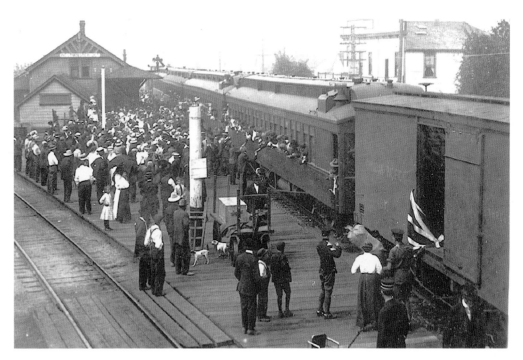

Port Coquitlam's young men gathered at the train station before heading off to fight in World War I.

In 1914 this contingent corps was ready to be called up when needed.

The war brought a brief shipbuilding boom to the city, as Pacific Construction Company won a contract to build five ships for the Greek government.

on the construction of the ship in a real estate investment that went badly. He returned to Nova Scotia and soon became successful in shipbuilding again.

Pacific Construction got an order from the government of Greece to build five wooden steam-powered cargo ships. Under the management of H.P. Simpson, the yard was expanded to handle as many as three hulls in various stages of construction at the same time. Up to four hundred men—carpenters, shipwrights, metal workers and other tradesmen—worked on the assignment during most of the war years, from 1914 to 1919, and Pacific Construction's payroll was almost $3,000 a day.

All five ships were launched on schedule. The hulls were 300 feet long, built entirely of wood, and were towed down the Fraser and around to Coal Harbour in Vancouver to have their boilers and engines fitted.

With the war's end, orders for ships stopped and the yard closed for good.

The busy men at Pacific Construction were a misleading indication of the economic impact of the Great War in PoCo. Their activity was feverish, but short-lived, and the war brought the city virtually nothing else in terms of employment.

The war did affect PoCo in smaller ways. Rose Phillips relates that her father, Don Chine (*chee*-nay), came here in 1913 from the town of Santa

Nicola in Italy's Reggio Calabria district and got a job with the railway. He wanted to bring his wife, Marie Giuseppa, over (they'd been married in Italy just before Don left), but the war intervened and Marie wasn't able to get here until 1920. "They lived right at Westminster Junction," Rose recalls with a smile, "and the first morning after she arrived, my mother put her hand out of the bed and felt water. The Coquitlam River had flooded overnight." Mrs. Chine didn't speak English at first, and when she was shopping she would indicate what she wanted by pointing at it. Rose was born in PoCo in 1923, her sister Phyllis (actually Filomena) earlier. The Chine children spoke Italian at home and English outside. "I've lost a lot of the Italian now," Rose says, "but if I'm in a roomful of Italians, it starts coming back!"

A drop-in centre was established in the basement of city hall (not far from the city jail, which was also in the basement) and there the members of the Women's Institute—whose president was Jane Kilmer, the chief engineer's daughter—and other volunteers rolled bandages and prepared dressings to be sent to the troops overseas. A short-lived group called the St. Andrew's Guild, made up of local Scots, was organized to help in the war effort, too. It sent clothing and other needed items overseas, then disbanded when the war ended.

The students of Central School "adopted" a Canadian prisoner of war and sent him socks and other small items of clothing. The boys and girls at James Park School contributed five dollars toward a Prisoner of War Fund, a not insubstantial amount of money to be raised by schoolchildren in 1918. Like hundreds of other Canadian towns, Port Coquitlam contributed its mite toward the great struggle.

Local organized sport tended to die out during the war, frustrating for a town whose football team had gone undefeated for all of 1914.

A man named Angus W. Keith, a broker, first pops up in PoCo's history in 1914 as an alderman. His council history is odd and fragmented: he was an alderman from 1914 to 1917, then mayor for one term in 1918, then he dropped out of sight, then he was an alderman again in 1922, dropped out of sight again, and then returned as an alderman from 1939 to 1943.

Another of the city's mysteries is the "Sabulite" factory. Sabulite is likely described somewhere, but details are sparse. We know it was an explosive of some kind, used for clearing stumps—and, says Lois Milne, also used in World War I weaponry—and that the plant

The Coquitlam City, *the first boat built in the PoCo shipyards, was an eye-catching vessel, but it came to grief on its maiden voyage. (Photo courtesy Edith Chambers)*

The Coquitlam Football Team, posed with its trophies behind Aggie Hall, was BC champion in 1913-14.

HISTORICAL FOOTNOTE

On August 28, 1915, the first train of the Canadian Northern Pacific Railway (soon to become the Canadian National) arrived in Vancouver. The line was on the southern side of the Fraser and had no direct impact on PoCo, but if you stood by the river you could see the CNR trains running along the other shore.

opened in 1914 "on Prairie Road at the Pitt River waterfront." We know that when the 1920 PoCo fire occurred there were fears the flames would reach a Sabulite chemical warehouse near the downtown, but aside from that we know very little. (The Sabulite Company wrote to council after the fire to assure them the materials stored were not explosive.) A March 21, 1914, clipping says the plant's main floor "will accommodate seven machines," and there will be a drying room for storage of calcium silicide and of sabulite. Calcium silicide is a deoxidizer and degasser for steel and cast-iron. But what is sabulite?

The war didn't stop growth completely. The University of British Columbia opened in 1915, and its Fairview location in Vancouver put it within reach of eligible local students. In 1915 a man named Percy Jackson and his family came to PoCo. The Jacksons are memorable because their home was the first in the city to be built north of the CPR line. It was on the east side of Oxford Street just a few steps north of Prairie. Percy was a milkman.

The Forrest family also arrived in 1915. Sam Forrest operated a tugboat service on the Pitt and Fraser Rivers, and more than eighty years later, Forrests are still occupied in that trade. More on the Forrests later.

PoCo's first-born baby was also on the move. You can tell where the David family lived. There's a street in the area named for them. It's near the top end of Coast Meridian. "We moved up there in 1916, when I was three years old," says Jim. "Dad had worked at Essondale cutting wood, then he got a job as a logger on Burke Mountain. When we moved he became a farmer and a strawberry grower. It was kind of crowded: six of us in a two-room shack. We started with ten acres and went up to forty later. We had some animals just for our own use. It was tough getting water at first, we had a windlass arrangement, then we got a pump."

In 1917, while the war was still raging, Robert Wilson moved his family here from New Westminster. They settled on the delta of the Coquitlam River and Wilson started a dairy farm—known to locals as the Wilson Ranch. He eventually sold it to Colony Farm (Wilson's silo is still there). With the proceeds he bought several properties in the downtown.

The seeds of a long-time PoCo tradition were sown in 1916 when Wynter Maxwell, a teacher at James Park Elementary School, started thinking about a springtime event that would bring students, teachers and parents together for a day of fun. "She hit on May Day as the perfect model for her event," says a 1998 booklet, "and a Port Coquitlam tradition was born." The growth of May Day is detailed in a sidebar in this chapter.

One other wartime item of note: The next time you pass by the Europe Bakery on Shaughnessy Street, give a thought to the historic significance of the site. It was there on January 11, 1915, in a house where the bakery now stands, that Port Coquitlam's first set of twins was born. They were John and Ethel, born to Harry and Christina Galer.

But now a theme emerges that will dominate PoCo's history for the next three decades: financial struggle. An economic depression settled gloomily all over the Lower Mainland and throughout British Columbia and the western provinces. Historian Margaret Ormsby writes, "British Columbia had suffered a serious disruption of its economic life with the outbreak of war. A fall in the price of copper and other metals had deranged the mining industry; lack of shipping had caused supplies of manufactured timber and of canned salmon to pile up . . . From the figure of 2 million acres in 1910 the sales of public lands fell to an infinitesimal total of 45,000 acres in 1914. In 1915, the government had to declare a moratorium on payments for Crown Lands as well as for timber and coal rights."

The treaty that officially ended World War I was signed June 29, 1919. But the joy felt at the return of the soldiers was severely tempered by continuing economic woe. By the end of 1916 the city's tax arrears amounted to nearly $145,000.

The shipyard closed in 1918 (its timbers were torn down and used for sidewalks in Pitt Meadows), and in September of that year Vancouver newspapers printed a listing from Port Coquitlam of properties available for sale as a result of nonpayment of taxes. The list took up *four pages* of tiny print. Most of the tax arrears were astonishingly low, many under $20, but people had no money to pay them. A late September auction of the properties attracted fewer than a dozen people, and they bought a mere 83 lots

The Jackson family arrived in Port Coquitlam in 1915. Mr. and Mrs. Percy Jackson (above) moved into the first home north of the CPR line. Percy (below left) and his brother didn't have to go far from the house to find open fields for hunting. (Photos courtesy Margaret Jackson)

Before the post-war economic downturn, city engineer John Kilmer posed confidently on an empty wooden sidewalk stretching far into the distance, surrounded by vast tracts of empty land ripe for development.

of the 1,300 for sale. Total proceeds of the auction were $3,545.53. The value of the land in city hands: $81,037.05. The *Vancouver World* commented that even at the low prices—in some cases the properties were for sale for less than 10 percent of their 1913 boom prices—the lots could not be sold.

Some of the names on the list of people giving up property are well-known in PoCo history: Langan, Lobb, Galer, Loftus Scott, William Routley . . . even city engineer John Kilmer's name is there. The broad and merciless sword of the taxman mowed down virtually everyone. The name of the Coquitlam Transfer Company, which had had grandiose plans, appears hundreds of times. The company seemed to have owned a third of the city, yet ended up flat on its back. Other names shown as owners of many lots: Charles Goodyear and Evelyn M. Goodyear, Fraser River Sand & Gravel, J.A.L. McAlpine, R.H.M. McAllister, H. and M.M. Boucher-James, H.R. Fullerton, North American Lumber Company, Pitt River Lumber Company, Thomas Corbett. Many of the property holders were speculators living in faraway England, who had bought the property after seeing CPR advertisements in their local news-papers. The more than 1,200 lots that didn't sell, however, would prove to be a valuable asset for the future of the beleaguered little city.

It needed all the help it could get. Hard on the heels of the financial slump came trouble of a different kind. A worldwide epidemic of Spanish influenza, which was killing millions in Europe, Asia and North America, arrived in British Columbia. Soldiers returning from the war unknowingly spread the disease all over North America. Ironically, despite the name of the disease, the outbreak had started in the US and been taken to Europe by soldiers. The virulence and suddenness of this strain of flu was frightening: a person who was healthy and vigorous in the morning could be dead by nightfall.

Port Coquitlam glumly awaited its turn. It came on October 5, 1918, when military author-ities commandeered the Aggie Hall for an emergency hospital; 160 returning soldiers had been stricken. Later, the vacant Terminal Hotel was also used. The first person to die from the flu was a Private Johns, on October 12. Schools, theatres and bars were closed. The first civilian to succumb, John Raymond, died on October 26. Others followed, including pioneer Matt Marshall. Worldwide, the Spanish flu killed more than 20 million people, perhaps as many as 40 million, before it was vanquished. (Even the lower figure is higher than the num-ber of casualties in the Great War itself.)

As the flu epidemic faded in 1919, a new company was created in PoCo, a company still around more than eighty years later. Harry Galer went into business with a partner named Charlie Case and started the Port Coquitlam Transfer Company. They set up the company with two Giant trucks—the brand, not the dimensions. (An indication of the size of the town in those days: the company's phone number was 90. That's all: 90.) "In those days," Joe Galer, Harry's grandson, told the *Tri-City News*, in the 1990s, "if you had a truck you were considered wealthy." They trucked coal and other bulk materials around and, besides other work, won a contract to haul coal to the Boys' Industrial School at Essondale. "We hauled anything," says Harry's son John. "My dad hauled explosives from the Dominion Powder Plant. I remember hauling sawdust from Fraser Mills and sacking coal off the trains as they came in. The coal sacks weighed 100 pounds and we would pick them up and deliver them. Then we started hauling some lumber, too." One of the Galer drivers was a young fellow named Sam Waddell. When he retired in 1985, Sam had worked for Port Coquitlam Transfer and its successor companies for forty-three years.

This house, the home of Loftus Scott, was the first to get electricity. It was on Pipeline Road (now Westwood). (Photo courtesy Scott family)

Harry's company, now known as PoCo Building Supply, is the city's oldest . . . and his grandson Joe runs it. It originally opened at 2581 Shaughnessy, where the Royal Bank is today.

There was another economic "advance" in 1919. The US brought in Prohibition, and with the border less than 30 kilometres away, drinking establishments all over southern BC did a thriving business. Port Coquitlam got its share.

But these were mere blips. PoCo's economy was still ailing. Young G. Roy Leigh (half the entire civic staff, the other half being city clerk John Smith) was collector and assessor for a city where there was virtually nothing to collect. Instead of the fabulous expected revenues there was a $500,000 debt. The city was committed to build schools, build roads, provide water, but there wasn't even enough tax money to pay the interest on the sinking fund on the bonded debt. By 1920 some 75 percent of all properties in the city had reverted back to the city through tax sale. The remaining 25 percent were charged with payment of debt and maintenance.

In 1920 the federal department of labour reported that the cost of living for the average Canadian family (size not given) was $15.98 a week, substantially more than it had been before the war. At the same time, on November 2, 1920, wages at Fraser Mills were cut 10 percent. A month later they were cut by 20 percent.

But when other Lower Mainland municipalities (like Burnaby and both City and District of North Vancouver) went into receivership and had their councils dismissed and their affairs handled by an appointed commissioner, PoCo kept afloat. That was Roy Leigh's work. He played a hand, too, in winning provincial refinancing legislation for the city. Strict economy was practised. Salaries were lowered and the small city staff moved into a little back office, leaving the big one empty. The building's furnace went cold—a small, potbellied heater took

May Day

In 1916 Wynter Maxwell, a teacher at James Park Elementary School in Port Coquitlam, wanted to introduce some kind of springtime event to bring students, teachers and parents together for a day of fun. The old English tradition of May Day suggested itself. It was held only at James Park Elementary at first, but seven years later, Mrs. Tom Routley—president of PoCo's Women's Institute at the time—suggested a joint May Day involving both the city's schools, James Park and Central. "Held alongside the Coquitlam River and ruled over by May Queen Evelyn Mars, it was the first Community May Day." That 1923 event began a tradition that has occurred every year since and, in fact, has become the city's biggest and happiest annual event. Just about everyone gets involved. The 1999 May Day parade took more than an hour to pass, and the list of participating groups was six pages long. Not bad for a city of PoCo's size.

In 1924 May Day activities moved to the corner of Wilson and Mary Hill Road (where the courthouse is today), and a porch post on a woodshed there was used as the flower-bedecked maypole. By 1925 the Women's Institute had taken over the event, and May Day celebrations moved again, this time to Aggie Park. Until World War II, a volunteer crew from Essondale would come in and build a temporary May Day bandstand, but in 1946 a permanent bandstand was built. The May Queen's chair, kept at Wilson Centre, was donated in 1931 by a Mrs. Struthers. In the nearly seventy years since, the only change to the chair has been the trim. (A note on the Queen: There was a time when contest rules required that the May Queen be born in PoCo, but that restriction was eventually dropped.)

Besides the selection of a May Queen, chosen by lot from girls attending the city's elementary schools, there were races for the children, afternoon tea, a baseball game, a Royal Banquet, dances and more. By the early 1930s a parade had been added, and John Galer of the Port Coquitlam Transfer Company (now PoCo Building Supply) donated the use of a flatbed truck. The truck was decorated by members of the WI and served as a "royal carriage" to transport the young Royal Party to Aggie Hall. "Even the Second World War didn't stop the affair," says a city-produced booklet on May Day

May Day 1999 was a rainy affair.

history. "The Elks Club joined in, putting on races for the young fry and giving each child an ice cream cone."

The celebrations were held on a Friday, which had become an unofficial holiday, but they switched to Saturdays in the 1950s when School District #43 stepped in and disallowed the selection of Friday, a regular school day. By 1962 the WI realized the event had become too big to be handled by one group. "Following the advice of the city council," the booklet continues, "a meeting was called and eight organizations formed a new May Day Committee: the Women's Institute, the Royal Canadian Legion and Legion Auxiliary, the Elks Club and Royal Purple, the Kinsmen, the Lions and the PoCo Band Auxiliary. Mrs. Elmer Routley, the president of the WI, became chairman."

May Day kept growing. Celebrations moved from the Aggie Grounds to McLean Park in 1967 and were held there for four years before moving to the Arena. In 1970 the City provided a professional float, which was not only featured in the annual parade but was also taken out of town to community events with the Royal Party. Since 1993 the May Queen has been joined by an Ambassador, a young boy also chosen by lot from a local school. Evelyn (Mars) Hay, the first May Queen, now lives in Vancouver and was one of the attendees in 1998 when the city held its seventy-fifth May Day and invited every May Queen it could locate.

From a single-day celebration, May Day grew to a weekend event, then a four-day event, and in 1998 became a week-long celebration of community pride and spirit.

May Queens and Ambassadors

1923 Queen Evelyn Mars	1954 Queen Lois Bloomfield	
1924 Queen Beatrice Osborne	1955 Queen Sylvia Luschnat	
1925 Queen Helen Berry	1956 Queen Ruth Langley	
1926 Queen Lucy Mabbett	1957 Queen Judy Kilthau	
1927 Queen Amy Colodin	1958 Queen April Wingrove	
1928 Queen Betty Hunter	1959 Queen Marlene Cave	
1929 Queen Victorine Young	1960 Queen June Levis	
1930 Queen Amelia Walters	1961 Queen Beverly Cuttnell	
1931 Queen Mary Morris	1962 Queen Louise Sweeney	*Port Coquitlam's maypole in 1920.*
1932 Queen Evelyn Hemphill	1963 Queen Anita Luschnat	1985 Queen Cari Lecky
1933 Queen Jean Richmond	1964 Queen Dawne Friemel	1986 Queen Kimberley Fairclough
1934 Queen Doris Cunningham	1965 Queen Debbie Rieu	1987 Queen Debbie Jo Gill
1935 Queen Norma Lawson	1966 Queen Debbie Posart	1988 Queen Tracy Bradley
1936 Queen Phyllis Chilcott	1967 Queen Linda Ramsey	1989 Queen Amy French
1937 Queen Margaret Gardner	1968 Queen Joan Stamhuis	1990 Queen Jessie Urquhart
1938 Queen Pauline Talbot	1969 Queen Toni Hart	1991 Queen Talia Young
1939 Queen Helen Gordon	1970 Queen Joyce Butler	1992 Queen Sabrina Shong
1940 Queen Blanche Cole	1971 Queen Cathy Goddard	1993 Queen Jemma Bond
1941 Queen Ida Watt	1972 Queen Lori Jacobsen	Ambassador Tony Ramos
1942 Queen Nancy Ogilvie	1973 Queen Chris Graham	1994 Queen Elisa Nightingale
1943 Queen Shirley Brewer	1974 Queen Diane Jansen	Ambassador Kristopher Hardjono
1944 Queen Donna Hartwig	1975 Queen Mandy Connell	1995 Queen Jennifer D'Alessandro
1945 Queen Margaret Hall	1976 Queen Coreen Morton	Ambassador Nick Palidor
1946 Queen Jean Davison	1977 Queen Lisa Hanson	1996 Queen Kelly-Jean Timms
1947 Queen Carolyn Ogilvie	1978 Queen Tina Robins	Ambassador Darren Miller
1948 Queen Sheila Wald	1979 Queen Debbie Clifton	1997 Queen Samantha Lowe
1949 Queen Noreen Marshall	1980 Queen Venae Harder	Ambassador Adam Watson
1950 Queen Karen McLellan	1981 Queen Candace Poole	1998 Queen Christine van Beekum
1951 Queen Jean Fletcher	1982 Queen Michelle May	Ambassador Sean Bird
1952 Queen Marjorie Edwards	1983 Queen Tammy Lambertus	1999 Queen Stephanie Briggs
1953 Queen Glenda Rae	1984 Queen Antonietta DiBauda	Ambassador Ryan Keefe

Many Port Coquitlam residents commuted to work at Fraser Mills. The sawmill continued operating through hard times, though often with reduced wages.

its place. The top floor of city hall was completely empty and stayed that way for years. (The mayor's office and the council chambers occupy the space today.)

It would not have been a happy time for Arthur Mars, James's brother, who, back from war service, was elected PoCo's fourth mayor in 1919. He held office until 1924, through the most difficult times in the city's history.

In eastern Canada, individual bondholders began to receive letters signed by G.R. Leigh, who, said a newspaper story on his 1954 retirement, "set down conditions exactly as they were, man to man, and honest." Leigh asked for interest to be reduced to a straight 3 percent from the usual 5, 6 and 7 percent. City payments dropped from $38,000 to $18,000 annually. Bonds were refinanced to mature in 1962. Painfully, slowly and steadily Port Coquitlam began the long journey back to financial stability.

Then disaster struck again. (PoCo was not having a good decade.)

Shortly after noon on August 5, 1920, a fire started in fire chief Dick McKinley's apartment on the upper floor of Kelly's Hall—PoCo's first city hall, which was now the town's fire hall. The fire got out of control . . . and began to burn down the fire hall. The city's fire engine, a modern $8,000 #10 American LaFrance "combination chemical hose and ladder truck of the best type," was pulled from the building and saved. The first building to actually go up in flames was the Coquitlam Hotel—sparks from the fire hall had drifted into its upper floors.

There was insufficient hose to function properly, and a hurried call was put in to New Westminster's fire department. It was there in fifteen minutes and took charge of all the fire-fighters.

"Shortly before 1 o'clock," the *Province* reported, "the flames leaped the Dewdney trunk road and set fire to the CPR freight shed. This structure was soon wiped out and employees of the CPR were valiantly fighting to keep the flames away from the passenger depot." They succeeded, although it got a severe scorching. "Had it caught," said the *Province*, "the recently erected factory of the Gregory Rubber & Tire Company would have been in danger, as only the double tracks of the railroad separate the two buildings."

The flames spread to the little downtown district, which was then on the Dewdney. Soon, most of the downtown—a modest side-by-side collection of a dozen small wooden buildings—was destroyed. "So hot was the bitulithic pavement on top of which the hose was laid," said the *Vancouver Sun* of August 6, "that with the weight of the water the hose sank into the road material and suddenly burst into flame."

"All business was suspended in the city," the *British Columbian* reported the next day, "merchants in other sections of the settlement locking their stores, and CPR switching crews coming up from the yards, all to render assistance. Too much credit cannot be handed the ladies of the city, many braving the heat of the flames and the streams of water in order to

Canadian Western Lumber's company town at Fraser Mills, one of Port Coquitlam's neighbours.

assist the less fortunate citizens in removing household goods. The Pitt river road reaching to the Essondale boundary was lined on both sides with autos filled with merchandise or household effects and whole families could be seen lugging whatever they could lay their hands on away in order not to be caught napping should the wind veer."

The "streams of water" referred to came courtesy of surrounding fire departments and other volunteers: Port Moody helped, so did Maillardville and, as mentioned, New Westminster.

The fire was under control by two o'clock, two hours after it had started.

But its repercussions went on much longer.

The fire added to the financial woes of the little city. Because it had started in the city's own fire hall, the city was liable for damages, and soon the claims began to come in. The list of losses was long: the fire hall itself; the thirty-five-room Coquitlam Hotel, owned since August 1, 1910, by William Routley and a Mr. Martyn (and uninsured); D. Smith's pool room; Craig & Sorbie's blacksmith shop; W. Selby's garage; the Blue Funnel Bus Line office; Wilson's Shoe Store; the *Coquitlam Star* printing office and plant; CPR freight sheds; several barns; and three houses. There was damage to the Royal Bank, the post office, the CPR depot and Dr. Sutherland's office, and the top floor of Jake Rowland's Cement Block was scorched. Rowland's three-storey building was credited with blocking the advance of the flames.

Fire crews and volunteers came from Port Coquitlam and neighbouring communities to fight the 1920 fire (above), but much of the town was left a smoking pile of ash.

The total losses ran to about $250,000, equivalent to many millions today.

There was, happily, no loss of life nor even injury. Lillian Rowland—married a year and just nine days away from the birth of her first child—had to help her husband Douglas carry the family furniture down the back stairs and out of harm's way.

At the central office of the BC Telephone Company the operators remained at their posts, even though some of them were shocked (literally) when the phone lines and the electrical lines came crashing down together.

Looters were busy in the days following the blaze. From the *Province* of August 7, 1920: "Mr. Martin of the Coquitlam Hotel got out of the bar-room a quantity of cigars and tobacco and innocuous fluids which were hurriedly placed on the side of the railway track. He estimates $200 worth was nefariously annexed."

The Coquitlam Hotel, shown here in 1910 with a troop of the BC Horse lined up in front, was one of the casualties of the fire.

Even worse than the financial impact, perhaps, was the embarrassment. Buried within the September 1920 minutes of PoCo's city council meeting is a furious reference by Mayor Arthur Mars to the man who investigated the fire for the provincial government. The essence of Mars's reaction is that if Fire Investigating Officer J.A. Thomas's report as summarized in the September 13, 1920, *Province* newspaper accurately reflected his views, then Thomas was "unfit to hold office." The fury was understandable: Thomas's report was devastating. He placed the blame for the fire on the city council. They had failed, he said, to have a volunteer fire brigade organized and had failed to enforce the city bylaws "respecting the use of stovepipes through partitions and roofs."

According to the *Province*, "If it was not for the seriousness of the loss occasioned to many citizens, declares the fire investigation officer, the story of the Port Coquitlam fire would read like a village comedy. When the fact that the firehall was burning was discovered by several aldermen and citizens, they ran upstairs and then downstairs, dodging about the fire engine, but made no attempt for some time to pull the equipment from the hall. There was a hydrant within a few feet of the door, but no one thought of making use of it by attaching a hose to it. The greater part of the city's hose was hanging in the tower of the hall, where it subsequently burned.

"The fire chief, Mr. Thomas says, admitted that in addition to that position he also filled

The Myrtle Hotel on Dewdney Trunk Road (now Kingsway) was not in danger during the 1920 fire, but it was swept away by the 1921 flood.

the offices of chief of police, tax collector, pound-keeper, license collector and other positions so numerous that he had forgotten them." For assistance in case of fire, the investigator said, Chief McKinley depended on anyone he could pick up. "There had been no fire drill for the past six years," Thomas continued, "and the evidence of the chief was to the effect that he had never had a day's training in fire fighting in his life."

Thomas concluded that in his experienced opinion the fire had started when smouldering soot escaped from a hole in the stovepipe and ignited the building. He concluded, "I earnestly recommend that a volunteer fire department for this city be at once organized, and that the present chief, because of his many other duties, should be relieved from this work. A competent man should be appointed by the council to the position of chief of the fire department."

Details are meagre, but the city was taken to court by various people who had suffered losses, and after three trials, the last two of which it lost, Port Coquitlam paid out an indemnity totalling $60,000. (It's not clear why that settlement was so much lower than the cost of the damage. Perhaps private insurance covered much of the damage, or maybe it was simply a case of the city not having enough money.)

The newspaper coverage of the 1920 fire gives us a starting date for one of PoCo's major industrial plants. In its September 13 story the *Province* made a passing reference to the "recently opened" Gregory Tire and Rubber Company. This was a substantial $69,000 three-storey plant, directly north of the railway tracks at Westminster Junction station, which made tires and tubes for farm machinery and bicycles. A 1920 report from Mayor Arthur Mars says, in part, "The outlook for 1921 is bright, and with the rubber works in full running I think we are justified in complete confidence in the future."

The late Keith Milne, at his wife Lois's behest, drew up a brief history of the Gregory plant and its successor (where he was employed). From this we learn that the Gregory plant ran until 1926, when it closed under circumstances that are still murky. One version is that the owner skipped town, another that it simply went into bankruptcy. Perhaps both are correct. In any event, the building sat empty for nine long years. The supervisor at the plant was a young man named Robert Percival Ogilvie, father of long-time PoCo resident Nancy

Ogilvie, source of much information in this book. (Her father died in 1942 at age forty-five, when Nancy was twelve.)

"When troubles come," said Hamlet, "they come not single spies but in battalions." After years of economic depression, a flu epidemic and a disastrous fire, PoCo next experienced severe flooding on the Coquitlam River. On October 28, 1921, the CPR's bridge and the adjacent bridge carrying the Dewdney Trunk Road were knocked out by a gigantic log jam, and half the city was under water. People were transported across the Coquitlam River on an aerial cable. (Mary Galer remembers being carried on that cable.) St.

You needed a boat to get ice cream during the 1921 flood.

Catherine's Anglican Church was torn off its foundations, floated away and ended up perched on a downstream sandbar. Residents in the three-storey Myrtle Hotel thought they were safe until the whole structure began to tremble violently. They stampeded down the stairs and out the door to safety as, with a huge groan, the entire hotel was wrenched off its foundations and sent sailing downriver. An onlooker said the hotel looked "like an ark" as it disappeared into the distance. Sinclair's Jewellers and Jack Baumgartner's barbershop were also swept away. Jeweller John Sinclair kept dashing back into his building to save stock and got out with just seconds to spare when a strong wave washed his shop away. (Some of these places had moved across the river after the 1920 fire. Out of the frying pan and into the flood!) Colony Farm was completely inundated, and there was substantial crop and dike damage.

"This," said historian Edith Chambers, "was the lowest point in the city's history." The CPR sent sleeping cars as temporary shelter for those forced from their homes, and brought in emergency food supplies.

Port Coquitlam's financial situation had now become so dire that the city was forced to sell its cherished fire engine in late 1921 and replace it with a converted dump truck. (And it paid dearly for that move the next year when another fire hit the downtown.) The city teetered on the brink of bankruptcy.

But it didn't tip over.

One result of the flood was that several shops and other businesses rebuilt on the east side of the river. That changed the location of PoCo's "downtown" to Shaughnessy Street. A fire

Locals survey the damage of the 1921 flood. The force of the waters twisted the rails of the CPR bridge.

station with one bay and attached living quarters for the chief was built on Shaughnessy to be nearer the new business district.

It's been more than seventy-five years, but John Galer still vividly recalls another incident that happened in 1921. He was six years old and accompanying his dad, who was delivering a drum of gas to the ferry. Harry Galer cranked the truck, it sparked . . . and proved to be in gear. The truck pushed him through the railing and he grabbed on for dear life, with the rear tires of the truck up in the air, spinning furiously, while little John sat open-mouthed in the cab and gripped the seat. "A fellow pulled me out, and another man pulled my dad up. He was in hospital for a while because of that." Harry Galer was on council at the time, so that adventure got a lot of attention.

In September 1922 a second sale of properties seized for tax arrears was held. Five lots sold for a total of $300. Another fifty-four lots were redeemed by their owners. And 480 others became city property.

There was one tiny but thrilling spark of light that year: On July 29 the Wild Duck Inn football team won the Imperial Cup, defeating Sapperton Athletics 6-2. That made them the provincial champions. Sports had returned as a major factor of PoCo's life: in 1924 the city won the Dewdney Baseball League's P.D. Roe Trophy, and in 1932 a PoCo team won the BC provincial baseball title.

Radio was an exciting new phenomenon, and 1922 was the year CFQC went on the air in Vancouver, the first radio station in west-

The ferry dock where Harry Galer was almost run over by his own truck.

Cars were becoming a more common sight by the 1920s, driving on the left side of the road or, as in this case, the Pitt River Bridge.

A May Day queen and her attendants, seated on the bandstand.

The city band played at May Day and other city functions.

ern Canada. It's known today as CFUN. New stations began popping up regularly, and PoCo caught the radio bug just like everyone else.

Travel to the outside world was becoming slowly but steadily easier. On January 1, 1922, motorists in Port Coquitlam and the rest of BC made the scary switch from driving on the left side of the road to the right. Mind you, with financial conditions as they were, there weren't that many cars in PoCo! Nancy Ogilvie remembers occasionally walking with her family to New Westminster even as late as the 1940s.

Pacific Stages Transport (which later became Pacific Stage Lines) began running in 1924 from Vancouver to Port Coquitlam and Port Moody. Dewdney Trunk Road—still the only paved road in the area—and Pitt River Road—which was "just a dirt road, and bush all the way"— were declared secondary provincial roads about this time, and that was good because it meant PoCo was responsible for only 50 percent of the upkeep on the sections of those roads within its boundaries. Cars still crossed the Coquitlam River bridge on planks.

In 1923, after years in which the city had been financially battered, hit by fire, drowned by floods and attacked by deadly influenza, Port Coquitlam began to celebrate May Day. No more fitting symbol of the little city's resilience could be imagined. For nearly eighty years the tradition has continued without pause.

This was also the year Port Coquitlam paid tribute to the men it lost in World War I with the construction of a cenotaph that was inscribed with their names and placed in McMitchell Park. On November 7, 1968, with the names of the dead of World War II added, the cenotaph was moved, to be placed prominently in City

Hall Park. A plaque commemorating the Korean War has been affixed to the cenotaph's base.

The Holstein herd at Colony Farm now numbered a substantial sixty-two, and the milk output for 1923 reached almost a million pounds. Among the more notable cows was Colony Grebegga Valdessa, two years old, who produced 28,371 pounds of milk, a world record for her age group. The farm's Holsteins were a famous feature until the herd was auctioned off in the 1980s.

Harry Galer, who had been a hard-working alderman on PoCo council for several years (1913, 1914 and 1918 to 1921) was elected mayor in 1925 and began one of the more remarkable records of service in BC civic life. He would be mayor for the next twenty years. One of the men who succeeded him as mayor was elected to council in 1926. Charles "Bouquet" Davies, nicknamed for the often-present flower in his lapel, served twenty years as an alderman—all but one under Mayor Galer—then spent the following ten years as mayor himself.

In 1926 the BC Provincial Police took over local policing. PoCo had had its own tiny force (two men) since 1913. A September 1926 report by Constable W.J. Hatcher of the BC Provincial Police, Westminster District, regarding the policing of Port Coquitlam includes a statement of expenditures for the month. Salary was $106.50, office supplies totalled $12.75, travelling expenses amounted to $6.30, equipment was 60 cents and "prisoners meals" cost $2.64. There is no indication of how many prisoners were fed that month. An interesting excerpt from the report relates: "At times the auto traffic is very heavy on the Dewdney Trunk Road, a count at different times shows that from 250 to

The Colony Farm Holstein herd grazes on the farm pasture with barns and outbuildings in the background. (Photo courtesy Morven Reid)

Port Coquitlam's World War I Dead

In 1923 Port Coquitlam paid tribute to the men it lost in World War I with the construction of a cenotaph inscribed with their names and placed in McMitchell Park.

George Bates	J. R. Middleton
J. E. St. Pierre	Arthur L. Hartree
James Redpath	Reginald Marshall
Walter Wigmore	David Baird
Thomas McQueen	J. McDonald
Walter L. Raynes	John Bruce
Benjamin Seaborn	George Reid
Alexander Masson	D. McDonnell
D. Judd	James Taylor
H. Bradley	Harry Oatway
Frank Vint	Thomas A. Smith
Frank Upham	William J. Hunter
Rod Allison	

The Dukers and Garveys, two early PoCo families, take their car out for a spin.

The BC Police paddy wagon struck fear into the hearts of PoCo criminals after the force took over local policing in 1926.

300 an hour pass along this highway, especially on Sunday afternoons and evenings."

In 1926 a wooden truss bridge was constructed over the Coquitlam River to link the busy Dewdney Trunk Road with Pitt River Road. (That stretch of the Dewdney is now part of the Lougheed Highway.) The new bridge, which replaced the old plank bridge that had been closed for two years for reasons of safety, was painted red. The "Red Bridge" was a prominent PoCo landmark for more than fifty years and later gave its name and its original colour to the modern, handsome, four-lane replacement. For a time the bridge was painted black, then white for better visibility, but it was always known as the Red Bridge.

Now another family prominent in PoCo's history arrives. The Laking family came to town from Cloverdale in 1928. John Laking went first to work at the Pacific Shingle Mill, but soon got a job as an attendant at Essondale, which was growing steadily. The patient population at the end of 1926 was about 1,200. Ida Laking got a job as a matron at the Boys' Industrial School, where Valleyview Hospital is today. They had six kids (Phyllis, Vernon, Bill, Betty, Noreen and George), one of whom, George, who was two months old when the family arrived, grew up to become a popular and friendly PoCo alderman and mayor, serving his city for twenty-two years. George Laking was also the co-ordinator for the 1988 book *Port Coquitlam: City of Rivers and Mountains*, published to commemorate the city's seventy-fifth birthday.

Another man who came to town in 1928 was George Graham, who bought a garage on Kingsway, near the CPR tracks. He named it Graham's Garage and started fixing local cars. He had a Ford Model A wrecker (what we'd call a tow truck today), and around about the early '30s he also started the first local cab company. It was called Coquitlam Taxi, and his regular fares included schoolchildren from outlying areas, and railway workers. Port Coquitlam's Graham Street is named for him.

Of all the people who have served Port Coquitlam as members of city council, none come close in terms of longevity to the astonishing record of Jane Kilmer. "She ran for office first in 1928," wrote Bud Elsie of the *Province* in 1963, "when she went to city hall with a friend and someone shoved nomination papers in front of her. She signed them and won. And she has continued to win every time, except for a two-year spell in 1946–48 when she lost by three votes." Jane Kilmer, born in Durham, Ontario, was the first woman elected to PoCo council (beating Vancouver to that distinction by nine years) and was on council, with a couple of breaks, for a span of just under forty years. (Her actual terms on council add up to thirty-four years, and in all that time she missed only about ten meetings.) She is the longest-serving woman alderman in BC history. Ms. Kilmer gave up a career in insurance sales to serve the city. She told Bud Elsie she had spent nearly ten years "nagging, jawing and nattering" at council for a city library before one was finally built in 1962. Ms. Kilmer must have spent an inordinate amount of time at city hall: she also worked as a secretary there. Though she never married, she assumed the care of four children when her sister-in-law died. Kilmer Elementary School is named in her honour.

Gene Boileau opened his barbershop on Shaughnessy in 1928, and that was the year the Melody Kings formed. The orchestra—a charming oddity in a country bouncing its way through the brief and tumultuous Jazz Age—consisted of Tom, Jim, Winnie and Bessie David, with Tom on fiddle, fifteen-year-old Jim on accordion, Winnie on drums and Bessie at the piano. The little band played at social events, dances and weddings and was a fixture at PoCo's May Day celebrations from 1928 to 1938, bravely making music as the western world began to plunge into the Great Depression. "During the early '30s," says Jim, "we played in Pitt Meadows, Haney, Mission, Fort Langley . . . all over. You got in for 50 cents, we each got $5 for playing. No amplifiers

Jane Kilmer (below) is shown above with her 1937 city council colleagues. Back row from left to right are W.C. Leacock, Jane Kilmer, Edgar A. Valens, and Assessor G.Roy Leigh.
In the front row are Mayor Harry Galer,
City Clerk John Smith, Charlie S. Davies
and John Orr.

then, of course. We'd play old-time and modern, reels, schottisches, foxtrots, waltzes." It was at one of those dances fifty-seven years ago that Jim met Elsie Waddell, whom he would later marry. (Waddell Street in PoCo is named for Elsie's father, Sam.)

Still more went on in 1928: the waterworks foreman, Jack Aplin, was appointed fire chief (the force was still volunteer). For the first time the fire chief did not have to be the police chief as well, since that function was now filled by a member of the BC Provincial Police.

Change was happening everywhere. Vancouver became a very much bigger neighbour on New Year's Day 1929. When the city amalgamated with the municipalities of Point Grey and South Vancouver, the population went from just over

The classroom building (above) and a view of the grounds and gardens of the Boys' Industrial School, near Essondale, where "incorrigible youths" were sent.

HISTORICAL FOOTNOTE

In 1925 Charles and Martha Lovell moved from Agassiz to Port Coquitlam, to live at 910 Pipeline Road. They are mentioned because they raised five daughters, named for the flowers their mother loved: Daisy, Rose, Lily, Violet and Pansy.

The shingle mill was a source of employment for some Port Coquitlam residents until it was shut down during the war.

117,000 in 1921 to about 247,000 in 1931. Vancouver had become the third largest city in the nation.

Donald McLean, who had been witnessing the region's changes for nearly eight decades since his arrival as a child in 1853, died May 4, 1929. To honour the memory of one of PoCo's earliest pioneers, the city's schools closed for the day.

There was still a steady flow of newcomers, including two Japanese families—the Mitsui and Suyehiro families—who arrived in Port Coquitlam in 1929. Masumi Mitsui and his family established a poultry farm on Laurier Avenue. Kantaro and Haruyo Suyehiro purchased 8 hectares (20 acres) on Back Ditch Road (now Cedar Drive), where they moved with their five sons (Kanichi, Hisaji, Hiroo, Goro and Shiro) and three daughters (Shizui, Sumako and Misaye). They had come in 1906 from Japan to Vancouver, where Kantaro

The Blue Grouse

In her book History of Port Coquitlam, *Edith Chambers relates a great story from the 1920s, a story of a long and leisurely Sunday afternoon stroll. "People used to go for walks oft-times up the mountains," she wrote, "following tracks laid by the logging companies …"*

Blackberries grew in profusion along these trails. One such Sunday, a trio came slowly back from an enjoyable stroll. As they walked, casually chatting, one, carelessly and without thinking, threw a rock ahead of himself.

It was one of those one-in-a-million shots, for at the same moment a Blue Grouse poked his head out from the grass, and the rock and the grouse met. Result: one dead grouse. This was a double mistake. First, it was illegal to kill Blue Grouse, in or out of hunting season, and this was out of hunting season. Secondly, the Game Warden in those days was a force to be reckoned with. He guarded his territory jealously.

Three very worried people picked up the grouse and discussed the problem of how to dispose of it. While doing so, the guilty party idly plucked at the dead bird, scattering feathers along the route. Finally it was decided that, as the bird was already dead, the only thing to do was to take it home and cook it …

Monday noon, three hungry people sat down to enjoy their forbidden bird. Then through the window the Game Warden was seen making his way toward the house. Panic struck the trio and, very quickly scooping the portions off each plate, the wife hurriedly placed them in a dish, covered them with a freshly ironed tea-cloth, and rushed out the back door, passing the warden on his way in. They sat through a tense (and birdless) lunch, listened to the Warden's version of some wicked person who had not only killed a Blue Grouse, but had had the temerity to leave its feathers scattered along the way. All shook their heads while also shaking in their shoes, for none of them could remember just where the feather-plucking had ceased.

Finally, much to their relief, the Warden left, still breathing vengeance on the culprits if he ever discovered them.

When he was safely away, the husband said, "Alright, Woman, let's eat."

Then and only then did the "woman" remember what she had done. In her haste to hide the evidence she had thrown bird, bowl and freshly ironed tea-cloth down the outdoor toilet.

worked as a commercial fisherman and later bought a candy store on East Hastings. Canada was not particularly welcoming to these immigrants. In 1928 the federal government had decreed that Japanese could not vote in Canada and were denied entry to professions such as medicine and the law, even if they were citizens.

By the end of 1929, however, a decade of hard times had begun for long-time residents and newcomers alike.

FIVE

A New Depression, A New War, A New Dawn

I t was like a big
family, everyone
knew everyone else.

—*Nancy Ogilvie*

A mysterious October 1929 event called a stock market "crash" in faraway New York City launched a continent-wide financial cataclysm: companies failed, business empires crumbled, banks closed and a vast army of unemployed formed on both sides of the US-Canada border. The Great Depression had begun.

Canada was not immune to it, and like thousands of other small towns in both countries, Port Coquitlam began to be battered by the Depression's effects. Wanda Frey's family lived in PoCo during the 1930s, and she remembered those years when she talked to the compilers of the book *Coquitlam*. "Times were very tough during the Depression. My mother [Alice Ross "Nanny" Heckbert, introduced in Chapter 2] was always very neighbourly, and was well known in the area. Everybody called her Nanny. She would always have something to eat for anybody who came by. The house we lived in was up from the railroad tracks, and the hobos used to get off the trains, and they would come up by the creek which was on our property. They would then come up to the house and ask for things to eat, and my mother would always give them something. I remember that well. The hobos would have bonfires down by the river."

Mary Pekrul, whose father-in-law Reinhold "Roy" Pekrul ran a big berry farm near where PoCo's Fire Hall #1 and work yard is today, has talked to many old-timers who remember picking raspberries on the Pekrul farm. You'll find Pekrul Place in that area. The house would frequently be visited by transients who, besides getting something to eat in the Pekrul kitchen during those lean years, might be offered a temporary job on the farm. When World War II started, Roy Sr. went to work in the shipyard. Mary, a widow today, married Roy's son, Roy Jr., who worked at Burnaby's Continental Can Company.

May Queen Mary Morris in 1931. (Photo courtesy Margaret Jackson)

Nancy Ogilvie recalls a rundown collection of lean-tos where transients would stay while en route through the area. It ran from the site of Mary Hill Secondary to the CPR tracks and was called Hobo City by the locals. "All the kids would walk around there. We never felt unsafe, never got in trouble." The men would knock on doors, looking for work, a meal, some spare change. "We never locked our doors back then, and I don't remember ever hearing of something being taken or of anyone being harmed in any way."

Rose Phillips recalls that, as a child, she sometimes had to step over people sleeping on PoCo sidewalks. They had nowhere to go. Rose's parents, Don and Marie Chine, had an acreage, a big garden and seven cows, so there was always milk and cheese and produce to feed themselves and to sell. Other memories were good, too: Rose was a flower girl at the 1930 May Day celebrations.

In spite of the Depression, business continued strongly at the Wild Duck Inn. In 1930 Will Routley added the Tudor Revival touches that are now so familiar, and the following year he added a hundred-seat pub.

And locals hadn't lost a sense of humour. From the front page of the *Coquitlam Herald* for January 14, 1934, comes this excerpt, part of an article headlined THE TOURIST TRADE: "In a recent issue of the *Sun*, considerable stress was laid on getting more tourists. Now if the writer lived in Port Coquitlam his heart would rejoice for the income of tourists is great. Almost every freight train carries from a dozen to 150 passengers, principally at night, young and old and either sex."

The Depression didn't curtail the reading habits of British Columbians, either, and may even have intensified them. For one thing, J.C. McChesney established the *Coquitlam Herald* in the midst of the Depression. And the Fraser Valley Regional Library started in 1930, thanks to a grant from the Andrew Carnegie Corporation, which had been financing the construction of libraries all across the US and Canada. When the Carnegie funds were exhausted four years later, the library's first director, Dr. Helen Stewart, set about to keep it going. One result, says a brief history of the FVRL, was a 1934 referendum in which "residents were asked to vote whether or not they wished to support the library through local taxes. Even though the vote was held in the middle of the Great Depression, 20 of the original 24 areas voted YES and the Fraser Valley Union Library became the first regional library in British Columbia and in North America." PoCo's Terry Fox Library—with 62,000 volumes—is part of the system today.

The 1931 mid-Depression census showed that Port Coquitlam's population was 1,312, an

John Wingrove (seated) raised his children after his wife died. Their names appear throughout PoCo's history as May Queen, fire chief, athlete, alderman . . . (Photo courtesy Lillian Wingrove Reid)

The Wingrove family home during the 1930s. (Photo courtesy Lillian Wingrove Reid)

increase of just 134 in ten years. Most other places in the Lower Mainland showed more rapid growth. PoCo needed industry and better connections to the outside world. But after nearly fifteen years of uninterrupted misfortune, and now enduring the Great Depression with the rest of the world, the little city would stay little for a time.

Like reading, sport thrived during these dark days. There were times when it must have seemed that every one of those 1,312 Port Coquitlamites were playing lacrosse. To quote *Port Coquitlam: City of Rivers and Mountains*, "Doug Rowland had been involved in lacrosse either as a player or manager since 1909, and was fondly referred to as 'The Father of Lacrosse in Port Coquitlam.' Bill Wingrove remembers first playing lacrosse on Mr. Rowland's land when he was about 12 or 13. 'Sure, that was where we first played, all of us kids, down on Rowland's field.'"

In September 1931 the Canadian Amateur Lacrosse Association established box lacrosse as its official game, and in 1932 Reginald "Pop" Phillips brought the box version to BC. Will Routley sponsored lacrosse teams in PoCo all through the 1930s, right up until his retirement in 1943. Port Coquitlam took to "boxla" with special intensity and affection.

Bill Wingrove remembered the hard work he and other local kids did to prepare the site for the construction of PoCo's first lacrosse box. "The schoolyards had to be cleared and levelled," he said. "Everybody helped!" That famous box, at the southwest corner of Mary Hill and Wilson, was upgraded in 1956 and named in honour of Doug Rowland. It and city hall are the only official heritage sites in Port Coquitlam.

Another man who helped in the early establishment of lacrosse in PoCo was Linton Osborne, who came to the city in 1921. In 1972 Lint Osborne's widow, Annie, accepted a civic medallion presented by Mayor Bruce Scott in tribute to Lint's many years of service to the community.

If sport was important in PoCo, so was the church. Until 1934, Catholics in Port Coquitlam had to travel to Sapperton to celebrate mass at St. Michael's with Father Finnigan. Then, says a church history, mass began in one of the parishioner's houses and in several places around town, including the Elks Hall and the Commercial Hotel. "A Chinese vegetable market," the history continues, "situated on Coquitlam Avenue, now part of the Lougheed Highway, was put up for sale with 'FOR SALE—CHEAP' painted on one of its walls. This store was snapped up by the parishioners for $400." It was the Depression, so economies were practised. The little

The Depression didn't put an end to community outings, like the one pictured here. (Photo courtesy Lillian Wingrove Reid)

building was "meticulously" torn down, and the parishioners, happily volunteering their time and effort, saved every board, every nail and practically every shingle. "These were the materials with which the original church was built." Father Finnigan named the church Our Lady of the Assumption. A lean-to was added as living quarters for the parish priest. That lean-to is still around, used as the kitchen in the old church hall. The first marriage was performed in the church January 6, 1937, with Father Finnigan presiding over the union of Daphne Voss and Patrick O'Daire. The first baptism (Raymond Peter Joseph Maisonneuve) occurred January 13, 1938. The church was formally blessed the following May 22. It served for seventeen years, until, with the growth of the parish, it became too small and a move was necessary.

The extra booze business brought to southwestern BC by thirsty victims of Prohibition ended in 1933. After fourteen long, dry years the Americans repealed the law. Now they could drink in their own country. Other great changes were happening, many sparked by the convulsive effects of the Depression: in the US, a president named Franklin Roosevelt was elected; here in BC, provincial electors voted the Liberals in, headed by Premier Duff Pattullo, while over in Germany that same year, a man named Adolf Hitler became Chancellor.

PoCo continued to be bedevilled by its rivers. An example: Bill Morrill, a steam engineer who settled here with his wife Rosina in the early 1930s, got a contract in 1935 to deepen the Coquitlam River to reduce the dangers of flooding. He had hoped to get a steam shovel built for the work, but the contract wasn't big enough, so he had to be content with wheelbarrows

HISTORICAL FOOTNOTE

Harrison Hot Springs had become a haven for people seeking relaxation, and that was good for PoCo because when Pacific Stage Lines laid on a route between Vancouver and Harrison Hot Springs, one of the stops en route was here. It was another link to the world outside.

Pacific Stage Lines ran a bus from Vancouver to Harrison Hot Springs and back, stopping at Port Coquitlam on the way.

and shovels and a small work crew. Then a sudden and unexpected overnight rise in the level of the river swept all his equipment away!

In 1935 one-tenth of the working-age population of Canada was unemployed. The following year one and a half million Canadians were on relief. PoCo had plenty of company in its misery, but a small ray of hope shone on March 23, 1935. In the middle of the Great Depression an American named E.S. Bellows purchased the empty Gregory Tire and Rubber plant and set it up as a branch of Huntington Rubber Mills of Canada, a major manufacturing firm. The factory would be active with varying degrees of intensity for the next forty years. The purchase contract, incidentally, stipulated that only white labour would be hired.

The history of the Boy Scouts and Cubs in PoCo begins in 1937 when Bud Stewart and H.L. Vanderveen began to organize youth activities. Vanderveen was killed during World War II, but when Stewart returned from the war he was determined to start a Boy Scout troop. At a Parent–Teachers Association meeting in 1946 he put forward this idea, and someone in the audience, pointing to local resident Morven Reid, said "Morven used to be in the Scouts."

"That was true," Mr. Reid says. "In 1929 when I was fifteen I attended a Boy Scout

Jamboree in Birkenhead, England—I was born in England in 1913—and there were 50,000 Scouts there from all over the world. I saw Lord Baden-Powell there, and the Duke of Windsor visited, too. So at that Port Coquitlam meeting a committee was set up and I was put in charge of it. They wanted to get Cubs going, too, and a Miss Sones was chosen to run that committee. But she wouldn't do it by herself, and the fellow who was named to assist her moved to Edmonton, so I helped her, too. I worked for seven years getting the first Port Coquitlam Boy Scout troop set up. They wore the Stewart tartan neckerchief—that was for

This aerial view of the now-vanished Huntington Rubber Plant (right foreground) also shows the railway junction that gave birth to Port Coquitlam. (Photo by Aero Surveys Ltd.)

Margaret Jackson was captain of the local Girl Guides in 1939. (Photo courtesy Margaret Jackson)

Mr. and Mrs. John Smith in the 1940s, after John's retirement from the position of city clerk. Frances Smith was PoCo's first female school trustee.

Bud Stewart—and my wife made a lot of them for the boys."

That first troop is still going more than fifty years later. Local Scouts focus on health and fitness, outdoor training and wilderness survival. (In 1999 the troop approved the purchase of snow-shoes for these activities.) A fine tradition of the local Scouts, with Girl Guide participation, is an annual torch parade.

In 1938 G. Roy Leigh succeeded John Smith as Port Coquitlam's city clerk. Smith had held the office for twenty-five years, and Leigh had been his right-hand man for the entire time. (Leigh was clerk for sixteen years; Robert E. King followed him for another thirteen and Ron Freeman for twenty-four years after that. Susan Rauh succeeded Freeman in 1992. Just five city clerks in eighty-six years . . . and considering Susan Rauh's youth, that might stretch to a hundred years!)

The Agricultural Hall was always in use. Bob and Dorothy Urquhart became caretakers of the hall in 1939 and continued to care for it for more than twenty years. Dorothy remembers arranging for church services there in the morning, and dances and socials at night. It was a versatile meeting place. The Urquharts were pretty versatile, too. They operated the dog pound and collected licence fees.

John Galer started working for his dad at Port Coquitlam Transfer in 1939. (He's still dropping in more than sixty years later!) There was a pace to life in PoCo then that old-timers sometimes pine for. "It was a one-locomotive town back then," John Galer says, laughing. You'd crank the telephone to call the grocery store and order your week's provisions, to be delivered by "John," in a van, while "Jim," driving a team pulling a covered wagon, brought fresh fruit and vegetables to the few folks who didn't have their own gardens or who didn't grow what he could bring. Baked goods and dairy products were delivered, too. Most of the locals had gardens, some with chickens, so there were always lots of eggs to be had.

PoCo old-timers also recall the royal visit of May 1939. What they couldn't have known at the time was that the visit to Canada of King George VI and Queen Elizabeth (now the Queen Mother) had been carefully timed to raise morale and consciousness of Britain in the months leading up to World War II. At 9:15 on the morning of May 29 some two thousand people from Port Coquitlam, Port Moody, Maple Ridge and New Westminster jammed the junction platform for a glimpse of the royal couple. Their schedule was heavy, so no stop was planned, but both PoCo and PoMo councils had asked that the train at least slow down. It did but, alas, the king and queen could not be seen as the train rumbled through. "Little Peggy Wingrove, May Day's 'Miss Canada'," waited with a bouquet of flowers and a

Dorothy and Bob Urquhart (seated) with Mayor Bruce Scott and Alderman George Laking at Bob's retirement party in December 1972.

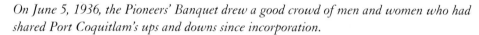

On June 5, 1936, the Pioneers' Banquet drew a good crowd of men and women who had shared Port Coquitlam's ups and downs since incorporation.

Stephanie Stewart (now Friesen) at her father's Wally's Garage.

Port Coquitlam erected this arch in New Westminster to welcome King George VI and Queen Elizabeth in 1939.

"neat little speech," but the flowers went unseen and the speech was not heard.

Two days later, however, the royal pair were in New Westminster and a lot of locals got to see them there. Port Coquitlam had erected an arch at the corner of Third Avenue and Second Street. There were twenty-six arches in all, and the king and queen passed under each one of them. Japanese Canadian veterans, who had acquitted themselves splendidly for the Allies in World War I, had an arch, and PoCo's Masumi Mitsui was among the Canadian-Japanese Society members gathered there. Some 350 Port Coquitlam school children were among ten thousand gathered in Queen's Park Stadium for special activities.

Three months later—September 1, 1939—Hitler's armies invaded Poland and World War II began.

There was one similarity between the two world wars within Port Coquitlam: no real war industry developed. Just as they had done one war earlier, members of the Women's Institute sewed bandages, quilts and other needed things for soldiers overseas. Annie Osborne, who volunteered not only for the WI but for the Red Cross as well, recalls a drive for blood donations in which thirty PoCo citizens got on a bus to go to the Red Cross clinic in New Westminster. Residents had to register at city hall for ration books supplied by the Wartime Prices and Trade Board for commodities like tea, coffee, sugar and butter. Nylon stockings were virtually impossible to obtain: nylon was needed in parachutes.

Local children helped: they sewed or collected scrap metal. Some remember drilling at school with broomsticks, an early and informal beginning to military training. There was a "Broomstick Brigade" under Mr. Brand at Central School, twenty-seven bright and eager boys ready to do their bit. A photo shows them happily crammed into a school hallway. Second from the right in the front row is young Japanese Canadian Shiro Suyehiro, whose parents had been in BC for more than thirty years, in PoCo for ten. Shiro had been selected out of all the school to lower the flag to half-mast on the death in 1936 of King George V.

A Grade 8 class at Central School made a soldier's quilt, each student making one of the patches and putting his or her name on it. Kay Grootendorst recalls the Quebec-based 22nd Regiment (the famed "Van Doos") going through on a route march. During a brief break one of the men asked Kay for a glass of water, and when she handed it to him, he smiled broadly and said, "Merci, mam'selle!"

"I was twelve years old," Kay says. "That was exciting!"

Port Coquitlam was at a strategic node on the railway, so extra precautions were taken. The federal government placed civilian guards at the Pitt River Bridge and stationed soldiers in the area. Merchant Marine men were billeted at the Terminal Hotel. A lot of PoCo women joined the New Westminster-based Queen's Park Drill Ambulance Corps. John Galer joined a local detachment of a military group called the Pacific Coast Militia Rangers. It had been formed by Melvin Clerihue, a driver for Port Coquitlam Transfer (owned by Harry Galer, John's father), and John Hellier, a foreman at the Minnekhada Ranch.

In 1940, Leading Airman Vic Coulter of 826 Squadron, Fleet Air Arm, stood confidently at Eastleigh, near Southamptom, not long before leaving for the Middle East. He was severely wounded in service, and received a Gallant Conduct Award. Vic, now eighty-two, lives in PoCo today. (Photo courtesy Vic Coulter)

Ian Clerihue, Mel's son, recalls those times. "My father was the local head of the Pacific Coast Militia Rangers. He'd been a veteran of World War I and they made him lieutenant of the Port Coquitlam detachment of the Rangers when World War II started. Every city had its own detachment. They had uniforms and weapons. I remember they wore what were called 'Bone Dry Coats,' great heavy things like canvas. Every now and again the men would take the Port Coquitlam Transfer truck and go up Pipeline Road to the rifle range, and one week they might practise with Bren guns, the next week with Sten guns. I was in cadets at the time and we would go up with them. The Rangers would have mock battles on Burnaby Mountain, just getting ready in case there was an invasion." The Rangers got an okay from council to set up an indoor rifle range in the Agricultural Hall. An air-raid siren was set up atop city hall. (It doubled as a fire siren.)

Starting about 1939, Mel Clerihue was also the manager of PoCo's government-run liquor store. (His customers called him "Doctor" Clerihue in thirsty gratitude.) He was the president of Branch 133 of the Canadian Legion, too. A busy man! His wife Colena, one of the earliest telephone operators in town, headed the Legion's Ladies Auxiliary.

The 1941 census showed that Port Coquitlam's population was 1,539, an increase of just 227 people in ten years. The little city was growing with agonizing slowness. But there was one place where you could count on a good, lively crowd. Oral and Myra Ticehurst bought the Good Eats Cafe on the Dewdney Trunk in 1941, and Oral "Pop" Ticehurst endeared himself to a generation of locals by not only providing good, plain and wholesome food, but also

Pop's Cafe, near Coquitlam Station and the old Westminster Junction, was a popular PoCo hangout in the 1940s and '50s.

by cashing their cheques in times of need. In 1947 Pop put up a new building on the Dewdney Trunk near the CPR station, and called it Pop's Cafe. He was already familiar because of his Good Eats Cafe, and the new spot was an instant success. It became a favourite PoCo hangout. Pop Ticehurst ran the Good Eats Cafe until his untimely death in 1952 at age fifty-six, and the family ran it for another fifteen years. The Ticehursts' oldest son, Ross, and Andrew Morgan, a son-in-law, managed the cafe from 1945 on. They sold a lot of ice cream. Nancy Ogilvie worked at Pop's after school and remembers developing a bad case of "ice-cream elbow."

John Galer became chief of the twenty-man Port Coquitlam Volunteer Fire Department the same year the Good Eats Cafe opened. He held the post for twenty years—but he certainly didn't do it for the money! The pay was ten dollars a month and two dollars a call. "From the age of six I used to go on the fire calls, anyway," says John. "Sometimes we'd have three of our company trucks sitting idle while we were fighting a fire. It cost our company [Port Coquitlam Transfer] more than what the city paid us, that's for sure." That selfless service to the community marks the company, now PoCo Building Supply, to this day. It's famous for support of local good works.

Near the end of 1941 the war came closer to home. Japan attacked Pearl Harbor in the Pacific on December 7, 1941, and the Allies added a new enemy. Canada declared war on Japan the same day, a full day before the US did. The immediate effect in British Columbia was a heightened suspicion and fear of its Japanese residents. (That was intensified in 1942 when a lone Japanese submarine lying two miles off the coast lobbed twenty-five to thirty shells toward a lighthouse at Estevan Point on the west coast of Vancouver Island. The gunners had poor aim, missing the station and the nearby settlement of Hesquiat.)

The light on a Stanley Park monument to Japanese Canadians who had fought for Canada in World War I was turned off on December 8, 1941, and the federal government began to remove Japanese Canadians from the coast. Some were sent to camps in the BC Interior, some to Alberta. Even those born in Canada were not exempt. The book *Port Coquitlam: City of Rivers and Mountains* tells some of the story. Mayor Harry Galer, a friend of Kantaro Suyehiro—who had been farming here with his family since 1929—offered to speak on his behalf, but as a civic politician Galer had no real power in this situation. (Ironically, the two oldest Suyehiro boys had volunteered for Canadian Army service and been turned away.)

Young Shiro Suyehiro, a member of the Broomstick Brigade at Central School just a few months before, and who had been chosen to lower the flag to mark a king's death, remembers the family had to leave for Alberta on very short notice. The janitor at Central kindly let Shiro and his brothers and sisters clear out their desks on the weekend. Shiro went to the blackboard and chalked a message to his classmates: "See you when I get back." He did not return until 1972.

The Suyehiro family left their farm on Cedar Drive and the next day stepped off the train in Coalhurst, Alberta. They were

Names of local men killed in World War II were added to the cenotaph, which is now located in City Hall Park.

Port Coquitlam's World War II Dead

The names of the Port Coquitlam men killed in World War II, commemorated on the cenotaph, are:

S. W. F. Baker	F. Meehan
H. Barnum	J. G. Millership
E. R. Berkey	A. H. Spinks
D. Davison	C. Tran
J. Earland	F. Treichel
W. Krivac	H. L. Vanderveen
R. Lonsdale	J. Zappia
H. McTavish	

The Forrest Family

The Forrest family has been associated with tugboating on the Pitt and Fraser Rivers since 1915, when Sam and Hilda Forrest arrived. Their two children, Harvie and Eve, inherited the business in 1935 when Sam died. "I was eighteen and my brother was sixteen," Eve told writer Vicki Jensen for the 1995 book *Saltwater Women at Work*. "We inherited a pile of debts and a second tugboat without an engine." Their home was a big floathouse on logs moored a hundred yards out on the Pitt, at the foot of Pitt River Road in PoCo.

They had the *Harvie W*, which their father had built, and they had the *Old Faithful*, the boat without an engine. The two kids went further into debt ($3,000 in mid-Depression) and bought an engine from J.B. Hoffar's famous shop on Georgia Street in Vancouver. "There it sat on the floor, this great hunk of iron. It was a Fairbanks Morse and taller than we were. We had no choice but to take it. Neither of us knew the first thing about running it, so Hoffar's let us have an engineer to start us out . . . There was no manual, no nothing."

Eve worked the *Harvie W*, while Harvie handled the bigger boat. They started getting log-towing work, took on a deckhand or two. One day, when both boats were out, Eve was at home taking care of her ailing mother when she saw a yacht out on the Pitt just as the tide was beginning to flood. She knew the boat was in trouble and got a reluctant neighbour (he was afraid the boat owner would have no money for the tow) to go out and tow him to a safe spot. "When the fellow came home from towing the boat, he told me 'The guy said to tell you thanks very much; his name was Brown and he paid me.'"

Later that night, the phone rang. It was Brown. "Send your boat up to Hammond Cedar to pick up some boom sticks and take them up to the head of Pitt Lake." That was the beginning of a business relationship that went on for years. There never was a contract.

In 1939 a seventeen-year-old Mission City-born kid named Ken Mackenzie started working for the Forrests. "They put a lot of trust in me," Mackenzie says, sixty years later. "I was put in charge of the *Harvie W*."

By 1941, after the purchase of a third boat, it occurred to someone it might be a good idea for Eve and Harvie Forrest to get master's papers. It seems their boats were of a tonnage that required that. So

when this indomitable brother-and-sister team wasn't working on the river, they took their courses. They passed with no problem, and the Pitt River Towing Company was born. Eve Forrest was the first woman in British Columbia to get a master's ticket.

Her father hadn't believed in women bothering with education beyond Grade 8, but Eve had her heart set on going further. She took correspondence courses, then began attending Grade 12 classes at Connaught High School in Vancouver. "I thought I'd die a thousand times being

Nel and Harvie Forrest, June 26, 1944. (Photo courtesy Nel Forrest)

twenty-four in Grade 12 . . . In the end I was ten credits short to graduate because I didn't have any electives. Mr. Calder was the principal, and he said, 'If they give credit for music and arts and all these things, I can't see why you couldn't get credit for your navigation papers.' He wrote Victoria and they agreed. So I was off to the University of British Columbia, then Queen's (in Kingston, Ontario). I missed the river terribly.

"Eventually I married, became a doctor and had five children."

Dr. Eve Forrest Gulliford, a remarkable woman, died at age eighty on March 9, 1997.

Now we have to back up a bit: At UBC Eve had been a member of the Student Christian Movement (SCM), and that's where, in the early '40s, she met Nellie Coyle. They were the same age and became fast friends. Nel (she spells it with one "l") had been born December 3, 1916, in Okotoks, Alberta, but grew up in Calgary. She moved to BC in 1941, when she got a job as secretary in the SCM office at UBC. There she met Eve Forrest, who talked a lot about her boats in Port Coquitlam and her house on the water. "You should come out and see it," she told Nel. So on New Year's Eve, 1942, after yet another invitation, Nel took the Interurban out to New Westminster, where Eve met her at the station.

Nel's story of her arrival in PoCo is funny, charming and gives a good picture of what life was like in PoCo more than fifty years ago.

The Forrest family on their boat Gulfcoaster *in 1969.*
(Photo courtesy Nel Forrest)

She told the story to Anita Saari for inclusion in a book privately printed for the family. What follows is from that reminiscence.

Eve met me with her car at the Westminster Station and we drove out to Port Coquitlam, the road winding all over the place. I thought I'd come to the end of the earth. Port Coquitlam at that time was about 2,500 people. It was just a little tiny rundown poor little village with few paved roads. They had received a city charter in 1913 and by 1919 they had lost all their buyers and had almost ended up in bankruptcy and stayed that way for the next 25 or so years.

When we were downtown it seems everybody stopped at Pop's Cafe, which was sort of the town meeting place. It was the place where Eve and Harvie's deckhands had their cheques cashed, because there was no bank. Eve went to New Westminster to do the banking, but the fellow who ran the cafe, Pop Ticehurst, was the banker for the town. He always had a chunk of bills in his pocket big enough to choke a horse—and he never had a bad cheque.

While we were having tea, of course I met Mrs. Ticehurst and Mr. Ticehurst. I was tremendously impressed with them and in later years called her "Mom." She lived to be 93 and I had the privilege of giving the eulogy at her funeral because of the relationship that lasted all those years.

Eve said to one of the boys, "Go and send for my brother, he's in there working on an engine—tell him we're here. I want him to come in for tea." So off he went . . . and in came this black apparition—as greasy as any human being could be and covered with soot from top to bottom, with a big grin on his face. I wasn't sure whether this was a human being or not. This, of course, was Eve's brother and everyone called him "Pop" because when he was a little wee guy he used to pop up everywhere and so the name stuck. He was two years younger than I was and two years younger than Eve and his name was Harvie.

Eve and I had our tea and came on down to this float house. Never had I seen a float house. I was a "prairie chicken." The house was attached by a walkway at the end of Pitt River Road. And there it sat, out there in the river—this great big house—the same one we're sitting in now. It was a huge big thing, two storeys with seven-foot ceilings and a third peak at seven feet on top of that. It was just sitting on logs and floating on the water. And so we walked down the ramp, and the last bit of the ramp was over the water and the planks jiggled. We couldn't walk on two, we had to walk on one. So we made it across with me probably doing a fair bit of screaming and on to the float house.

All the deckhands were in the house, and Nel helped Eve make dinner. "In those days, the deckhands worked on the tugs 24 hours a day and if they weren't out they slept in the house. There was one room that was the deckhands' room and one room that was Eve's and one that was Harvie's." Later the deckhands went off to celebrate New Year's.

Nel continues: "Eve and I had planned to have a poetry reading between us, sit by the fire and have music and records. That was going to be our New Year's Eve. We were all set to do this in front of a beautiful fireplace . . . Harvie had a date. He fooled around getting ready for his date for a long, long time. It must have been nearly 11:00 p.m. before he left and he was back at 1:00. We were amazed to see him back so soon. It must have been the shortest date ever!

"Then he started to court me."

By the end of January, one month after they met, Harvie produced an engagement ring. "You are absolutely crazy," Nel told him. "You don't even know me and I don't know you and I will not accept the ring." So he put it back in his pocket.

"Each time we'd go out, he'd say 'Put this on, put this on.' 'No, no, no.' But by the middle of March I was wearing the ring."

Nel and Harvie were married in Calgary on June 26, 1944, a date chosen because it was her parents' own anniversary.

The length of the honeymoon was the time it took to get back, which was 24 hours . . . we got off the train right in Port Coquitlam. Almost immediately Harvie was out on the tugboat. He was leaving and very quickly I was alone in this big old house out on the water. Also, almost immediately—because I was very subject to hay fever, which on the prairies was much later in the year, but out here everything was in full bloom—within hours I was swamped with hay fever. The next morning the young man who came with the speedboat to take the scalers out from the house every morning saw me with very red eyes, and mopping my eyes and nose, and he said, "That's all right, dear, it'll be o.k."

"It's hay fever," I said, "I'm not crying."

Harvie and Nel were married until his death in 1978.

Nel soon found her sea legs. "I learned a great deal about tugboating as it was done on the river in those days."

The hours on the tugboat were very, very long. They didn't ever stop from Sunday night until whenever they got finished on Saturday. It was just a constant run bringing things down the river from Sumas, where they were brought from the upper river to the Mission Bridge and then on down to here. The tows were very, very long and took much longer than they would ever take today. They would use two boats on them, sometimes more, but usually two, one on the bow and one on the stern. The tow would be so long that when the bow of the boat was in the Pitt River here, the stern of the two with its light on was away back in the Fraser.

They would bring that tow up into the Pitt, always against the tide or they would never have been able to stop it because they didn't have enough power. The power on the *Wayfarer*, which was the biggest tug, was 75 horsepower with a three-to-one reduction, and that's no power at all in today's version of a tugboat, which has

1,000 to 1,500 horsepower. They used the river, and the force of the river would do the work for them.

Harvie was a master at reading the river and understanding where the eddies were and where the easy places were, how to turn, how to correct it.

Ray and Mike Forrest (left) and a cousin with a sixty-pound spring salmon caught in the Fraser in 1954. (Photo courtesy Nel Forrest)

He was an expert on that river in almost everybody's opinion from those he worked with. It looks so easy when you see a little tug out there just chugging along, but with those logs behind them it was a tremendous thing to manage.

In 1946 Harvie and Nel bought a small sawmill that was on the land near their floathouse. The mill was owned by Pop Ticehurst of Good Eats Cafe fame, who knew very little about running sawmills. Pop Forrest, a rather younger Pop, often gave him advice. Finally, senior Pop said to junior Pop, "If you know so damn much about this sawmill why don't you buy it from me? I'm ready to sell." The Forrests asked Nel's father to lend them $10,000. He did, and they found themselves the owners of the mill, which they ran for the next ten years. There were fourteen mills in PoCo at the time, and all were busy. Most of them were small operations with from two to five workers. The Forrests usually had four.

On August 18, 1948, Ken Mackenzie and Harvie Forrest started up Harken Towing. They had just one boat, the *Harken No. 1*. In 1949 Ken bought out Harvie's share of the company and began to expand it. Today, Harken Towing is one of the major tugboat companies in BC. Harvie, meantime, continued running the mill, began to build houses and, with Nel's help, started planning the Port Palladium roller rink.

refused food at the local cafes, and no one would give them lodging. So Mr. and Mrs. Suyehiro and their eight children slept in a CPR baggage car. They were awakened the next morning by railway police and an RCMP officer who asked why they had been sleeping there. They explained, at which point the RCMP officer took them to a spot in town that prepared breakfast for them all. The family found work on sugar beet farms, but later most of them moved to Ontario.

Another Japanese Canadian PoCo farmer, Masumi Mitsui, a World War I veteran who had won medals for outstanding bravery at Vimy Ridge, had his home and properties seized by federal authorities in 1942. Mitsui was forced to move to Greenwood in the BC Interior, and later to St. Catharines, Ontario. When the war was over, Mitsui moved to Hamilton, Ontario, to be near his children.

In a moving ceremony on August 2, 1985, Mr. Mitsui, who had been invited back to BC from Ontario for the occasion, was escorted to the Stanley Park monument. The frail old man, ninety-seven, quietly turned the monument's light back on. On April 22, 1987, Mitsui died, the last surviving Japanese Canadian World War I volunteer. He was ninety-nine.

Mayor Charlie Davies.

At the time, some Canadians protested the removal of the Japanese, but most were indifferent to the action, more concerned about the Asian threat and the war and jobs.

Around 1944 the federal government asked the Huntington Rubber plant to begin producing self-sealing tanks for aircraft. That work continued until the end of the war in 1945, when the staff was reduced to six. Imagine! Just six people at work in that big three-storey plant. Things would again pick up slightly toward the end of the 1940s.

The war in Europe ended May 8, 1945; the war in the Pacific the following August. Stores and factories in PoCo closed on VJ Day to celebrate, and locals waited for their sons and daughters to come home. Some would not return.

The year after the war ended, PoCo held a civic election that was notable for a couple of reasons: it brought in as mayor the very popular Charlie Davies, who had been an alderman for twenty years, and it returned to council for a second term Rosina Morrill, only the second woman to win a seat, and the only woman on the '46 council. (Jane Kilmer didn't run that year.) Rosina's husband Bill had died, and she had to find work to provide for her four kids. She became a nurse's aide at Essondale . . . but with not enough income to afford a car, she had to hitchhike to work! (One wonders how many city councils in Canada had members who hitchhiked to work.) Eventually the hospital started a bus service for its employees, but it was tough to juggle working, raising a family and sitting on council.

The new bandstand in Aggie Park was first used for May Day 1946.

Young George Laking, later to become a Port Coquitlam alderman and mayor, had his own transportation woes at the time. He didn't have a car, and he was courting Jocelyn Huth, an Essondale nurse-in-training, who lived in residence at the hospital. George had to take a cab out to the hospital every time he wanted to see her, and the fare was 50 cents, no small amount back then. (George and Jocelyn were married in 1949.) As a fifteen-year-old, George had started working for the Canadian Western Lumber Company in 1943, doing odd jobs at first. "Within six months I was sawing shingles. Then they shut down the shingle mill, and I went to plywood for four or five years.

"They had as many as 2,200 people working at that mill, but when Crown Zellerbach bought them out in '53 they were down to about 200. I got hurt in 1951. I was sawing shingles and the equipment broke. I didn't want the saw to fall on my feet, so I grabbed it, wrecked my back. I was off for one year and nine months. Three months I was lying on a Foster bed, didn't move, couldn't wash myself. The neurosurgeon, he tells me he didn't think my right leg would ever work. I said, 'You just leave me alone. I'll *make* it work'." And George did. His recovery included going to what was then the Workmen's Compensation Board in Vancouver. He drove in for therapy every day for five months. "The WCB doc said he didn't think I should go back to work. I told him, 'I'll go nuts if I don't'." He went back. When George retired from Canadian Western on April 30, 1991, he had been there "forty years, eleven months exactly."

To the hard-working and serious Port Coquitlam of the 1940s, Karl and Clara "Babe" Jacobs brought a touch of glamour and excitement. They had come to town in the 1930s and owned several rustic cabins situated near the Coquitlam River. It was said that Mexican-born Clara Jacobs had been a Hollywood actress, and it appeared she was still playing the role. "Heads would turn . . . when they saw Clara Jacobs, in long scarf and dark glasses, driving her beautiful old car, complete with rumble seat," wrote a town historian in *Port Coquitlam: City of Rivers and Mountains*. Karl's brother was rumoured to be a movie director, and there was also talk that Karl had been a Hollywood stuntman . . . and one of the first referees in the National Hockey League. (A researcher aches to know how Karl and Clara met.) Their collection of cabins, formally Steelhead Ranch, was informally known as "Hollywood Hideout," and local legend says that many stars of the silver screen stayed there from time to time, including Errol Flynn. Sadly, in 1961 this scenic vacation retreat was washed out when the Coquitlam River flooded. The Internet Movie Data Base, which has details on every movie ever made and all the people who worked on them, shows no Clara or Babe Jacobs in its vast data bank (and no chronologically correct Karl Jacobs), but perhaps she's listed there under her maiden name or a screen name.

This entry in the 1946 May Day parade drew attention to the "Gay 90s Revue," put on by a local theatre group. (Photo courtesy Edna Sabatine)

Now and again a fact in a city's history pops up that gives a delightfully clear picture of what it was like in earlier days . . . like hunting parties within city limits. Nancy Ogilvie, a member of the Port Coquitlam Heritage and Cultural Society and a treasure trove of information for this book (and who, incidentally, was the 1942 May Queen), recalls that her family, armed with the proper licences, occasionally made trips to "the flats," now the Broadway industrial area, to shoot pheasants for Sunday dinner. "The birds were in abundance in those days. We wore big hipped wading boots, and I remember we'd get hung up sometimes on the barbed wire fence." Her dad raised and trained hunting dogs, including golden and water spaniels, Labrador golden retrievers, Chesapeake Bay retrievers, Irish setters and pointers. They'd be put to work in the hunt, during which young Nancy—carefully taught by her father—would get some shooting in herself.

"We had 1,500 people here in 1942," Nancy says. "It was like a big family, everyone knew everyone else." She recalls swimming with friends in the "beautiful unpolluted waters of the Coquitlam River, where deep holes formed as the river made its way to the Fraser and the sea. It is true that you could actually walk across the fish in the river bed at spawning time." Long-time PoCo resident Don Gillespie recalls fish swimming in ditches alongside some city streets all the way up to Prairie Road.

It's possible there were more fish in Port Coquitlam than people! The city's population continued to inch up with agonizing slowness. No new schools had been built in PoCo for thirty years, and for a few years the upper floor of Aggie Hall was used for classrooms. Long-

In the late 1940s the Variety Club put on stage shows for Port Coquitlam.

Founding members of the Port Coquitlam Order of the Royal Purple #10 receive their twenty-five-year pins in 1972.

time resident Morley Deans remembers taking Grade 4 there. But enough growth occurred in the region to spark the creation, in 1947, of School District #43. It comprised all the schools in Coquitlam, Port Coquitlam, Port Moody, Anmore and Belcarra.

Another newcomer sprang up in 1947: on February 13 the Port Coquitlam Order of the Royal Purple #10 held its first meeting. This well-known service organization, founded in 1914 at an Elks' convention in Moose Jaw, is affiliated with the Elks Club—itself a Canadian institution since 1912 and an American one since 1868. The women of Royal Purple in PoCo have been engaged in good works for more than fifty years, including raising money to buy hearing aids and other equipment for deaf children. The order also helps parents who need to travel from remote areas for their children's medical care, donates money for kidney dialysis, gives bursaries to high-school students and helps support seniors' housing.

It was about 1947 when production at the Huntington Rubber mill picked up. "Over the years," former employee Keith Milne wrote, "the plant produced gaslines for chainsaws, baby bouncers, wheel coverings, vibration pads for heavy machinery, dam seals for hydro dams in BC, Quebec and the USA. They also made tank lining and muzzle covers for guns for the Department of Defence."

It was busy, too, at the Gilley Brothers quarry on Coquitlam Mountain. Lifetime resident Jim Jacobi worked for seventeen years in that quarry, starting in the late 1940s. He drove truck, worked a jackhammer, worked as a "nipper" (prying rocks loose after blasting), loaded barges with rocks and did lots of other hard work. "The quarry had its own generator," Jim says. "The water to run the generator came down from Monroe Lake—you can see the waterfall from town. A fellow named Ted Kay activated the waterwheel up there; it took two hours for the water to get down to the generator. We'd put symbols on the generator to show how much water we needed, and Ted would use a telescope to look down and see the symbols. If it was a foggy or a misty day it got difficult!"

The new service club and school district, and the upsurge in work, got more attention than the arrival the same year of John and Christina Galer's baby Joseph. "When I was born," Joe recalls, "my family was actually living at the fire hall." Joe's father had been appointed volunteer fire chief in 1941, and the family business, Port Coquitlam Transfer, was right next door to the fire hall, then on Shaughnessy—which made for considerable savings in time when responding to a fire. John's sister, Mary Galer, said, "Every time there was a fire in the city, our house got the first call."

One of the great PoCo stories concerns John Galer. When the fire department needed a new fire truck in 1949, it bought a LaFrance in Owen Sound, Ontario. John went to Owen Sound with fellow firefighter Harry Hammond, and they drove the truck back all the way from Ontario to Port Coquitlam. In 1959, ten years after the initial ride across Canada, John and Harry did it again with a second truck. But that's only half the item. In 1998, at age eighty-two, John drove the 1949 truck in the May Day parade. (The mileage on the truck was still fairly low: over half of it was racked up on the trip from Ontario.)

Along about this time, 1946 or '47, Fred McCallum and his family came to Port Coquitlam from Tisdale, Saskatchewan. Fred bought the Morrison and Rodgers grocery store on Shaughnessy (located at what is now the parking lot adjacent to and north of the Masonic Hall) and converted it to a Red & White store, part of a well-known BC chain at the time. "The Morrison and Rodgers store was run by two old gentlemen," says Maida Smyth,

Fred McCallum (right) retired for a second time on December 2, 1972, when he left his job at the post office.

HISTORICAL FOOTNOTE

A light note: among the people elected to Port Coquitlam council in 1948 was one A.L. Alderman. For three terms, PoCo had an Alderman Alderman!

The 1948 flood waters lapped at the CPR bridge over the Coquitlam River (above) and crept up the walls at Wally's Garage (below).

McCallum's daughter, "and it must have been there a long time. For one thing, the telephone number was 1. They sold groceries, dry goods, a little bit of hardware, that sort of thing. Dad was cleaning out the warehouse and he found mouldy old high-button shoes and canned rabbit meat intended for First World War military use. Anyway, in 1952 he closed the Red & White store and built a Super Valu across the street and south a bit, where the Loonie Store is today. The video store next door used to be his parking lot. That Super Valu was the first cash-and-carry supermarket in Port Coquitlam; up to then everyone had been used to charging their groceries."

Fred McCallum, who served a term on PoCo council in 1958, retired at about the same time and sold the store to Al Nichol, who in turn sold it to a Chinese couple. Here's a delightful historical coincidence: in 1981 Chuck Lohm and his wife Beverley bought the Shop Easy store at 2535 Shaughnessy. Beverley Lohm is Fred McCallum's granddaughter. On September 28, 1998, the Lohms converted the Shop Easy into . . . a Super Valu! To complete the circle the Lohms asked the chain's headquarters to give the store the same number, 61, that Fred McCallum's original Super Valu had. Done!

By the way, Fred McCallum didn't take to retirement. A friend at the post office asked him to come in to help during the Christmas rush, and he liked it so much he kept working there for another fifteen years. Another postal employee, hired by postmaster Charlie Davies, was Nancy Ogilvie. She recalls taking out-of-town mail down to the CPR station in a wheelbarrow. "One time," she says, wincing, "I put eastbound mail on the westbound train."

Now, yet again, the city's rivers attacked. The 1948 Fraser River flood is still counted as the greatest natural disaster in British Columbia's history, and Port Coquitlam was right on its banks, flanked by two other rivers prone to flooding. On May 28, 1948, the gauge at Mission—long used as the "early warning system" for Fraser flooding—read 23.4 feet (7 metres). The danger level was 20 feet (6 metres). The water continued to rise, at one point by an inch (2.5 centimetres) every hour, and on May 30 the dike at Matsqui collapsed. All up and down the lower valley, men, women and children were loading sandbags and patrolling the dikes. The area near Colony Farm was flooded, and residents of the Indian reserve there had to be brought out in rowboats over the fence tops. Water on the highway in front of Essondale was two feet deep. PoCo resident Art Castle remembered seeking out a CPR boxcar loaded with sand and helping "lads from the high school" pack sandbags to carry to the river's edges.

Barnston Island, in mid-Fraser just off PoCo's shores, was completely submerged. Five houses on Pitt River Road west of Shaughnessy had to be abandoned and their residents housed elsewhere. But PoCo was a small part of the havoc: throughout the valley, dikes failed, two thousand homes were destroyed and sixteen thousand residents were evacuated. Total damage from the flood was more than $20 million in 1948 dollars. If the same flood level was to occur today, say experts, the damage would approach $2 billion.

This book began with an admiring reference to beautiful Lions Park. The Lions were established here in November 1949, and since then the club has done a mountain of good work. The park itself was financed by them in 1951, and the next year, in tandem with the Red Cross, they began annual Port Coquitlam Blood Donor Clinics. By 1986 the club was collecting more than 30,000 pints (17,048 litres). Today the Canadian Blood Service handles the clinics.

In 1950 the "Vedder Fishing and Hunting Club" was born,

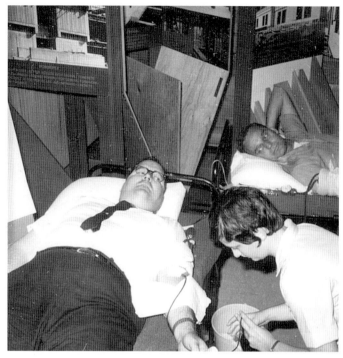

Alderman Bruce Scott at a blood donor clinic in 1970, eighteen years after the Lions and Red Cross held their first clinic.

The Golden Ears barbershop in 1971, not much different from the way it was in the '50s.

The Forrests and the Flood

During the 1948 flood, the Fraser River carried all sorts of flotsam: whole trees, great chunks of riverbank, houses and barns, dead cows and horses. Much of that refuse was piling up alongside the Forrest family's floating house at the foot of Pitt River Road. "Our house, which was a marker for river traffic," Nel Forrest recalls, "with its lights always on, was soon in danger from the high water."

The water crept up the two sets of pilings on each side of the house. The house was tied to the pilings by a heavy wire rope and heavy shackles. The protection from the moving refuse was rapidly being lost as the pilings were more and more covered by the rising river water. So we had to make plans to move the house up on to the shore. The authorities had stopped all tugboats or other craft from working or moving on the river in order to prevent damage to the dikes from the wash of the boats. Our tugs were tied to a railing across the end of Pitt River Road (much like horses in the old movies). We had to search for a very small tug down the river and get a special permit to allow it to come up the river.

The *River Dee* travelled in back eddies and close to the shore to get up to us. By June 1, 1948, the river water was swirling right over the tops of the pilings. My husband and other workers had a very difficult time to get the cables freed, as the shackles were away down under the water, holding down the float of logs on which the house sat, while the river pushed it up. The power of the river was amazing and frightening.

Finally, they were able to chop the cables and the tiny little tug pushed the float slowly and steadily, with lots of help from that wild river, in towards shore. The little boat continued to push until the huge logs which made the float under the house finally struck bottom and stuck there. Our house has been in that same spot for all the years since.

spawned by the habitués at Gene Boileau's popular barbershop. Complete with card and billiards tables as well as a lunch counter, the club became a popular spot for the men in the city. In 1951 the Golden Ears Hotel, still a fixture on Shaughnessy Street, was built around the club. The barbershop was kept and so were the lunch counter and billiards tables. Gene's son Jim—who later became the city's fire chief—began working in the barbershop with his father in '51. After the Beatles became international superstars in the mid-'60s, Jim had to take courses in the new hairstyles popularized by the Fab Four.

But something else besides hairstyles was changing. In the early 1950s PoCo—after decades of slow and sleepy progress—began to look and feel just a little different.

SIX

Growth at Last

Port Coquitlam was a microcosm of the BC economy. "There was fishing, farming, commerce, manufacturing . . . a little bit of everything."

—*Dave Barrett*

By 1951 the City of Port Coquitlam recorded an official population of 3,232, the first time in its existence the city had had a marked jump in population. That 3,232 figure was just over double the population of ten years earlier. PoCo was still tiny compared to other places in the Lower Mainland (Coquitlam had 15,697 residents), but its growth was no longer static.

In fact, it was on the verge of exploding. And a major factor in that growth was the 1951 arrival of the Lougheed Highway. Running parallel to the CPR line, the new road cut diagonally right through PoCo. It would change the city forever. Many of the people already living here still worked for Essondale or for the CPR, but now new people who worked in other, more distant places began to settle here because the new road gave them faster and easier access to Burnaby and Vancouver.

The easier access also began to attract industry. After years of isolation and economic malaise, Port Coquitlam was turning into a busy, active and attractive city. PoCo's board of trade launched a campaign to make the city "a better and brighter place to live so that every resident is happy and proud to say they live in Port Coquitlam," reported the *Coquitlam Herald* of July 4, 1952.

The impact was immediately evident: from 1951 to 1961 PoCo grew more rapidly than any other city in southwestern BC. The population at the 1961 census was 8,111, or just over 150 percent of what it had been ten years earlier. (As a point of comparison, Coquitlam grew by a paltry 85 percent in the same period.) But this was just the beginning.

More people meant more schools. Viscount Alexander Elementary, named for Canada's Governor General at the time, opened in 1951 at the corner of Flint and Prairie. It's an indication of PoCo's slow start in growth that Viscount Alexander was the first new school built in the city since 1914.

Locals recall the shows put on at the school and other locations by the Port Coquitlam Variety Club. It started in 1951, too, and put on musical and comedy shows of all kinds. The Port Coquitlam Variety Players went on to perform at the Haney Correctional Institute, Essondale and seniors' residences.

A year later, in 1952, PoCo got its own roller rink when Harvie Forrest taught himself how to make a Quonset-style hut. (The original Quonset hut, named for Quonset Point, Rhode Island, where it was invented, was a building with a semi-circular arching roof of corrugated metal. They could be built quickly and were developed as shelters and storage depots during World War II, when thousands were built.) Forrest used wood from his sawmill, which he bent into the required shape. Apparently he swung a deal with the contractor of Viscount Alexander school, who came to him for lumber. According to Nel Forrest: "The contractor needed lumber. He came to Harvie and Harvie said, 'You have the equipment to hold up my beams, and I've got the lumber,' so they did a 'horse trade,' and he supplied the lumber for the school and the beams were up and all of a sudden we had an instant building, which jarred the City Council somewhat."

The Forrests' plan was to build two Quonset-style buildings with the space between them devoted to a lunch counter, change rooms and restrooms. There was to be a dance hall on the upper level of the second building. "Out in the auditorium," says Nel, "we couldn't afford to buy the special heaters that were used in roller rinks at that time. We built four electric heaters into the wall where the kids would put on their skates. Once they were on the rink they didn't care whether it was warm or cold." The fire marshall okayed the plan.

The roller rink and coffee shop opened in May 1952 (the second building was still just a shell). Ads asked people to submit names for the complex, and the winning name was "Port Palladium." The Forrests put in a sound system and piped in music for the skaters. The rink was open late on Tuesdays and Thursdays, and it was also open Sunday night, a rarity for the time. "As long as it was a club it could be open," says Nel, "so we made it a Sunday night club and people had to sign up to be members of the club and of course that was our biggest night, always."

There was no public transit at the time, so if you couldn't drive to the rink or get a ride, you had to walk. Harvie Forrest would drive his little truck around and pick up people—mostly youngsters—who wanted to skate. A lot of the Sunday night trade came from Dutch people in the Pitt Polder area just across the Pitt River Bridge. The rink was doing okay. (Morley Deans remembers as a kid running around on the roof of the Palladium—a no-no!)

In December 1953 the insurance for the building came due. The Forrests had insured with a PoCo firm and, PoCo being the small town it was at the time, knew their insurance man as a friend. It was as a friend that he came to see the Forrests and told them, "You know, until you get better established, your insurance rate is awfully high. Maybe you should drop it $5,000. It's not going to burn anyway because it's laminated, solid beams, there are no air spaces. Why don't we lower it $5,000 and that will make it easier for you."

So on December 15, 1953, Harvie and Nel dropped the amount of their insurance to $20,000. Exactly one month later the Port Palladium burned to the ground. A girl coming out of a late movie saw the smoke, turned in the alarm and phoned the Forrests at home. It was about midnight. Harvie thought at first the caller was playing a prank, but when he was convinced she was serious he dashed downtown just in time to see the Palladium's roof cave in.

Harvie and Nel Forrest's Port Palladium Roller Rink provided recreation for PoCo's kids— and adults—for twenty months before it burned to the ground. (Photo courtesy Nel Forrest)

HISTORICAL FOOTNOTE

An irresistible story from the early '50s tells of a fellow who moved to PoCo to build himself a home. He bought a lot on what was a completely empty block and was told he could buy the entire block if he wanted to. When asked why he didn't, he replied, "I just didn't have the $5,000."

The Coquitlam District Music Festival began in 1953 and is still going strong. These photos show (above) the 1972 Music Festival Committee, with Mary Routley at far left, and the Senior Citizen's Choir of Port Coquitlam in competition at the 1971 Festival (below).

The fire department's hydrants were frozen, and the water they had on their truck wasn't enough. "We lost the whole thing," Nel says. "There was not a six-inch piece of wood left in the building . . . It was a terrible blow."

There was worse to come. The Forrests had left the running of their lumberyard to a "nice old man" who had done similar work on the Prairies. When the W.A.C. Bennett government announced an impending 4 percent sales tax, the lumberyard went into overdrive. People were buying everything before the tax came into effect, and the month before the tax was imposed should have been a bonanza for the little company. Instead, because the Prairie man had been overwhelmed and confused and had let a lot of material leave the yard unbilled, the Forrests found themselves in a hole. They closed the doors.

"It was a terrible month," says Nel Forrest. "We were so broke and don't even remember the next two years, it is just such a blur." To help make ends meet, she looked for and found work as a substitute teacher and Harvie got a six-month stint with Northern Navigation on the McKenzie River. They survived.

In 1952 Mayor Charlie Davies—president of PoCo's 1912 provincial championship football team, alderman from 1926 to 1946 and mayor since 1947—stepped down after twenty-nine years as the city's postmaster. His son-in-law Malcolm Rae (after whom Rae Place and Rae Street are named) succeeded him.

Another sterling tradition was thriving by 1953 when a children's musical festival, started a couple of years earlier by Mary Routley and Beryl McLeod (of McLeod's Music Store on Shaughnessy), became the Coquitlam District Music Festival. Mary Routley was the first secretary of the organization and held that post for an astonishing twenty-five years. At first performers were all from PoCo and concerts were held in local homes, but the festivals became more and more popular and eventually grew to include all the schools in School District #43 (Coquitlam, Port Coquitlam, Port Moody, Belcarra and Anmore.) By 1961 there were five hundred entries, featuring vocal, instrumental, dancing, band, orchestral and speaking performances.

In 1953 John Oughton was first elected to council. Oughton would be a councillor from 1953 to 1955 and mayor from 1956 to 1959. Another future mayor was first elected to council in 1954: Robert Hope (whom everyone, of course, called Bob) was an alderman in 1954 and 1955, then mayor from 1960 to 1966. While he was mayor, Bob Hope retired from his job as the CPR's yardmaster to spend full time at his civic duties.

An era could truly be said to have ended in 1954 in Port Coquitlam when G. Roy Leigh retired. An excellent *Vancouver Sun* story of April 17, 1954, was headlined FOR MORE THAN 40 YEARS G.R. LEIGH HAS GUIDED DESTINY OF PORT COQUITLAM.

"If the heart and character of Port Coquitlam could be wrapped and delivered in one packaged personality," wrote reporter Vera Martin, "it would have to be in the person of G.R. Leigh, city clerk, who retired the last day of March. Even before the city of PC was incorporated forty years ago, this man who wears his dignity as a garment had his hand on the helm of affairs. Through flood, fire and complete financial disaster, he kept it there, steady and serene, until prosperity gradually broke like the dawn . . . Second in command to City Clerk John Smith at the time, it was acknowledged that he was the power behind the desk.

"When other municipalities went into receivership this one kept afloat."

G. Roy Leigh had been an exemplary public servant. He was the first president of the Municipal Officers Association of BC, secretary of the school board from 1919 to 1946, at which date School District #43 was incorporated, and he had been named a Justice of the Peace in 1925. At the time of his retirement he was stipendiary magistrate for the County of Westminster, a judge in the Juvenile Court and a police magistrate. "In his own city he was both 'His Worship' and a 'Dutch uncle' to the young folk coming before him whom he scolded roundly . . ."

"Roy Leigh was always very well mannered, well spoken," Nancy Ogilvie recalls. "He reminded me of old country England. I don't remember an accent, he came here as a boy, but he had that *style*." (Nancy's mother, Dorothy Gordon, who had taught at Central School from 1922 to 1924, was an administrative assistant to Leigh from 1942 to 1946. Mrs. Gordon's husband had died in February 1942 at age forty-five, and to support her family she had to find work at a time when a mother working outside the home was a rare phenomenon.)

Leigh was a member of the BC all-star cricket team in interprovincial play "and is today," Martin wrote, "the only life member of the Brockton Point Cricket Association." It turns out he had been one of the stalwart players in that 1912 provincial championship football team.

Robert King, thirty-six, who had worked under Leigh for seventeen years, succeeded him as PoCo's city clerk on April 1, 1954. Leigh agreed to remain in the city hall in an advisory

The BC Provincial Police enforced law and order in Port Coquitlam from 1926 to 1956, working out of an office in city hall, which also held the jail. This photo shows, left to right, Ken Jensen, Game Warden Frank Urquhart, J.P. Stone, Jack Cave, and John Dowsett.

capacity. With King's appointment, a change in title was made to firmly indicate that the city clerk was the chief staff person of the municipality. PoCo followed the lead of several other BC municipalities and appointed King clerk-administrator. He served in that capacity until he left the city's employ in 1967. In late 1999, eighty-two-year-old Bob King still lived in the Port Coquitlam area.

By the mid-1950s the presence of the Lougheed Highway had worked another change in Port Coquitlam: a new downtown. The centre began to shift to the south. This underscored a persistent problem for the city: traffic moving between the northern and southern halves of PoCo sometimes had to wait long minutes for the CPR's trains to go by. (It wasn't a new problem: John Galer, along with a lot of other city old-timers, remembers scoldings from his par-

ents when he would impatiently run across the tracks to beat the trains back in the 1920s.) The crossing remained a problem until the 1962 opening of the Shaughnessy underpass.

In 1955, for the first time in more than forty years, PoCo borrowed money for city improvements. The city's seven thousand inhabitants okayed the borrowing of $125,000 for improvements in the water system.

PoCo's growth in population naturally affected its churches, too. Our Lady of the Assumption Catholic Church moved in 1955 from its first location to the present one, two acres of land purchased from the city on Grant Avenue near the Coquitlam River. (The original church had become far too small: latecomers had to stand outside or go to other parishes.) The site of the new church was dedicated by the co-adjudicator archbishop of Vancouver,

The CPR may have helped give birth to Port Coquitlam, but by the mid-1950s its level crossing was causing long waits for drivers whenever a train went through town.

Our Lady of the Assumption Catholic Church moved to a new location with an expanded church building in 1955.

the Most Rev. M.M. Johnson, on Sunday, May 29, 1955. The first wedding occurred just two days later when Dick Bodnarchuk married Rochelle Wild. The first baby baptized in the new church in early January 1957 was Greg Rieu, whose mother Zelle is still very active in church affairs. She kindly provided a history of the church, which explains that "the unique cross-shaped design of the new church was an inspiration of Monsignor Kane's, who had seen a similarly designed church in Agassiz, built by architect Peter Thornton."

A bridge carrying the Lougheed Highway across the Pitt River opened in 1957, and that brought excitement to PoCo because the new bridge was officially opened by Premier W.A.C. Bennett. This was, so far as we can tell, the first official visit to Port Coquitlam by a premier in more than forty years. This was also the year the Huntington Rubber mill staff grew to a record twenty-five people, and the Port Theatre closed.

The Port had been managed by Mr. and Mrs. Lilly, who

both had backgrounds in vaudeville. Maida McCallum Smyth worked at the Port as book-keeper and in the little box office selling tickets for the evening shows, which were always sold out. "We had three different double features every week," Mrs. Smyth recalls, "and I remember we even had a crying room, where people could take their babies and still hear and see the movie through a big window. I remember that room because my husband used to come in and we'd sit in there after the night's last tickets had been sold and watch the show. Our first projectionist was Elmer Canning. Three men owned the theatre: Joe Pregler, Mr. Miller and Mr.

Port Coquitlam in the 1950s, looking northeast over the Coquitlam River. (Photo by Aero Surveys Ltd.)

Centennial Pool, built to celebrate the hundredth anniversary of BC becoming a colony, has been a favourite spot for kids since it officially opened in January 1958.

Kincaid." When television came in, that spelled an end to the Port. The theatre building still stands on the east side of Shaughnessy just north of McAllister. For a brief time in the late 1990s it housed a rowdy nightclub that was eventually shut down by city hall. As 2000 dawned, plans for the building were still unformed.

Now development in Port Coquitlam really began to accelerate. There had been a start on residential development on Mary Hill (when it was apparently called St. Mary's Heights) in the city's early years and later, but world wars and the Great Depression had scotched the plans. In 1957 all that changed dramatically. Yorkshire Trust announced plans to construct 1,100 homes on Mary Hill, a project that would top $20 million—equivalent to something like $150 million today. It was a huge boost for the city. Three-bedroom homes in the development would sell for $15,000 to $16,000 with down payments as low as $975 and 6.25 percent financing.

In June Charlie Davies, former mayor (the wheels for the project had begun to turn during his term in office), turned the first sod to launch the project while the serving mayor, John Oughton, and Yorkshire representatives looked on and beamed. Later, developer Norm Hullah took over the project.

There was more to come in 1957. A $2.5 million school construction program was proposed, and Cedar Drive Elementary and Mary Hill Elementary were built under that program.

PoCo was really chugging. It was the first city in BC to complete its 1958 Centennial project (celebrating the hundredth anniversary of BC's union with Vancouver Island as the colony of British Columbia)—on June 15, 1957, when a $35,000 swimming pool was opened on the Agricultural Hall grounds. The pool, which immediately became a favourite with local kids, officially opened January 3, 1958. PoCo citizens raised $7,000 of the total cost, with the balance of the funds coming from the provincial government.

Fred McCallum sold his SuperValu store—which he had established in 1952 as the city's first supermarket—in 1957. The next year he ran for council and was elected.

Esco Ltd. began construction on its Canadian Alloy Steel Foundry in 1957. Esco, a US-based firm, selected the 8-hectare (20-acre) site at 1855 Kingsway because of its accessibility to the CPR's main line. Esco had been in Vancouver's Marpole district for two years, but now the Marpole office building was cut in half, the two halves were put on a barge and floated up the Fraser to a site near the plant where they were reconnected. That same

Esco Ltd. opened its $1.25 million Canadian Alloy Steel Foundry in 1958 (left and above) and is now one of the city's largest employers. Its office building (top) was floated up the Fraser to Port Coquitlam.

In 1958, May Queen April Wingrove and Mayor John Oughton placed a wreath on the cenotaph to honour the local men who died in the two World Wars.

Rick Mabbett, "the Pot-Hole King," was on city council, with two one-year gaps, from 1960 to 1983.

office building is still being used today. The $1.25 million Port Coquitlam facility, which opened in January 1958 with a staff of fourteen, could manufacture 150 tons of castings a month. By 1980 Esco had expanded its plant three times and was employing 250 men and women. In 1992 Esco's plant received an environmental award from the Chamber of Commerce for its extensive recycling efforts. Between 1995 and 1997 the company invested $5 million in the facility on new equipment and more work space, and capacity went from 50 tons a day to 90. In 1998 Esco received a special city commendation for forty years of operation. With 220 employees in 2000, it is one of the ten largest employers in the city. It's engaged in aggregate crushing, mine crushing, mine milling and casting industrial rail parts.

What were house prices like in PoCo in 1958? A two-bedroom house on 5 acres (2 hectares) of land sold for $8,450 and a three-bedroom home on a 99-foot (30-metre) corner lot closer to the city sold for $8,950. The most popular lots, 1.6-acre (.6-hectare) blocks, cost from $2,050 to $2,300 depending on their location. As a point of comparison, the average weekly wage in Canada that year in the manufacturing trade was $66, so the $8,450 cost cited was equivalent to 128 weeks of work.

Mabel Madaski and her son Mel bought the Port Coquitlam Bowladrome in 1958. It had been opened in 1950 by the Froland and Beattie families . . . and, according to *Port Coquitlam: City of Rivers and Mountains*, had met with some resistance. "The city was apprehensive," say the writers, "that it might attract people of 'questionable character'!" Exactly the opposite happened, and the Bowladrome became a favourite haunt of local families. The original owners sold the lanes to Bud Sowerby in the mid-1950s; then the Madaskis bought it and enlarged it. Brian Madaski, who started as a pinboy for his parents, now manages the lanes.

In the late '50s a fellow named Jack Campbell and his wife Norma arrived in PoCo from the Peace River district. They went into the hotel business, owning and operating the Golden Ears Hotel for many years and turning it into a centre of social and business life. In a few years newcomer Campbell became one of Port Coquitlam's more prominent mayors.

The Galers, on the other hand, have been a part of PoCo for as long as the city itself has existed, and in 1958 John Galer, son of the man who had been the city's longest-serving mayor, stepped down as fire chief and got himself elected to council. He won four elections in a row, then decided to concentrate on his business affairs. In 1962 he won a Good Citizenship Award from the city. Perhaps he should win a Good Traveller's Award, too. A

June 21, 1992, story by Myra Ross in *Coquitlam Now* tells how "John Galer does countries: 43 in four years . . . He writes their names on a worn and folded piece of paper kept in his wallet. The list includes Turkey, Hawaii, Mexico, Brazil, Argentina, Spain, Fiji and the Greek Islands, his favorite." (Galer was succeeded as fire chief by Jim Boileau, who was voted in by his fellow volunteers and was chief until 1961, when Bill Wingrove took over. Boileau and his men had a new two-bay station at 2352 McAllister to work out of, a block and a half from the old station.)

In 1958 Port Coquitlam's fire department had two trucks and a brand-new building to work out of. Volunteers, from left to right, were Maurice Wingrove, Howard Smith, Jim David, John Galer, Kim McLennan, Albert Osborne, Bill Wingrove, Harold Bradford, Jim Boileau, John Campbell, Roy Routley, Dave Perugini, Art Wingrove, Bob Gillespie, Sam Waddell, George Bracewell, Bill Battistoni.

One of Port Coquitlam's most prominent women, Ada Irvine, teacher and latterly principal at Central School for forty years, died in 1958. She had started teaching at the Junction Schoolhouse, where her father R.D. was principal, in 1906. In the late 1930s one of Ada's students was the already-mentioned Shiro Suyehiro, who had a real talent for art. Ada was so impressed by one of young Shiro's paintings that she drove all the way into Vancouver to the museum and asked the staff to display it.

The next year, 1959, was a major milestone in PoCo's education history. Port Coquitlam High School opened on 6.5 hectares (16 acres) on the north side of town. Kids from Grades 8 to 12 attended and enjoyed a quarter-mile cinder track, tennis courts, a cafeteria and a full-sized gym with bleachers. The high school was a centre for schooling in PoCo for forty years.

PoCo's fire department bought two new fire engines in '59 and increased its volunteer force to twenty-five men. The department bought a used '57 Chevy panel truck the same year and converted it for use as an emergency inhalator vehicle.

In 1960 Eric "Rick" Mabbett was first elected to council and quickly made his mark with a sharp eye for the quality of the city's infrastructure. "Rick Mabbett used to be affectionately called the 'Pot-hole King'," retired city clerk Ron Freeman remembers, "because he noticed the little things around town that weren't being done: filling potholes, cleaning sidewalks and so on. He was a good guy." Mabbett, a native son, worked for the provincial public works department as a supervisor at Essondale. He left council in 1968 because he was expecting a transfer out of the area. When he got a promotion rather than a transfer, he jumped back into the civic race and romped home a winner. He kept winning until 1983, with one other one-year gap, for a total of twenty-one years on council. "Mabbett's wife Edna was a real sports fan," Freeman says with a chuckle. "She'd wear a Walkman to fancy city

The 1961 Coquitlam River flood caused more damage to the city than the 1948 Fraser River overflow, even though the latter covered more ground. The torrent shifted the Red Bridge slightly on its foundations and washed away an excavating crane, trees and sections of road, among other things.

dinners to keep up on the Lions or whoever. She rode a bicycle. A nice lady."

Another notable election in 1960 saw a twenty-nine-year-old social worker named Dave Barrett gain a seat in the provincial legislature as MLA for Dewdney, which took in PoCo. Barrett and his family lived on Mary Hill Road at Western Drive from 1964 to 1972. He recalled Port Coquitlam as a "microcosm" of the BC economy: "There was fishing, farming, commerce, manufacturing . . . a little bit of everything." He also remembered, with pleasure, that locals were "heavily engaged" in local politics and had a friendliness and an openness he still recalls with fondness.

That community spirit was called on the next year. The January 15, 1961, upsurge of the Coquitlam River illustrates the vagaries of flooding in the Port Coquitlam area: the 1948 Fraser flood had been far greater in scope, but the 1961 flood did more damage to PoCo. The weather had been unseasonably warm (up to 54 degrees Fahrenheit, about 12 degrees Celsius), and nearly 25 centimetres (10 inches) of rain fell overnight. The result was dramatic. Stand at the corner of Pitt River Road and Shaughnessy and look west toward Riverview Hospital. Now imagine that whole area covered with a sheet of water, which in some areas near the river was almost a metre (3 feet) deep. A massive dam of splintered trees and debris piled up against the old Red Bridge, forcing the water behind it even higher and slightly shifting the bridge on its foundations. The torrent of water gouged out a new channel for the river, cutting off Steelhead Ranch on Chester Street and washing out a section of road near Scott's Gravel Pit. "The company had been working near the Coquitlam Bridge and left a dragline [an excavating crane with a bucket dragged toward the machine by a cable] on the riverbank overnight," relate the authors of *Port Coquitlam: City of Rivers and Mountains*. "The floodwaters rose so rapidly that by morning the bank had been washed away and the dredging equipment, weighing in the neighborhood of 20 tons, was washed down to the Red Bridge!"

Chief Coquitlam performs a good-luck dance on November 6, 1961, to inaugurate Port Coquitlam's "Jeep" mail delivery service, the first in Canada. Mail carrier W. Charlton delivers the first letter, from the Postmaster General, to Mayor Robert Hope.

It took more than a year to completely clear the river. With prompting from PoCo council, BC Hydro agreed to lower the level of Coquitlam Lake by 3 metres (10 feet).

A discovery made as a result of the flooding was the river's overlapping jurisdictions. The provincial government's minister of highways, Phil Gaglardi, sent in a crew to remove the log jam in the Red Bridge area and was also asked to finance repairs to the bridge. It was, of course, on a provincial secondary highway. When it came to removal of the silt in the river, responsibility was assumed by both the District of Coquitlam and the City of Port Coquitlam. Then Mayor Bob Hope asked the federal government to dredge the Coquitlam River south of the Red Bridge, because that section of the river was in *its* jurisdiction. It made for a lot of committee meetings.

By the end of the 1960s new flood control measures were in effect—including a dike built in May 1967 at the Red Bridge itself. Provincial and federal funding was granted for more extensive dike work.

Financial peril, fire, flood, influenza, the Depression . . . was there anything PoCo hadn't experienced yet? Yes. The list of woes was extended just after midnight on October 13, 1962, when Typhoon Freda hit the southwest coast with winds of 130 kilometres per hour (80 miles an hour) and knocked out PoCo's power for several days. Because of the length of time people were left without electricity, PoCo firefighters brought many home deep-freezes to the station and plugged them into the fire hall's auxiliary power system. The little city had plen-

By late 1962 the new Shaughnessy Street underpass was almost completed, promising a shorter travel time between the northern and southern halves of Port Coquitlam.

HISTORICAL FOOTNOTE

The purpose of the Shaughnessy Street underpass was to link the commercial core of the city with what was then a predominantly residential north side. It worked. But it didn't work for everyone. Lois and Keith Milne were at an Elks dinner and heard a northside resident tell Mayor Hope she would never go to the Port Coquitlam Recreation Centre. The mayor asked why. "Because I would have to go through that underpass to get there."

ty of company in its misery: the entire Lower Mainland was buffeted. Seven people were killed, a fifth of all the trees in Stanley Park were blown down, and houses and buildings sustained varying degrees of damage over a wide area.

In spite of these disasters, the Port Coquitlam area's potential as a major industrial site was becoming daily more evident: it was on a big navigable river, a major highway ran right through it, the CPR was literally in the middle of town and land costs were lower than those in the more urban areas to the west. That potential, and memories of the disastrous 1948 Fraser River flood, inspired the city's board of trade in 1962 to resurrect the old idea of a canal connecting Burrard Inlet to the Pitt River. The waterway, which would serve double duty as a flood-control measure and a new route for export trade, would be 61 metres (200 feet) wide and 10.7 metres (35 feet) deep. A committee was struck and got as far as a meeting with Canada's external affairs minister, Howard Green. He liked the idea a lot. It didn't hurt that Green was Member of Parliament for a Lower Mainland riding, Vancouver-Quadra. But even with the interest of three oil companies (Imperial, Shell and BA, all of whom had fuel storage facilities on Burrard Inlet), the canal could not be shown to be cost effective and the idea died on the drawing board.

If they couldn't get a canal, they could get an underpass. In 1962 the north-south flow of PoCo's traffic was immensely improved with the opening of the Shaughnessy Street underpass.

The underpass is not viewed with as much affection today (with PoCo's population about fifty thousand) as it was in 1962, when there were fewer than nine thousand people, but the opening was a major occasion in the city's history, ending years of frustrating waits by motorists and pedestrians as the CPR's trains crawled by. A banner announcing "The City Underpass Week" was draped across the entrance, and the audience was seated right in the middle of Shaughnessy Street. A plaque at the south entrance notes the $450,000 project was officially opened December 8, 1962, and names the official party:

> Mayor Robert Hope. Aldermen: S.R.H. Evans, Miss Jane Kilmer, R.E. Nacht, E.W. Mabbett, George Wingrove. City Clerk: R.E. King. Works Superintendent: J.S. Robbins.

Besides being a good year for drivers, 1962 was a terrific year for PoCo and lacrosse. The New Westminster O'Keefes gained three junior players from PoCo that year, and their 1962 lineup was, according to sports historian David Savelieff, "one of the greatest clubs in the history of the sport." The O'Keefes won the Mann Cup in just four games on the road, the only club ever to do so. The team's three newcomers were Mike Gates, Charlie Saunders and Gordon Stidolph. In 1965 they moved over to the newly formed Coquitlam Adanacs in the Senior "A" Division . . . and Mike Gates really hit his stride. He captured the Ed Bailey Trophy for Outstanding Rookie in 1961, went on to be named a First All-Star *six times* and won the scoring title three times. During his eleven years in the sport, Mike scored a total of 113 points in 427 games. He was elected to the Canadian Lacrosse Hall of Fame in 1977. Today, Mike Gates is a long-time (and frequently poll-topping) PoCo councillor: he marked twenty years on council in 2000, and he recently pushed for the lacrosse box at the new Terry Fox Secondary to be named for his former teammate Gordon Stidolph. (PoCo pioneer Jim David recalls lacrosse games with Gates. He laughs. "Mike played goal for us. He was a great player when he wasn't fighting.")

Other sports were popular in the area in the 1960s. In 1965 Port Coquitlam High School won the Coquitlam Track and Field Championships, which took in all the schools in District #43. And during the 1960s Don and Alice Bitcon became known as "Mr. and Mrs. Soccer" for their efforts in promoting children's soccer in Port Coquitlam. Minor soccer became so popular that several teams were formed, and the city has produced a lot of excellent soccer players over the years. An undated clipping from

Young lacrosse players like these are inspired by PoCo's long line of successful boxla stars, including Mike Gates, Charlie Saunders and Gordon Stidolph.

the *Coquitlam Herald* named a few: Scotty Coutts, Bill Wingrove, Tom David, Alec Sales, George McMyn, Todd Sloan and Harold Routley. In 1987 Don Bitcon and John Watkins organized a reunion to bring former junior players together with their team-mates. The Bitcons' legacy is still alive and well, but Don says that today his only involvement is watching his grandchildren play.

One of those soccer players, Bill Wingrove, became Port Coquitlam's first paid fire chief in May 1964. He had already been the volunteer chief for four years, but the city was getting too big for an all-volunteer force. The Wingrove family—there were a lot of them—has been prominent all through the city's history. The name pops up everywhere, including on PoCo's map: Wingrove Place runs off Oxford near Kwayhquitlum Middle School.

An excellent indicator of PoCo's accelerating growth in the mid-1960s is Ford dealer Metro Motors, a genuine success story. Metro was opened by Glenn McKone in April 1965 at the corner of Lougheed Highway and Hastings Street. McKone opened a

Soccer is another popular sport in the city, which has a legacy of champion teams dating back to the era when it was known as football. Bill Wingrove (right) was a soccer player who became Port Coquitlam's first paid fire chief in 1964.

body shop exactly a year later, a new showroom the year after that, and doubled the staff to forty-four the year after that. Today Metro's vice-president and general manager Layne Magnuson heads a staff of 110.

The death in 1965 of Port Coquitlam's William Charles Hughes completely changed the look of one important part of the city. Hughes had come out from Manitoba in 1947 and delivered farm-fresh eggs to local homes and businesses or sold them right at his Cherry Blossom Farm itself. The farm was at what is now the corner of Broadway and Kingsway. When Hughes died, his son Charles developed the farm into thirteen industrial lots. "The farmhouse is still standing," he says, "and being used for industrial offices." Hughes Place, a block east of Hastings near Westwood Park, is named for Charles's father. (Incidentally, Charles Hughes was in the first graduating class at Port Coquitlam High School.)

Port Coquitlam's estimated population at the 1966 mid-census was 11,121, an increase of just over 3,000 in five years. And 1966 was the year provincial redistribution split the big Dewdney riding in two, with the eastern half retaining the name Dewdney, while the western half became Coquitlam riding. Dave Barrett continued to represent the latter, which still included PoCo.

There was shock and sadness in December 1966 when popular mayor Bob Hope died in office. More than three hundred people attended his funeral at St. Catherine's Anglican. The

Metro Motors drew crowds to see its selection of Ford vehicles—or, as in this case, to meet the mascot of Vancouver's new hockey team, the Canucks.

honorary pallbearers included Reeve Jimmy Christmas of Coquitlam, Mayor Harry Douglass of White Rock, Mayor Al Howe of Port Moody, Reeve Peter Jenewein of Maple Ridge, Reeve O.A. Austring of Pitt Meadows and Reeve Clarence Taylor of Delta. Making Mayor Hope's death especially poignant was the fact that, because of PoCo's growth, the top floor of city hall—which had been unoccupied for fifty-two years—had just come into use. A new council chamber, a committee room and the mayor's office were installed on that top floor.

A February 16, 1967, item from the *Vancouver Sun* reported that a "committee has been appointed by city council to compile Port Coquitlam's early history." The members were Robert E. King (he was city clerk at the time) and Mrs. King, Mr. and Mrs. J.E. Duncan, Mr. and Mrs. E.J. Routley (presumably this was Elmer Routley, Harold's brother) and Stuart Thomas. A later story in the *Vancouver Province* on August 25, 1967, adds Mr. and Mrs. D.D. Bennie to the list. That would have been Doug Bennie and his wife. He was presented with a Good Citizen's medallion by PoCo's board of trade in March 1967 for his community service activity, much of it with the Boy Scouts. We don't know whatever became of this project, but perhaps Edith Chambers made use of its findings for her 1973 history.

In 1967 Larry Pollock, who had joined the city staff in 1965 as treasurer (he had earlier performed that function for Fort St. John), was appointed clerk-administrator and also retained responsibilities for the city's finances. A year later, recognizing that the volume of administrative work was increasing, Pollock became city administrator and Ron Freeman was hired to attend to the duties of the clerk's office as city clerk. Pollock left the employ of the city in May 1981 and went to Oak Bay on Vancouver Island, where he served as administrator for eleven years until retirement. He died in 1998 at age sixty-five.

Ron Freeman, on the other hand, was with PoCo for twenty-four years of solid service. He had served in Kelowna as assistant city clerk for six years and had been an elected member of the Kitimat Municipal Council for seven years (1955 to 1962) before that. "The first bylaw I placed on a Port Coquitlam council agenda was #896, considered on September 23, 1968," he recalls. "The last one was #2655, which received first reading March 23, 1992. That meant that 1,760 bylaws were prepared for consideration by council while I was city clerk."

"Municipal politics is the most interesting," Freeman says, quoting Mayor Jack Campbell, "because you're involved in *everything*. And the clerk is privy to everything going on in the city. It's really interesting. Sometimes you have to tell the council they can't do certain things. For example, at one time they wanted to increase the speed limit on the stretch of the Lougheed Highway that runs through the city. I told them they couldn't do that, that's a provincial decision. The clerk can act as an ombudsman if a member of the public has a grievance. Let's say he wants to fill in a ditch and he can't get approval; I might go to Alderman so-and-so, who's head of the public works committee, and put his case for him.

"You also have to be prudent. I'm the kind of guy who, if you ask when Christmas will be this year, will tell you, 'We-l-l, it was on December 25 *last* year'."

"One thing I realized right off the bat after getting elected," Councillor Mike Gates says. "When Ron Freeman talked, you listened."

In February 1967 a by-election was held to fill the vacant mayor's chair, and Golden Ears Hotel owner Jack Campbell—a resident for just seven years—won. Being a mayor was not a new experience for Campbell: he had earlier served two terms as mayor of Sexsmith, Alberta. His years in office in PoCo were marked by a boom in residential development and surging population growth: from 1961 to 1971 the city's population grew from 8,111 to 19,560. Campbell was a popular mayor, coming back and winning each mayoralty race until 1971. "He was a friendly fellow," says former councillor John Keryluk. "His nickname was Pidge. He'd walk down Shaughnessy, talk to folks, stop for a coffee." Retired city clerk Ron Freeman concurs. "You'd be with him at a restaurant for a coffee or a business meeting, he'd talk to the waiter or waitress and sooner or later some connection would come up. The cook used to work for him, or the waiter knew someone from his home town. The connections were almost uncanny. He was a real people person, he loved to talk to people."

Oops!

One of the oddest stories in Port Coquitlam's history was unearthed thanks to long-time city clerk Ron Freeman. In 1969, shortly after he became clerk, Freeman made an astonishing discovery: The city's land titles from tax sales had never been properly registered in the Land Title Office.

"The procedure on tax sale," says Freeman, "requires that a 'Tax Sale Notice' be filed when the tax sale has been held and then, after a one-year redemption period has expired, an application is made to the Land Title Office to have the title transferred.

"This second step, with almost all the tax sale land, had never been taken—in some cases, for more than forty years! This meant that each property was *still registered in the name of the former owner*, and a note had simply been made on the Land Title records that the land was subject to tax sale proceedings. The actual transfer of title had never been completed. The Assessment Department of the City, as it was at that time, merely changed its internal records to show it was city-owned land and it was forgotten.

"To say I was astounded at this lack of completion is understating the case. Even at that early time the land was worth a great deal of money—today it would be in the tens of millions of dollars. With staff changes over the years and the pressure of daily business it was simply a subject to which no one had turned their attention. It took several years to clear the records, and we were very lucky to encounter a sympathetic Land Title Registrar who allowed us to complete the proceedings with only very sketchy information.

"The exact year the tax sale for any particular property had taken place, the amount of taxes that had been due, or any of the other details, could only have been determined by a prohibitive amount of research through dusty old record books. There were hundreds of lots. Fortunately, the Registrar saw this to be the case and took pity on us."

In one memorable case, Freeman says, a particular tax sale lot had been sold by the city to a third party by way of a deed that remained unregistered. "This only came to light when this third party wanted to sell the property and the purchaser discovered that the vendor, apparently, did not own the property. As far as the purchaser could tell from the Land Title Office records, some other person did; and worse, the property had been sold to the City for taxes! The resulting confusion was truly amazing."

Another new face on council in 1967 was George Laking, who won by acclamation two years after his initial attempt (which he lost by twelve votes). "I campaigned on the lack of industry in town," he says. "In the industrial area south of the tracks there were two industries. Two! There was nothing in terms of recreation, just a couple of playing fields. The city wasn't moving. It was basically dead." Shortly after Laking joined council, Mayor Campbell asked him to chair a planning committee. The existing committee had resigned, complaining it wasn't being listened to. Laking came back after two weeks and advised "no more planning committees." Instead, he recommended an *advisory* committee to advise council. Done. "I don't care what anybody says," Laking says, slapping his knees briskly for emphasis, "you have to go out in the community and *talk to people*."

Canada celebrated its hundredth year in 1967, and during March a Centennial Banquet was held at the Golden Ears Hotel. Fifty Port Coquitlam pioneers sat down to dinner. (The Golden Ears itself was in the news the following year when it added six new rooms and opened PoCo's first dining lounge.) On June 29, 1967—the last day of the school year—the Robert Hope Centennial Pool, named in honour of the late mayor, was opened in Yorkshire

Park on Mary Hill. The park itself was later named for Hope. Another construction project completed in 1967 was the Red Bridge dike, a further safeguard against the sometimes erratic behaviour of the Coquitlam River.

And on August 21, 1967, the first sod was turned for the Port Coquitlam Recreation Centre. The Parks and Recreation Commission had recommended the city build a recreational complex with an ice arena, change rooms and a seating capacity between 750 and 1,000. A public vote approved the $325,000 project, and soon there was a facility—the Port Coquitlam Recreation Centre—for hockey, figure skating, lacrosse, roller skating, basketball and ballroom dancing. The building opened in 1970, designed by architects Carlberg Jackson Partners to allow for later expansion. It has undergone a couple of upgrades since then and is heavily used to this day, though it must be said that because the centre was on Wilson Avenue, on the south side, some PoCo residents on the north side were unhappy. This dissatisfaction came back to haunt Mayor Campbell in 1972.

The Elks Hall was refurbished in 1970 and continued to be a gathering place for men and women (in the Order of the Royal Purple) doing good for the community.

With memory still green of the thirty-seven years in which no new schools were built in Port Coquitlam, the situation had dramatically changed. Now there weren't enough being built! The provincial government put a freeze on school construction in 1968, and suddenly PoCo's schools were full to bursting. In September 1968, at the beginning of the school year, some 1,400 students from Centennial Senior Secondary sent letters to Premier W.A.C. Bennett, drawing his attention to the city's overcrowded classrooms. They were backed up by Coquitlam MLA Dave Barrett and local union tradesmen. Funds were squeezed out and School District #43 was able to build several new schools adjacent to new subdivisions. (One of these schools was George Pearkes Junior Secondary, opened February 20, 1970. It has since become Minnekhada Middle School.)

Port Coquitlam High School expanded in 1968. The inclusion of science facilities and the industrial education wing transformed the building. That was also the year of the first annual "Youth in Action Day" at the high school. Local businesses sponsored the event, and a mock city council was elected by the students. The "Mayor" was student Kathy Whiting. She and her council proposed that a street in the Cedar Drive area be named after the school's popular student counsellor, Al Wright. The real city council agreed. Wright Avenue runs east off Cedar Drive a block north of Prairie. It might be the only street in British Columbia named as a result of a suggestion by students.

Growth wasn't confined to schools. Annie Osborne tells a story about the occasion when the city opened up a new street and named it for her. "I went out to have a look at it," she says. "The next time I went, there were eight houses on it!"

A long and distinguished life and career came to an end in 1968 when Harry Galer, PoCo's longest-serving mayor (1925 to 1945) to that time, died at age ninety-four.

When Harry was mayor, and up until 1968, there were five councillors on council. But now the growing size of the city prompted PoCo council to ask for provincial approval to increase its size to six members. Approval was immediate, and the increase took effect for the 1969 council. For the record, the mayor was Jack Campbell and the six aldermen were Dr. Robert M. (Bob) Heffelfinger, George R. Laking, G.R.A. MacDonald, Eric W. (Rick) Mabbett, L. Bruce Scott and J.B. Young. Two council members, Laking and Scott, were later mayors themselves. (Several PoCo councils have had two future mayors amongst the councillors; none has had three.)

The city reached another milestone the next year, when the Port Coquitlam Fire Department hired five paid firefighters to add to the twenty-five volunteers. (This was also the year the Essondale Fire Department retired its truck after forty years' service.)

The Port Coquitlam Recreation Centre (above) and George Pearkes Junior Secondary School (below) both opened in 1972 to meet the needs of the rapidly expanding community.

A newcomer to PoCo in 1969 was nine-year-old Mike Farnworth, who arrived with his family. Farnworth, who was elected PoCo's MLA in 1996, was born just outside Liverpool, England. "My family decided to move, but we couldn't decide between Canada and New Zealand. So we literally flipped a coin. Heads to Canada, tails to New Zealand. It came up heads." They moved to Montreal just in time to experience the most violent period of the FLQ crisis. "If we'd wanted to move to where bloody bombs were blowing up," Farnworth says now, "we'd have gone to Belfast!" The Farnworths moved to BC, and young Mike took to PoCo immediately: he and his chums discovered a secret hideout near the south end of Shaughnessy—"before they pushed [the road] through"—that they dubbed Elephant Island for an

oddly shaped cedar tree there. "There was a natural tunnel through a rotted-out tree, a very private place, kids'd go there to play and swim." The views of Colony Farm and Mary Hill were great, with vine maples a blaze of colour in the fall and later with snow covering the mountains. When he was elected to council in 1984 at age twenty-four, Mike Farnworth was the youngest councillor in the city's history.

Speaking of politics, in 1969 Coquitlam MLA Dave Barrett became leader of the opposition in the BC legislature and quickly became a thorn in the side of Premier W.A.C. Bennett.

That year the Port Coquitlam District Boy Scouts started their annual PoCo Trek, a tradition that has unfortunately lapsed. The idea was to give participants (not just Boy Scouts, but Girl Guides and Brownies and any interested individuals or groups) an opportunity to enjoy the wholesome activity of walking through Port Coquitlam and along sections of the PoCo Trail, and to make a small donation to promote the local Scout movement. By 1978 there were six hundred "Trekkers." Former alderman Phil Ranger would like to see the Trek revived.

People were keen on physical fitness at the end of the '60s. In 1970, with the encouragement of Mayor Campbell and the city's recreation department, a Port Coquitlam track and field club developed. To quote *Port Coquitlam: City of Rivers and Mountains*:

PoCo Boy Scouts and supporters set off on the PoCo Trek in 1972.

Through the efforts of Ron and Dorothy Davis, Elaine Cramer, Bob and Lois Holm, Mike Forrest, Kay Whiting, Ted and Norma Barrett, Judy Watkins and Art Castle, the Poco Pacers Track and Field Club was founded. By October of 1971 more than 70 individuals and 14 businesses and organizations worked to promote the club's activities.

Coaches received their training from the BC Track and Field Association clinics, and famous track and field stars like Debbie Brill. Elaine Cramer explained the purpose of the club was to "encourage children to enjoy the sport of running and Olympic-style track and field." Approximately 60 athletes between the ages of six and 20 were involved, including both Doug Alward and Terry Fox, who displayed exceptional skill in track and field events even at the ages of 11 and 12.

Doug Alward was to become Terry Fox's driver during his national campaign, and the background and training provided by the club no doubt was a factor that contributed to the eventual success of the Marathon of Hope.

(For more detail on Terry and his magnificent campaign, see the story and sidebar in the next chapter.)

On March 23, 1970, an outdoors group called the PoCo Trail Blazers presented plans for a terrifically exciting project, a 25-kilometre (15.6-mile) nature trail that would completely encircle the city. The idea had come from Harold Routley, a PoCo resident since 1906 and a city council member in the late 1950s. The board of trade liked the idea and found lots of support, including from the BC Dyking Commission (much of the trail would be built atop the

Port Coquitlam students compete against rivals from other cities' high schools in a 1973 track meet.

city's dikes). Among those involved in the proposal were Helen Busch and Elaine Eisel, Clyde Griffiths of the city's Parks and Recreation Department, Hans Kappel, Barbara Murphy and George Shaw of the board of trade, George Lank of the Burke Mountain Trail Riders, Central School Principal Glenn MacDonald, Hanne Mortil, Phil Ranger (himself an alderman from 1971 to 1980), Charles Saunders, the Community & Ratepayers' Association of Mary Hill and, of course, Harold Routley.

Phil Ranger has a theory about Routley's brainchild: "Harold worked at the railway bridge over the Pitt River," he says. "I'll bet he sat there looking at the dikes one day and conceived the trail idea right there."

Not long after Routley had the idea, a trio of civic-minded guys who all happened to live

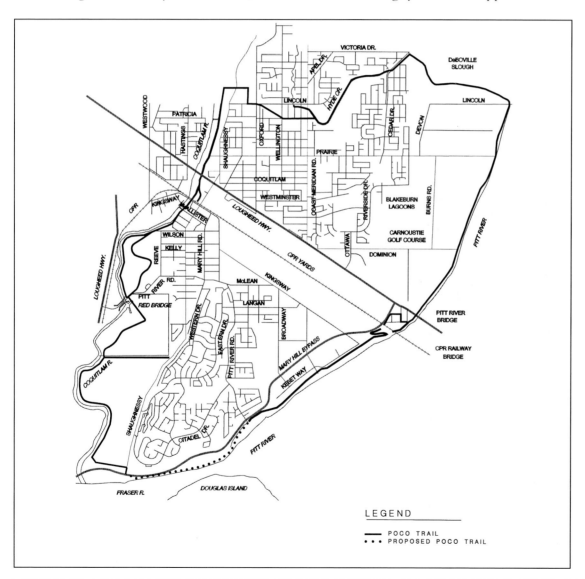

A map of Port Coquitlam showing the PoCo Trail and its proposed extension. (Courtesy City of Port Coquitlam)

on Claudia Street in the Mary Hill neighbourhood got together to help build the trail. Phil Ranger, Alex Docherty and Charles Saunders dragooned others into service as the Trail Blazers, and a group of sixteen people went to work with machetes. "It was hands on," said Saunders. "Wheelbarrows, shovels, blood, sweat and tears." Phil Ranger laughs as he recalls one particularly brutal session. "We were whacking away at the bush on an uphill stretch. The Hydro power line was right above us, so we knew which way we were going. Well, we worked like mad on that stretch. Two days of hard, sweaty work. We came by the next day and Hydro had clearcut the whole right of way."

The Trail Blazers described the original route proposal: "Starting at the Red Bridge (Pitt River Road) the proposed trail would run south on the dyke along the Coquitlam River to Colony Farm, east along Colony Farm, cut across Mary Hill along the Hydro easement, and follow a natural trail to Pitt River. From there it would run north on the dyke along the river to Twin Bridges, west along the Hyde Creek diversion to the Coquitlam River and south on the dyke along the river to the Red Bridge." It would also give access to 8-hectare (20-acre) Marshall Island. The Trail Blazers hoped the trail would be used by hikers, walkers, cyclists and horseback riders, and envisioned areas along the trail that could be developed with playgrounds, boat launches and picnic areas.

Over the years, residents hacked and sawed their way along, raising money by holding dances and other events. By the end of 1998, the city was able to point to a number of enhancements. The eastern end, where users have to come onto the Mary Hill Bypass to go under the CPR's main line, wasn't part of this upgrade, but the path was lowered under the Kingsway railway bridge, where the low clearance was hazardous to heads. A section from Lions Park to Wilson was paved, and a more prominent entrance to the trail was created.

This splendid nature walk, now maintained by the city, is one of PoCo's greatest treasures.

SEVEN

Moving Forward

W hen I decided to
do it, I knew I
was going to go all out.

—*Terry Fox*

According to the 1971 census, Port Coquitlam's population was 19,560, an increase of 8,349 in five years. Besides celebrating that growth, the city also celebrated the hundredth anniversary of British Columbia's entry into the Canadian Confederation. The provincial government offered per capita grants to assist communities with local events and projects, and PoCo joined in the fun. Pioneer medallions were also presented to BC residents who were either born in Canada or were living in Canada prior to 1897.

Not everything called for a celebration. A yellowed clipping from the era shows that in 1971 PoCo council established a special committee to look into the subject of low-cost housing. It seems a study revealed that 56 percent of the city's population earned less than $8,000 a year. In fact, some 20 percent of the Port Coquitlam workforce earned less than $479 each month. "Council is aware," the committee's report read, "that families earning less than $8,000 a year have difficulty in affording ownership of any type of home and therefore most must seek rental situations. This committee feels it is necessary to offer the option to purchase a home." The report recommended continuing the city's policy of attempting to spread low-income families throughout the community rather than concentrating them in a "ghetto."

About that time the Greater Vancouver Regional District (GVRD) got involved in housing. During the 1970s the GVRD's member municipalities—Port Coquitlam among them—recognized there was a desperate and growing shortage of affordable rental accommodation to meet the needs of people with lower incomes, sometimes called the "working poor." Some households at the time were paying more than 30 percent of their gross income on shelter. The federal government created subsidized housing programs through Canada Mortgage and Housing Corporation (CMHC), but more needed to be done. So municipally elected officials, including PoCo's, established the Greater Vancouver Housing Corporation (GVHC), a non-profit subsidiary of the GVRD. The GVHC increased the supply of housing stock throughout Greater Vancouver by developing subsidized rental

Westwood was another of the new schools that sprang up in Port Coquitlam in the early 1970s to take in students from the city's growing subdivisions.

housing under the various federal programs available. To avoid a concentration of social housing in any one municipality, the GVHC took a regional approach to increasing the rental supply. This meant rental units were distributed more equitably throughout the region, and it eliminated the need for separate housing departments in each municipality.

Under this program, a rental housing project at Prairie and Coast Meridian was built in PoCo, followed by another on Kingsway, just across the river on the McAllister footbridge. The co-op housing at Pitt River Road and Shaughnessy was built in the early 1980s.

The 1971 civic election brought in three new faces for the '72 council: lawyer Stuart Leggatt; Michael Thompson, an insurance broker; and high-school teacher Phil Ranger. Long-time alderman Rick Mabbett was squeezed out, but he got back in the following year. At the end of the twentieth century, Stu Leggatt is a justice of the BC Supreme Court, Mike Thompson is still in insurance and Phil Ranger, after

Port Coquitlam high-school students were aware of events happening far from their home, including the 1971 US nuclear bomb test on the Alaskan island of Amchitka.

Aldermen Ron Nacht (left) and Jane Kilmer in a May Day parade.

thirty-four years as a shop teacher at Killarney Secondary in Vancouver, is retired.

Leggatt, originally from New Westminster, started practising law in Haney, but moved in 1957 to a one-man office on PoCo's Shaughnessy Street. "There was a lot of motor vehicle work," the judge recalls today, "criminal defence, wills, contracts and so on. Port Coquitlam's the CPR's western freight terminus, so there was railway work. I was busy." But not too busy to run for school board for District #43, where he served for eight years.

"Then somebody, I forget who, asked me to run for city council. I sat on council in 1971 and '72, then I ran for a federal seat in New Westminster. I was an MP for seven years, until 1979. It was a big riding: it took in a large section of Burnaby, Coquitlam, Port Moody and New Westminster. It didn't include Port Coquitlam. I got tired of the travel back and forth and wanted to see more of my family, so I came back to run as an NDP MLA for Port Coquitlam/Port Moody. I could still practise a bit of law as an MLA, couldn't do that as an MP, and I wanted to help Dave Barrett out. He had just been defeated as premier by Bill Bennett, but he was still leader of the party. I was an MLA until 1983. Then I was appointed as a County Court judge." Judge Leggatt was appointed to the BC Supreme Court July 1, 1990.

A familiar PoCo figure departed in 1971 when Jane Kilmer died. Mayor Bruce Scott wrote a warm tribute to her in the *Coquitlam Herald*. "Known for her friendly ways and kind smile, this dear lady spent her whole lifetime in serving our community. Her record of years of service as an alderman alone stands without parallel throughout the province." Her niece Cate Nicholson and Cate's husband Nick had been caring for her during her last years in the big Kilmer home. Jane Kilmer slipped away at age eighty-one. "We had hoped to buy the house," Cate says today, "but we couldn't afford it." The big eleven-room house was sold in 1973 to settle the Kilmer estate.

In December 1971 Alderman Bob Heffelfinger advised council he had been asked by Mrs.

Edith Chambers to inquire about the possibility of providing a temporary museum for historical items and also whether it would be feasible to have a small cubicle in Phase II of the Recreation Centre for such use on a permanent basis. Nothing came of that admirable initiative, and it wasn't until twenty-eight years later that the city's Heritage and Cultural Display Centre opened.

One piece of PoCo heritage demanded attention in 1972. Sometime in the past the CPR switched from using steam locomotives to diesel engines in its PoCo marshalling yards. CP no longer needed big, handsome Steam Engine 3716, so the company presented it as a gift to the city. The locomotive went into storage in the railway's False Creek yards. In 1972 the CPR called to say that 3716 was rusting away and what did the city want to do about it? PoCo had no facility to either restore or display the engine, so the city sold it to BC Rail for one dollar, with the understanding the company would restore it as a backup for the Royal Hudson. That beauty, named because it had pulled the train taking King George VI and Queen Elizabeth (the Queen Mother) across Canada in a 1939 royal visit, was being used for wonderfully successful excursions between North Vancouver and Squamish. BC Rail readily agreed, and today 3716 can often be seen on that scenic run. It came back to PoCo in 1988, marking the city's seventy-fifth birthday, and again in 1998 to celebrate the seventy-fifth anniversary of May Day.

There was a political upset in 1972. Bruce Scott, a millworker who had been on council for five years, and whose father Loftus Scott had been an alderman himself in 1920, was elected mayor that year, defeating incumbent Jack Campbell by just four votes—1,472 to 1,468.

Campbell told the *Vancouver Sun* that he blamed his narrow defeat on antagonism between the north side of Port Coquitlam and the south side, an antagonism he said began over the location of the city's recreation centre in 1969. A ratepayers' group called The Wrong Side of

Steam Engine 3716 spent years in the PoCo marshalling yards before it was retired to occasional service on the North Vancouver to Squamish run. It returned to Port Coquitlam in 1988 to celebrate the anniversary of the city and again in 1998 for May Day.

the Tracks formed in 1972 and kept the fires of dissent glowing. "I won both south side polls and lost both in the north side," Campbell told the *Sun*, adding that he'd had enough. "I am out of politics, but there is no bitterness." He also commented that during his tenure he had learned that a politician should not be decisive. "If he wants to keep people with him, he should stay in the grey area."

Ron Freeman recalls that Campbell's successor, Bruce Scott, was a pretty good mayor and "smartened the CPR up." The railway had tended to take the city for granted and would sometimes work as if it was a power unto itself. "Bruce convinced the CPR that we were not some little hick town in outer Slobovia," Freeman continues, "and we wanted their damn diesel oil out of our ditches, the grain off the yard area to discourage the pigeons, building permits for their buildings, and a general all-round recognition that there were some things the Railway Transport Committee did not have control of—we did!"

Not long after he was elected, Scott began excitedly talking about a major $7 million downtown PoCo project that involved the CPR.

Phil Ranger remembers that project. "The Greater Vancouver Regional District had been discussing 'regional town centres.' They had a map with little red dots. That's where the GVRD was recommending these centres would be. Well, we were promoting development, and the CPR had nearly 39 acres [16 hectares] where their roundhouse was sitting. The property ran from Oxford to Shaughnessy. Marathon Realty, the CPR's real estate arm, came to PoCo council and said 'We want that property to be one of those regional centres.' We thought that was a fine idea. I even had my students at Killarney build a model of the proposed site; they were really imaginative, even put a heliport in!" George Laking, mayor at the time, wasn't as enthusiastic. "They were planning a million square feet of office space, and two million square feet of living space, apartments." Laking was not in favour of such a massive addition to the city's skyline. But it all became academic when the neighbours to the west got it. "A developer named Ira Young tied up the area where Coquitlam Centre is today," says Ranger, "and that's where the regional town centre went. It was less complicated there: just raw land."

That colourful and venerable—and unused—CPR round-house later attracted the attention of the BC Railroaders' Association. The group asked Mayor Traboulay for his support to obtain it as a railway museum. Traboulay went with members of the group to see the CPR's local man in charge, Jim Bromley. "Mr. Bromley told us the roundhouse would interfere with the oper-ation of the railway," Traboulay said. "Nothing was to interfere with his operation of the railroad." During the early hours of the next morning the railway tore the roundhouse down. "BOOM!" says Traboulay. "Down it went!"   (A 1978 paper on the CPR's round\house by two UBC architecture students, Gregg Brown and Linda Moore, indicates it was being used less and less by that time. There was space for a dozen locomotive stalls, but only four were in use with the rest having been converted to workshop and storage space. At one time, say the authors, as many as thirty steam engines were operating out of the building.)

At left, a sketch of Phil Ranger's medallion recognizing public service. Mary Hill Baptist Church (above) and Hawthorne Lodge (below) were under construction in the early 1970s.

Causes for celebration: Harold and Mary Routley celebrate their fiftieth wedding anniversary in 1971 (above); Dave Barrett, the city's MLA, hands out honours at the Kinsmen Sports Carnival in 1971 (below); and BC Hydro extends bus service to PoCo in 1973 (right).

If the roundhouse wasn't so busy, the same couldn't be said for the city's thriving library. During his second year on council, 1972, Phil Ranger distinguished himself by suggesting the establishment of Friends of the Library. The group, active to this day, carries out library publicity programs, encourages the use of the library's resources and services, sponsors cultural activities and reflects the public's view to the city councillor who handles library matters. The Friends also arrange special displays and sponsor fundraising events for materials otherwise unavailable within the library's budget.

Another Ranger idea was the creation of a medallion to honour local people who had made exceptional contributions in public service. The first recipient was Port Coquitlam pioneer Harold Routley. No one deserved it more. The remarkable Mr. Routley had been active in a dozen local initiatives including the Elks Lodge, the Juvenile Athletic Association, lacrosse, soccer, the board of trade, Royal Canadian Legion and, of course, he had come up with the idea of the PoCo Trail.

In early 1972—further reflecting the rapid growth of the city—the courtroom, police office and the basement jail were moved

from city hall to a separate building. Later that year, extensive renovation of the building's interior began.

Moving from civic politics to provincial, 1972 was the year Dave Barrett, who had been representing Port Coquitlam (and Coquitlam and Port Moody) since 1960, was elected premier of British Columbia. Barrett defeated W.A.C. Bennett, who had set a record of twenty years as premier. The first physical evidence of Barrett's election locally was an anonymous hand-lettered sign set up near the creaky Red Bridge, nearly fifty years old. "We'z now," the sign read, "gonna get a new bridge." No, we'z ain't. Even though PoCo's MLA was the province's premier, the new bridge didn't go in until years after he left office. "In fact," said a PoCo councillor, "we didn't get a thing out of Dave Barrett when he was premier."

A milestone reached in 1973 was the advent of public transportation. BC Hydro had been operating a service from New Westminster to Maillardville, and Pacific Coach Lines had a low-frequency interurban bus service, so PoCo's transit service was dismal. That all changed when Hydro finally extended its bus service into the city. Within three weeks of establishing the serv-

The RCMP bought a new boat to patrol the rivers in 1973 (above), Len Traboulay attended his first council meeting (lower left) and construction started on the Hyde Creek Recreation Centre (below).

The Coquitlam Herald *covered news in PoCo and neighbouring cities from this unassuming office.*

Note the meat prices (99 cents per pound for ham) in this 1974 publicity shot for the U-Buy-Rite Market.

ice, extra buses had to be laid on. There was another benefit: far fewer hitchhikers.

The first full-length history of Port Coquitlam appeared in 1973 when Edith Chambers' *History of Port Coquitlam* was published. This informal look back at the city's past was timed to coincide with its sixtieth year and reflected the late Ms. Chambers' affection for her adopted city.

Another 1973 publication was a booklet titled *Birds of Port Coquitlam*. It was compiled by Richard S. Jerema and a small team who looked at the avian population of the city and discovered that our feathered friends have "neighbourhoods." Sparrows hang out most commonly north of the Lougheed in residential areas, starlings are most often present in the newer residential developments (where there isn't enough greenery yet for songbirds), the varied thrush is seen in the city's deciduous woods, while the open fields are home to savannah sparrows. Those seeking exotic birds will find thin fare here: the city's most counted birds are robins, starlings, the varied thrush and the black-capped chickadee. At the northern edge of the city, DeBoville Slough sees populations of mallards, wood ducks, buffleheads, mergansers, and other water-favouring birds . . . who have to keep an eye out for the occasional hungry coyote.

On March 6 the *Vancouver Sun* had a story on PoCo's birthday party, at which Mayor Scott had coffee and cake served at the public council meeting. One of the newly elected aldermen attending that ceremony was a thirty-eight-year-old Trinidad-born schoolteacher named Leonard Traboulay.

The irrepressible Jack Campbell decided, after Bruce Scott's two-year term, to forget what he had said about being through with politics. He ran for mayor again in 1974 and was easily returned, becoming the only PoCo mayor to serve separated terms. (Jack Campbell, by the way, was also a sometime columnist for the *Coquitlam Herald*.)

Along about this time the New View Society began operating in Port Coquitlam. It's a non-profit organization for mentally and emotionally disturbed people. Its home at 2050 Mary Hill Road is in a beautifully kept house.

The PoCo Valley Golf and Country Club opened in 1974. It was developed by the Tej Banns family, long-time residents of the area, who had been operating a dairy farm on the land since 1937. At its peak there were 140 cows on the property. Construction of the eighteen-hole course began in 1971 for opening in the spring of 1974. One thing Tej Banns recalls with real clarity: the first season they opened the golf club it rained. And rained. And rained.

One of the major original features of the course was a huge clubhouse made of cedar, said to be the largest all-cedar building in the world. "There was enough lumber in that building to build fifty houses," says Tej. Ron Talbot passes along a story about that big clubhouse. It seems he'd been showing a friend around town and, during their tour, had pointed out the unique structure. He phoned his friend the next day and told her, "It's a good thing you got a chance to see that building. It burned down last night." Luckily, no one was injured in the 1977 blaze.

Tej Banns and his family now live in Pitt Meadows, where they operate a lawn turf business and also grow cranberries. He sold the course in 1978 "to Jim Methven, the fellow who owned Johnston Terminals." That was the same year he quit the dairying business after forty-nine years

Jack Campbell's mid-1970s council (left to right): George Laking, Phil Ranger, John Keryluk, Campbell, Len Traboulay, Mike Thompson, Rick Mabbett.

The stunning cedar clubhouse at PoCo Valley Golf and Country Club.

working with cows. During that time he developed a special diet of minerals and vitamins for his cows, which resulted in some of them living to be twenty-eight years old, ancient for a cow. He began using the same diet himself, and at seventy seems in excellent health.

An average of twenty thousand golfers played the course in the first few seasons, attracted by green fees as low as four dollars per round. No Name Creek supplied the water to irrigate the course. Today, Carnoustie (it was renamed in 1979 after the famous course in Scotland) is host to an annual average of forty to fifty thousand rounds at $30 to $40 a round. Golfers enjoy an eighteen-hole course with clubhouse facilities that include a lounge, banquet room, full pro shop and a covered driving range as well as six racquetball courts, six squash courts and an exercise/weight room. Prime Minister Brian Mulroney visited Carnoustie in 1987.

A long-serving PoCo councillor was first elected in 1974. John Keryluk, a teacher and school librarian who'd started his career in Manitoba, marked the last of his twenty-five years on council in 1999, taking just a one-year break in 1982 for a run at the mayor's chair against Len Traboulay.

At about the same time, another councillor, Phil Ranger, decided to have some fun at Coquitlam's expense. Talk about amalgamation of the so-called Tri-Cities (Coquitlam, Port Coquitlam and Port Moody) pops up every few years, with much more enthusiasm for the idea in Coquitlam than in the two smaller cities, and Alderman Ranger decided to throw a cat among the pigeons. With great seriousness he proposed a boundary plan that greatly enlarged the size of Port Coquitlam, Port Moody and New Westminster. One unavoidable consequence of Ranger's redrawing of the map was that Coquitlam entirely disappeared, swallowed up by the three other cities. "Coquitlam is a big bedroom community," Ranger told the *Columbian* on January 10. "Let's divide up the bedroom." When that plan hit the fan, the screams in Coquitlam rattled windows all over the Lower Mainland. Talking about it today, Ranger still laughs delightedly.

That same year, 1975, the Drama, Art and Language facilities at Port Coquitlam High were updated and enlarged. And a plaque at the PoCo Recreation Centre at 2150 Wilson shows it was re-opened February 15, 1975, by

Some ringette players at the Port Coquitlam Recreation Centre, 1975.

Premier Dave Barrett. (The official title at the time was the Port Coquitlam Arena and Senior Citizens' Complex.) Mayor Campbell and council were there, of course. An additional ice rink had been added to the building, precipitating the celebration. The building was again upgraded and enlarged in 1999.

One of the popular activities in the centre is ringette, which had come to BC in 1974. PoCo embraced ringette with real enthusiasm. The 1992 national championships were played in PoCo and broadcast by TSN. Ringette is a fast-paced ice game, inspired by hockey and invented in 1963 by Sam Jacks, the director of Parks and Recreation for North Bay, Ontario. Jacks was looking for a sport played on ice but designed specifically for girls. Players use a straight stick to pass, carry and shoot a rubber ring to score goals. The ringette season runs from September to March.

Dave Barrett's tenure as premier—and as a representative for Port Coquitlam—ended later that same year when he lost the provincial election to Bill Bennett, son of the man he

The PoCo Senior Secondary basketball team that Terry Fox would have played for during his high-school career. This is the 1975 Ravens team.

had defeated three years earlier. He even lost his seat, but won a by-election the next year in Vancouver East and was leader of the opposition from 1976 to 1984. Barrett later went on to serve four years in the federal Parliament as MP for Esquimalt–Juan de Fuca.

In 1976 the Huntington Rubber mill finally closed. It had started more than fifty years earlier as the Gregory Tire Company and had operated most of that time at less than capacity. In 1978, empty for two years, the building burned to the ground in a fire deliberately set. The culprits were never caught.

On April 13, 1976, another old building, the Agricultural Hall, was demolished. It happened in the early hours of the morning, and some locals were furious. "But the fact is," says someone who knows, "the foundation of the building was defective. The city's own inspectors said it should go. It would have cost too much money to fix it and renovate it [$80,000], so the council decided to knock it down. They knew if they went to the public the debate could have gone on forever, and then the contractor was worried about demolishing it with

A Canadian Hero

He was born Terrance Stanley Fox on July 28, 1958, in Winnipeg and moved with his family to Port Coquitlam in 1966. "He graduated from Port Coquitlam High School," says Leslie Scrivener in her book *Terry Fox: His Story*, "with straight As but for one B in English." Then he went on to Simon Fraser University to study kinesiology. He tried out for the junior varsity basketball team, where his coaches noted that while other players maybe had better skills, young Terry Fox "out-gutted" them. He made the team.

In late 1976 Terry began to experience unusual pain in his right knee. He underwent a series of tests and on March 5 was diagnosed with a rare cancer of the bone called osteogenic sarcoma. To save his life, his leg would have to be amputated. He was eighteen years old.

The operation was scheduled for March 9. On the night before, Terry was visited by a crowd of friends and well-wishers, along with his family. Among the visitors was Terry Fleming, Terry's high-school basketball coach. Fleming brought a copy of *Runners World* magazine. He had marked a certain story, a profile of a one-legged runner named Dick Traum who had competed in the New York Marathon. The Traum story convinced Terry that he would be able to run again, and it inspired him to take on a challenge that would eventually raise hundreds of millions of dollars for cancer research.

His goal became nothing less than to run across the country and raise one dollar in research donations from every Canadian.

"I don't know why I dreamed what I did," Terry said once. "It's because I'm competitive. I'm a dreamer. I like challenges. I don't give up. When I decided to do it, I knew I was going to go all out." (He showed that determination when he participated in a wheelchair-basketball team from 1977 to 1980, a slot he got after being recruited by Rick Hansen. Part of Terry's self-designed exercise routine was to push his chair along Gaglardi Way, a long, steep climb up Burnaby Mountain toward Simon Fraser University at the top.)

After the operation and sixteen months of chemotherapy treatment, Terry began to train and, eventually, to run daily—painfully short distances at first, but increasing steadily as he developed strength and technique. His running style was his own: two hops on

his remaining leg, then a long stride on his artificial leg while lifting his torso and shoulders for leverage. After fourteen months of training he had obtained sponsorship and planned his route, and on April 12, 1980, he was in St. John's, Newfoundland. He dipped his artificial leg in the Atlantic, then turned his face to the west to run across the nation. Terry's dream, the "Marathon of Hope," began.

At first there was little media attention outside Port Coquitlam itself, but as he survived dangerous road hazards, semi-trailers that almost blew him into ditches, hailstones the size of golf balls, police barring him from parts of the Trans-Canada Highway, and trouble with his artificial leg, the image of this courageous young man and the story of his crusade began to take hold of the public's imagination. Media excitement built, and by the time he reached Ontario, Terry Fox was famous. He marked his twenty-second birthday in Gravenhurst, Ontario . . . a day on which he ran only 20 miles (32 kilometres), instead of the daily 26 he aimed for. The trickle of coins had become an outpouring of dollars—the Ontario division of the Canadian Cancer Society was getting five hundred pledges and donations a day. On Terry's arrival in Toronto, the Canadian media was overwhelmingly behind him. Terry Fox had become the news of the day.

As his popularity increased, so did the crowds. Schoolchildren lined the streets, contributing their allowances and pledges. Terry overcame shyness and became an eloquent public speaker, raising even more money. "Knowing that there are people who care about what I'm doing," he said, "that I'm not just running across Canada, that there are people who are giving money to help fight the disease that took my leg and to help other people who are lying down in hospital beds all over the world, it's a reward."

But as his run continued westward through Ontario, Terry began to be bothered by a persistent cough and pain in his chest. His last diary entry was made Sunday, August 31, 1980. On an early September day 18 miles (29 kilometres) outside Thunder Bay, Ontario, Terry's run came to a tearful end. "I tried as hard as I could, I said I'd never give up and I didn't."

His cancer had metastasized, spreading to his lungs. He had run in constant pain for 143 days, averaging an unbelievable marathon (26 miles or 42 kilometres) a day, and raised $1.7 million for cancer research. Now he was hospitalized. Canadians flooded Terry with messages of love and support ... and continued to contribute money to his campaign. The Port Coquitlam post office reported that during December 1980, Terry got more mail than everyone else in town—residential and business—combined.

By the end of December, largely because of a CTV telethon, a total of more than $24 million had been raised. Terry's goal of a dollar for every Canadian had been reached and exceeded. He had, as Leslie Scrivener writes, "more than doubled the National Cancer Institute of Canada's 1980 research allowance."

Terry died in Royal Columbian Hospital on June 28, 1981, a month short of his twenty-third birthday. His dedication, courage and selflessness are perpetuated through the annual Terry Fox Run and the Terry Fox Foundation. His parents, Betty and Rolly Fox, still work today to keep the Marathon of Hope alive.

The first Terry Fox Memorial Run was held September 13, 1981 at 880 sites across Canada with more than 300,000 participants. They ran, walked, cycled, roller-bladed, swam and wheeled—and raised $3.5 million. Unique ways were invented to raise money. Residents of a Newfoundland seniors home had a rocking chair "rockathon," raising money through pledges. One group of young people had Jello-bath "sit-ins." Canadian peacekeepers in Rwanda held a run. Beginning in the early '90s a deaf man in Prince Rupert began going door to door annually for the cause. He collected more than $39,000 in 1994 and was up to nearly $47,000 in 1995. That year there were more than 275 runs in fifty countries, raising more than $10.5 million, the most successful single-day fundraiser for cancer research in the world. To date, nearly $250 million has been raised, virtually all of which has remained in the country of origin to fund innovative cancer research, in accordance with Terry's wishes. There are now three hundred Terry Fox Run sites in fifty-two countrires, and over a million people run annually.

Terry Fox's honours and awards are too numerous to list in full here, but they include the following. He was named "Canadian of the Year" two years in a row and was made a Companion of the Order of Canada, Canada's highest honour; he received the Order of the Dogwood (British Columbia's highest award), the Sword of Hope (the American Cancer Society's highest award) and the Lou Marsh Award for outstanding athletic accomplishment. He was made a freeman of the city of Port Coquitlam. The Canadian government created a $5 million endowment fund, the Terry Fox Humanitarian Award, to provide scholarships in his honour, and he was inducted into the Canadian Sports Hall of Fame. In 1983 Burrard-Yarrows Shipyard in North Vancouver built an icebreaker named the MV *Terry Fox*. There is a Mount Terry Fox in the BC Interior, and the Terry Fox Courage Highway runs 83 kilometres (52 miles) between Thunder Bay and Nipigon, Ontario, commemorating the ending of the run. Canada Post has issued two commemorative stamps portraying Terry, and monuments have been erected at BC Place in Vancouver, Rideau Square in Ottawa and in Thunder Bay. His high school was named for him, and so is Port Coquitlam's public library. A statue of Terry by George Pratt stands in front of the library. Many schools, parks and roads continue to be named after him.

As 1999 drew to a close, the people of British Columbia overwhelmingly selected Terry as the most heroic figure of the century.

Once in a while someone special comes along who makes us aware of the needs of others. Terry Fox was such a man.

(An excellent video documentary, *The Life and Times of Terry Fox*, is available from the Fox Foundation.)

—*Written with assistance from Rita Woodman*

people all around. So they had it brought down in the middle of the night and got it over with."

Len Traboulay recalls that council meeting: "We met at 7:30, adjourned at 9:30, it was torn down at 4 a.m."

On March 9, 1977, Terry Fox, just eighteen, a gutsy and athletic graduate of Port Coquitlam Senior Secondary, had to have his right leg amputated six inches above the knee to stop the spread of osteogenic sarcoma, a rare and malignant bone cancer. Just three years later, Terry began a courageous run across Canada to raise awareness of cancer and funds for research into the disease. (See his story in the sidebar.)

Some years before Terry captured the Canadian imagination, the country's first "Participark" opened in PoCo's Robert Hope Park on April 1, 1977. With funding from the federal government's Participaction project, which aimed to get Canadians exercising and fit, local groups were encouraged to create these parks, which included exercise facilities for people of all ages. Port Coquitlam's Kinsmen Club pitched in, building an exercise station made out of cedar logs. The opening of the park was a major event, with Lieutenant Governor Walter Owen on hand, along with Premier Bill Bennett, federal fitness and sport minister Iona Campagnolo, Mayor Jack Campbell and a crowd of MPs, MLAs, aldermen, civic officers, Kinsmen officials, business people and sports figures. In terms of sheer VIP power it ranks as one of PoCo's major events. After the formal ceremonies, MCd by Alderman Phil Ranger, Premier Bennett and others jogged around the park while local kids provided hot dogs.

A second and up-to-date fire station opened December 10, 1977, on the north side at Toronto Street, and the older southside station (2353 McAllister) became Fire Hall #1. In 1979, while responding to what turned out to be a false alarm, the department's 1959 LaFrance pumper was totalled in an accident at the corner of Lougheed Highway and Shaughnessy. The department quickly bought a replacement.

Volunteers involved with the Pitt River dig examine some of the artifacts unearthed at the Kwikwitlem site. (Photo courtesy Val Patenaude)

The next year, Val Patenaude began an archaeological dig at the Kwikwitlem site on Baker Creek, near the mouth of the Pitt River. Several thousand local kids toured the dig while it was happening. Construction of the Mary Hill Bypass obliterated the site, but there are ten thousand artifacts from it in the provincial museum (see the sidebar in chapter 2).

There was another shift on city council in 1980 when George Laking, who had been a popular alderman for eleven years, ran for mayor against incumbent Jack Campbell. "I liked Jack," Laking says, "enjoyed working with him, but a lot of people were bitching, so I thought I'd try." He won, won again in 1981, then decided to step down as mayor and try to get back in as an ordinary alderman. He succeeded, and kept winning for eight more years. (His successor as mayor was Len Traboulay.) To the obvious question—why go back to being an alderman?—he responds "I could *do* that. Being mayor is another thing."

A favourite George Laking story concerns his old house, which he left the same year he became mayor. He and Jocelyn had been living on York Street, right across from McLean Park. "Well, they had no water in the park, y'know, for getting a drink or wetting down the dust. So they ran a hose from our house over to the park! We did that for a long time. Jo and I lived in that house for about thirty years. We moved a mile or so away in 1980, when the Lutheran Church bought the property. When they opened the church, they invited me to address them. I told the congregation I was standing in what used to be my living room!"

Where George shone on council was as a troubleshooter. "Jack Campbell would appoint me when there was trouble in a specific department: recreation, public works, industrial development. Same thing when I was on Len Traboulay's council. *"That* I could do." During Laking's tenure as mayor he was named chair of the Labor Relations Committee of the Greater Vancouver Regional District, which suddenly found itself in a major labour dispute. PoCo council didn't like the GVRD recommendations to settle the strike, called in protest against a broad range of issues, and convinced Laking to resign as chairman. (He was replaced by John Parks, a Coquitlam councillor.) The GVRD's workers, including those in PoCo, went on a strike that lasted thirteen weeks. "It was a hell of a time," says Len Traboulay, who was on council at the time. "There was garbage everywhere." Port Coquitlam and Surrey both withdrew from the GVRD bargaining unit and have never returned. Laking recommended that PoCo do its own labour negotiations. "We still do!" he says proudly.

The evening of October 6, 1982, brought a terrific opportunity for some Laking troubleshooting: a tractor-trailer cab sideswiped a car on the old Red Bridge and knocked out its main supports. The bridge fell to the river below, with the truck and several cars on it. Miraculously, no one was injured and traffic was rerouted through the downtown and the Lougheed. Coquitlam RCMP charged a Vancouver truck driver in the incident. "When the bridge was destroyed," Laking says, "we had an engineering firm come in to tell us how long the bridge would have lasted if it hadn't been hit. That was to tell the insurance company. I

Mayor Len Traboulay at Port Coquitlam's West Coast Express Station.

George Laking: Alderman, Mayor, Dynamo

phoned Alex Fraser, the highways minister, the next morning and told him what had happened. He said 'We'll get you a Bailey bridge.' We kept the Bailey bridge and used the insurance money to build a new bridge to take Kingsway over the Coquitlam River!" That latter construction was interesting: the entire existing Kingsway bridge was lifted and slid aside 14 metres (45 feet). Traffic continued to use it while the new bridge was being constructed.

A detachment of army engineers from Chilliwack came in to build the Bailey bridge. (This form of bridge, a military innovation named for the British engineer who invented it, is a temporary bridge formed of prefabricated, interchangeable, steel truss panels bolted together.) The Bailey bridge created its own set of problems: it was unable to support the weight of commercial or industrial trucks and it was subject to closure several times a year because of high water in the Coquitlam River. Nonetheless, this "temporary" bridge at one of the major entry points into Port Coquitlam remained in place for the next fourteen years.

By this point, Port Coquitlam's population (recorded in the 1981 census) was 27,535 and growing steadily. The years of stagnation were just a memory.

At the end of 1982 there was a major change on the Port Coquitlam council: a new mayor. His name was Len Traboulay, and he's still occupying the mayor's chair as the city enters a new century.

Leonard Macaulay Traboulay was born in Trinidad in 1934, the grandson of indentured servants and the son of literarily inclined parents who gave him a middle name commemorating the English poet and historian Thomas Babington Macaulay. He was bitten by the political bug very early in his life. "My mother was influential in the Presbyterian Church in Trinidad. I went to Sunday school. I was in every students group that existed: student council, the orators' group, you name it. I came to British Columbia in 1954 and started teaching in School District #41 in Burnaby. Before long I was vice-president of the Burnaby Teachers Association, and the president the year after that. I found myself co-chairing meetings of six hundred teachers; it was a steep learning curve." At a UBC dance on Valentine's Day in 1958, Traboulay met Joanne Ursulescu and "we were married exactly four months later, June 14, 1958."

Later that year the couple moved to Edmonton, where Len took teacher training at the University of Alberta. He taught at the junior secondary level in Edmonton: French, English

Literature, Social Studies, Office Skills. Then in 1964 they moved back to BC, where Len became a teacher at Moscrop Junior Secondary in Burnaby, teaching French to Grades 8, 9 and 10. "I was five years at Moscrop, and we were living in Burnaby. Then in 1967 we bought a house on Cedar Drive in Port Coquitlam. It stood on a quarter acre, and we bought it for $19,000. I was still teaching at Moscrop, but then I got a transfer to Cariboo Hill Secondary. I was there for seventeen years. In 1986 they had a need for French teachers at Burnaby Central, Grades 11 and 12. I was there to 1995."

Overcrowding at Cedar Drive Elementary caused students to use the gym and stage for classrooms in 1972.

The Traboulay kids, Trevor and Angela, were attending Cedar Drive Elementary. Now it happens that one of the hot education issues at the time was the number of students in a class: classes of more than forty were becoming the norm. In the case of Cedar Drive, the problems also included a playing field that was under water every winter. These and other issues prompted Joanne to join the Cedar Drive Elementary parents committee, and she soon became the chair. "In our living room one night," Len Traboulay recalls, "we had a host of neighbours. Joanne was talking about safety issues at Cedar Drive Elementary. For one thing, we needed a sidewalk along Cedar Drive. So I was sent to speak to council."

It's too bad that PoCo council meetings weren't being videotaped back then; that 1969 meeting would have been a treasure. Mayor Jack Campbell was presiding; two future mayors, George Laking and Bruce Scott, were on council; and another future mayor was appearing as a delegation.

"In 1970," Traboulay continues, "the Burnaby Teachers Association decided the president should be full time. I ran and won. Not long after, I ran for the Coquitlam school board [District 43]. My opponent was Dr. Michael Angus, who had delivered most of the babies in Port Coquitlam. I ran off my campaign literature on a Gestetner, painted up eight signs, put them up here and there. A high wind came up and blew 'em all down. Angus won, but not by much. Dave Barrett was in the audience when I ran for trustee. He came up to talk to me after the meeting. I ran again for school board in 1971, lost that time to Kay Whiting."

Then in 1972 a vacancy appeared on the Port Coquitlam city council as a result of Stu Leggatt's departure to run for a federal seat in New Westminster. "My opponent in that election," says Traboulay, "was Jack Whiting, the husband of Kay Whiting, who had beaten me in the election for school trustee!" A newspaper called the *Coquitlam Times* ran a positive piece on Traboulay, and it's evident he attributes much of his success in that election to the *Times* story. He won that 1972 election, and he's been winning ever since.

Eleven years later, October 29, 1983, Traboulay was on hand when Betty and Rolly Fox

officially opened the Terry Fox Library at Wilson Avenue and Mary Hill Road. A commemorative plaque was unveiled and a statue of Terry by George Pratt was placed in front of the building. The library is used intensively: in 1998 it circulated 408,251 items from the collection of 73,000 books, paperbacks, magazines, videotapes and audio books. Some 175,043 people visited the library, and library staff answered 49,417 questions. A remarkable statistic: 30,376 people have library cards, or 65 percent of PoCo's population! The council liaison for library matters in 2000 is Michael Wright, whose interest is genuine—and even personal: Wright's wife Thelka was a librarian. (Did you know: Michael Wright's daughter is one of the few people to be married in Port Coquitlam's council chambers.)

Betty and Rolly Fox flank Len Traboulay as he cuts the ribbon to open the Terry Fox Library (above)
In 1986 the high school their son attended was renamed in his honour (below).

Terry Fox's name lives on in many other ways: In 1986 the name of Port Coquitlam High School was changed to Terry Fox Senior Secondary School at the suggestion of Principal George Buckley. When the old school was closed in 1999 after forty years of service, the name was transferred to the modern new replacement. A memorable tribute to PoCo's most famous citizen occurred in 1987 when Rick Hansen, who had been paralyzed in a road mishap in 1973, began his Man in Motion wheelchair journey around the world. In the book on his own epic journey, Hansen made it clear that Terry Fox had been his inspiration:

> In 1980 my friend and basketball teammate Terry Fox set off on his Marathon of Hope. He was going

to run across Canada to focus attention on the horrors of cancer and to raise funds for cancer research. He wanted nothing for himself. He'd had cancer, it had taken his leg, and now he was going to fight back. That's what it was: a personal fight between one young man and this terrible thing that had attacked him. He would battle it one-on-one. He would show people it can be beaten, and in the course of the battle he would raise funds and inspire other people . . . I've heard and seen it written that cancer beat him. Not true. It only beat his body. It returned and raged through him this time, forcing a halt to his marathon after five months and finally taking his life. But [the cancer] didn't win. In life and in death Terry did what he'd set out to do: he rallied Canadians to a common cause as never before. The money poured in and is still pouring in, because every year, through memorial walks and other fundraisers, people remember the fighter who wouldn't quit.

Steve Fonyo's 1984–85 run across Canada was also directly inspired by Terry and raised a further $13 million for cancer research.

Another man inspired by Terry Fox is teacher Bruce Moore. (It's his words that open this book.) Bruce was Terry's counsellor and soccer coach during Grades 11

Wilson Centre is a place for seniors to gather for a visit or a game of pool . . . or for myriad other activities. It is always bustling.

and 12, and he has attended every one of the nineteen PoCo Runs held since they began. In June 1999 Bruce himself was diagnosed with cancer: non-Hodgkins lymphoma. That made the connection even stronger for him, he said. Besides, his son Greg (of the planning department in PoCo city hall) was co-chairman of the '99 Run, and Bruce's sister also had cancer. While Bruce undergoes chemotherapy, he keeps his eye on a big picture of Terry at the end of his hallway at home. "I see it every day." The 1999 PoCo Run, by the way, had a nineteen-year high of 6,500 participants and raised an estimated $47,000.

In 1986 Port Coquitlam got its first tiny taste of BC's increased moviemaking activity when a part of the movie *Housekeeping*, starring Christine Lahti, was shot here. Among the TV series that have used the town are *Viper* and *The X Files*, while other movies include *White Tiger* (1996), *Disturbing Behavior* and *I'll Be Home for Christmas* (both 1998).

PoCo's 1986 population was 29,115, an increase of 1,580 in five years. It became easier for residents and others to move around that year, too: the Mary Hill Bypass opened. Skirting the southern boundary of the city, the bypass is now used by thousands of cars daily.

One of the most recognizable of Port Coquitlam landmarks, Wilson Centre (at 2150 Wilson) re-opened in 1987. It seemed as if half the town came to celebrate the expansion of this recreational facility for seniors. Drop in just about any time and you'll find the Centre bustling with activity: exercise classes, crafts, talks and teas, and sales. Programs are offered in art, sewing, flower arranging, dancing, carpet bowling, cards and snooker. The centre also has a top-notch kitchen serving lunches Monday through Friday, and snacks every day.

There's another attraction at Wilson Centre: the people! Their tales of the city's early days and its more colourful characters would make a valuable, interesting, funny and heartwarming book.

EIGHT

The New Millennium

This is a terrific
place to live.
— *Len Traboulay*

A lot of seniors volunteered for a wide range of activities during the celebration of Port Coquitlam's seventy-fifth anniversary, its Diamond Jubilee, in 1988. Some of those volunteers, like Annie Osborne, then eighty-three, were older than the city itself! Some were still in school: the Jubilee logo was designed by Darren Janzen of Terry Fox Secondary School. The committee members in charge of preparation and events included William Hyde, C. Bowen, Audrey Leonard, Alan Edwardson, Councillor Mike Gates, former mayor George Laking, Joanne Traboulay, Shirley Armilotta and Rocky Layne.

In December 1987 the *Tri-City News* carried an appeal from Bozena Lukomska-Khan to the Polish community in Port Moody, Port Coquitlam and Coquitlam to participate as a group in the Diamond Jubilee celebrations. There was a huge response, and Mrs. Lukomska-Khan and others officially formed what is now the Polonez Tri-City Polish Association on March 11, 1989. The group meets regularly at Hyde Creek Recreation Centre and participates in PoCo's annual events (like May Day, Canada Day and the Harvest Festival), organizes social and entertainment events of its own, assists new Polish immigrants, and has sent aid to victims of floods and other natural disasters in Poland. The association has even established a Saturday School for Polish children, which meets at Archbishop Carney Secondary to learn Polish language, history and culture. It's a lively and committed group.

Another tangible result of the Jubilee celebration was the book *Port Coquitlam: City of Rivers and Mountains*, commissioned, as this book was, by the City of Port Coquitlam. We gratefully acknowledge that earlier book, as it made this one immensely easier to prepare. George Laking co-ordinated the project, and the volunteers who conducted the interviews and gathered and wrote the stories included Debbie Caron, Beth McWilliam, Dhorea Ryon and Diane Rogers. They in turn paid tribute to Edith Chambers for her 1973 book *History of Port Coquitlam*.

Locomotive 3716 was brought into town to help celebrate the Jubilee May Day. Told in one sentence, it sounds easy, but it took weeks of preparation. "There were negotiations at the highest levels of the provincial government, the CPR and BC Rail," says Phil Ranger, who chaired the 1988 May Day celebrations. "We were able to display

Port Coquitlam celebrated the seventy-fifth anniversary of incorporation with (among other things) a tree-planting ceremony at the Aggie Hall grounds, April 23, 1988.

3716 for the day at the West Coast Express station. And the CPR put two new super-diesel engines and a couple of their travelling museum cars on display."

Another Diamond Jubilee project was a city hall expansion. The lead architect on the project, Tom Annandale of Toby Russell Blackwell, had a job on his hands. "The inside of the building was pretty old—it needed extensive seismic upgrading, it didn't come close to meeting the code. Everyone was agreed on one thing: they wanted to keep the exterior as a reminder of the city's heritage." It was Annandale who had the idea to "swing the building around" so that its front entrance would be on Shaughnessy. "The council was very supportive," he says, "and so were Bryan Kirk, the city administrator, and city planner Carlos Felip. The building needed a better sense of entrance. It was easier to create a new one and orient the building to the park. Handicapped entrance was a factor, too. We replaced the stairs on the old, unused McAllister entrance and replaced the doors." The original plan called for even more new building than was ultimately put up, but it was decided to defer that expansion.

There was a medical building side by side with the original hall. It became the city library and then, when the Terry Fox Library opened, it became home—as it still is—to PoCo's parks department. Meanwhile, next door, Double V Construction started work on City Hall's renovation in early September 1987, while project architect Pat McTaggart supervised the changes. The original hall had been declared a Heritage Site in late 1985, so a great deal of care was taken to ensure the old-style appearance of the 1914 building remained intact and that the new construction reinforced and complemented the original design. While work went on, city hall was emptied of staff, who worked out of a building on Marpole.

Some of the agricultural land still within Port Coquitlam's boundaries is on Dominion Road.

During the Diamond Jubilee year Lois Milne, president of the Port Coquitlam Heritage and Cultural Society, arranged for a time capsule to be placed within the city hall grounds. The capsule is slated to be opened in 2013, the city's hundredth anniversary. Mary Hill Junior Secondary School also created a time capsule, but no one can remember where it is!

In 1990 council had the 486 hectares (1,200 acres) of the "Dominion Triangle" removed from the Agricultural Land Reserve (ALR), but not without a struggle. (Think of the Triangle as a wedge of pie pointing west, with its point where

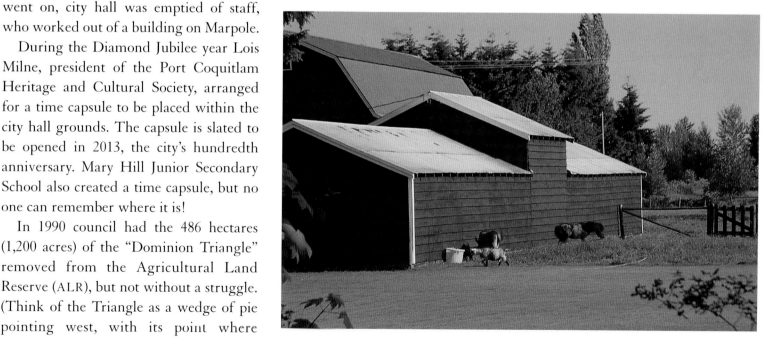

Lougheed Highway and Dominion Avenue meet. The pie's crust would run along the Pitt River.) The majority of landowners in the area approved of the removal, saying the land wasn't suitable for farming, being boggy with bad drainage. A few liked the place just the way it was. The Triangle is now an industrial area, and development continues along those lines. Nearly 109 hectares (270 acres) have been zoned for service, commercial, business park and industrial use. It is currently home to Art Knapp Garden Centre and Costco. In early 2000 one company took an option on 21 hectares (52 acres) within the Triangle, owned by PoCo businessman Jack Giesbrecht, and there was cautious talk that this company might privately finance a vehicular crossing of the Lougheed Highway. Such a project would do much to improve movement between the two halves of the city.

Back in 1990, around the same time the Dominion Triangle was removed from the ALR, the Burke Mountain Naturalists began an annual walkabout of Colony Farm to increase public awareness of the value of the farm as an ecological haven. (Long before it became a haven, it was a playground for some PoCo kids. Mike Gates recalls, "When we were kids we'd come down here, tease the bulls, ride the pigs.") A chamber of commerce report described the area: "On the banks of the Fraser River, surrounding the Coquitlam River, is a large expanse of level fertile ground that remains a part of the ALR. Although once extensively farmed, only small areas of the land are still in use for crops, and a small piece of land is also in use for the Forensic Psychiatric Institute. The majority of the land now lies fallow and has turned back to tall grass and wetlands since irrigation and drainage systems were stopped. Until a use that complies with the restraints of the ALR is found, it is likely this area will remain much the same for many years."

The decision to turn Colony Farm into GVRD-administered parkland (see the sidebar on the farm in chapter 3) meets the "restraints" of the ALR. Another change is actually a harking back to the farm's recent past: a small bridge over the Coquitlam River, linking the Port Coquitlam and Coquitlam sides, will be built to replace one that burned in 1995. (There remain 546 hectares [1,349 acres] of ALR land in PoCo, most of it concentrated along the Pitt River north of the Lougheed.)

The Forensic Institute, incidentally, was rebuilt only a few metres from where it was originally located. It opened March 14, 1997, to provide, in the words of the ministry of health, "a

HISTORICAL FOOTNOTE

Did You Know: There are 140 kilometres (87 miles) of roads in PoCo.

range of expert services to persons who are mentally ill and in conflict with the law. Services include assessments of mental status for the courts, clinical treatment and case management." The institute was designed to provide a high level of security within a "village" concept, with landscaped grounds, a rehabilitation centre and an adjacent farm. The main building includes separate units for those who require minimum, medium and maximum security. All buildings are either one or two levels and include the latest communications and security systems. The Forensic Institute replaces a hospital built in 1948 to accommodate mentally ill war veterans. The older building was demolished.

Colony Farm is a favourite spot for birdwatchers.

A new Mental Health Act in 1990 downsized Riverview to a 550-bed tertiary-care facility. This change was completed by 2000. It had an effect on employment in PoCo, although not as severe as it would have been if the city were not growing so rapidly.

In 1991 Port Coquitlam not only had more people than it had ever had before (36,773, an increase of 7,658 in five years), but it also had more land. On September 29, Douglas Island—in mid-Fraser River opposite Mary Hill—became part of Port Coquitlam. When next you drive across Port Mann Bridge, cast an eye on the island just to the east of the bridge. That's Douglas. (Barnston Island is just behind it.) Writing in *The Greater Vancouver Book*, Roger Parton says, "Until recently, 187-hectare [462-acre] Douglas Island—near the junction of the Fraser and Pitt Rivers—was the property of Canadian Forest Products. Purchased by the government for $4.5 million, it is an important foreshore marsh and river habitat. Its green space is clearly visible just upstream from the Port Mann Bridge, with a necklace of log booms fringing its shores. Its rich habitat and inaccessibility made it an ideal site for Ducks Unlimited to enhance an area where wildlife could thrive in relative safety . . ."

Douglas was one of the totally unzoned chunks of land in the GVRD. That meant anyone could build anything they liked on it, and that alarmed PoCo. (One plan involved building a bridge to the island and putting high-rises on it.) The province bought the island from Canadian Forest Products, and the city applied to have it brought within PoCo's borders. Other adjacent municipalities were asked if they were interested in acquiring the island and had said no. It was rezoned in 2-hectare (5-acre) lots to make development unwieldy. The island will remain undeveloped and will eventually become a park, developed and maintained by the city and the Greater Vancouver Regional District.

Out in Space . . . and Just Around the Corner

One of the most interesting companies in Port Coquitlam is International Submarine Engineering, at 1734 Broadway. ISE builds products for use in space, under the ocean . . . and at your neighbourhood gas station.

ISE started in Port Moody in 1974 as McIlhenny Offshore Surveying and Engineering, but by 1976 the name was changed by James McFarlane, the company's founder and still its president. ISE was established to design and build robotic submersibles. McFarlane had been in the Canadian Navy for eighteen years, engaged in building manned submersibles. After leaving the navy he had a notion to build a "revolutionary" tethered vehicle . . . but when he started he discovered that eight or nine companies were already doing it. So he began to concentrate on remotely operated vehicles.

Essential subsystems for these products are robotic manipulators, computer control software, and sensors, and these subsystems became the basis of ISE's products. ISE control products—some for use under water, some on land and some in space—are the common thread throughout the ISE product line. The company's customers include Shell Oil, Westinghouse, AT&T, Rockwell, Shin Nippon Kaiji , the US Navy, the Canadian Navy, the Canadian Space Agency (astronaut Marc Garneau has visited the plant), and NASA's Johnson Space Center in Houston, Texas. ISE's markets are in Japan, China, Singapore, the Gulf of Mexico, Brazil, France, Scotland, the USA and Canada.

McFarlane started with two people, then there were three, then four. Now he employs 110, and annual revenue is about $10 million. The range of products developed and made at ISE's 3,344-square-metre (36,000 square foot) plant is extensive, but one item that caught the writer's eye was the *Theseus*. It's about 9 metres (30 feet) long and looks like a fat yellow pencil fitted with small rudders. The *Theseus* is remotely controlled (though it has some self-guiding skills of its own, like the ability to avoid obstacles) and was developed to lay long lengths of fibre-optic cable under the Arctic ice pack. It successfully laid a fibre optic cable 175 kilometres (109 miles) long at depths of 500 metres (1,641 feet) under an ice pack that ranged from 2 to 5 metres (6 to 17 feet) thick.

ISE gets into the International Space Station, too. It has been devel-

Sea trials for the Theseus Autonomous Underwater Vehicle.
Photo courtesy ISE)

oping robots and software control systems for the Canadian Space Agency for the last ten years. These robots will be used for task verification and for training astronauts who will work on the space station.

ISE is in space, but it's also down to earth. In December 1999 the company announced a partnership with American Controls Inc. (ACI) to develop autonomous fuelling robots for automobile assembly lines. These robots will be developed for all major automobile manufacturing plants and are designed to work with a variety of moving vehicles on each line. One variation of these fuelling robots, still in development, would be used at your local gas station. When this system is in place, you will pre-register your vehicle and then every time you visit a gas station, you will drive up to the pump, where the system—using transponder tag technology and computer vision—will detect your car. A special "customer interface" will approach your car window so you can swipe your credit card and select the grade of fuel. A special arm will move over to your vehicle, open your fuel door, extend a fuel nozzle through your specially designed gas cap and fill your vehicle with fuel in under two minutes. When the system is finished fuelling, it will retract the nozzle, close the fuel door and send you on your way. You won't even have to get out of the car. It's called the Shell SmartPump™ and has already been tested in the US with hundreds of vehicles.

Company president James McFarlane may not use this futuristic

"The GVRD is monitoring the birdlife and wildlife on the island," says Janet Lee of PoCo's planning department, "and Ducks Unlimited is active there; they're creating nesting areas and maintaining drainage. The GVRD may put in a loop trail and a canoe beaching area and establish some educational programs." With the addition of the island, the area of Port Coquitlam is 28.76 square kilometres, or 11.1 square miles.

In March 1991, *Tri-City News* reporter Kate Poole wrote, "George Laking, Port Coquitlam council cowboy, hung up his spurs." On March 23 more than 170 people gathered to subject Laking to an affectionate roast. "His haircut, his campaign habits and his willingness to accept credit were favorite targets . . . 'Ever have one of those George Laking signs on your lawn?' asked Phil Ranger, fellow alderman from 1970 to 1980. 'He put them up in August and took them down in January.'" His penny-pinching ways did not go undetected. Said Alderman Mike Gates, "I think I'm the only politician elected on a smaller budget than George. He used the same picture for 23 years." His famous brush cut came

TLC in the OCP

People who live in cities should have a say about the direction in which the city goes and grows. That's obvious these days, but there was a time when it wasn't. Today residents exercise that say partly by electing people they believe will do the things they want done, and partly through what's called an Official Community Plan (OCP). Virtually every sizeable town in BC has an OCP, which provides the city with a guide for developing its land. If the policies of the OCP are followed, the city develops in the way the majority of citizens want. (Not everyone is going to be happy with all the results, but no plan ever devised satisfies everyone.)

PoCo's Official Community Plan is outlined in a plump binder of more than 170 pages.

In formal terms, the province's Municipal Act defines an OCP as "a general statement of the broad objectives and policies of the local government respecting the form and character of existing and proposed land use and servicing requirements in the area covered by the Plan." But there's more: the OCP also provides for the integration of environment, land use, transportation, community facilities and services into a broad strategy to direct the city's growth and development. So when major development is planned,

the council—advised by senior staff—ensures it follows the guidelines laid out in that binder.

The style couldn't be described as sparkling, but it is solid and gives real insight into the myriad factors that come into play with development. A sample, from the section on General Development Policies: "That rezoning of lots on a block for development be permitted only when remaining contiguous lots on that block, if consolidated, produce parcels of sufficient size to permit further development in accordance with OCP land use guidelines."

There are hundreds and hundreds of policies listed in the OCP, covering Residential Areas Policies ("That appropriate design criteria be followed so that new multiple-family developments are related to existing surrounding buildings"), Commercial Areas Policies ("That the City support development of the Pitt River Bridge Area with maritime sales and service, tourist commercial and marine related uses"), Agricultural Areas Policies, Parks and Recreation Policies, Community Services Policies, Roads and Transportation Policies and on and on.

Not much goes on in PoCo that isn't affected by the OCP, which the residents of Port Coquitlam, with their votes and their voices, helped to write.

PoCo's Coat of Arms

In June 1993, Port Coquitlam received an official coat of arms, presented by the Canadian Heraldic Authority. It is described here by Robert Watt, chief herald of Canada.

When completed, the arms of the City of Port Coquitlam took the place of the previous emblem, which dated back to the time of incorporation, March 7, 1913. The motto, BY COMMERCE AND INDUSTRY WE PROSPER, was an obvious choice for an expansionist and visionary community just before World War I.

The shield blends the themes of native and natural heritage and the railway. The central band or herladic fess used a special edge implying a conifer twig that was originally developed by a Finnish heraldic artist. Overall, the fess can be seen as a pathway, with the edge representing the city's green spaces and the continuing wealth and amenities flowing from local forests. The railway was highlighted through the use of the twin bands of gold, colour of commerce, and the red steam locomotive wheel. The name of the river from which the city takes its name, Coquitlam, meaning little red fish, is celebrated in the upper part of the shield.

The crest is set on a wreath of two of the city's official heraldic colours, white and green. It is composed of a mural coronet, emblem for municipal government, set with six anchors, three visible, which represent ships and maritime commerce and refer to the "Port" in the city's name.

The compartment on which the supporters stand is the grass of the city lands. The beaver supporters, coloured in the gold of commerce to echo the motto, are taken directly from the old emblem on city hall. They have patriotic and thematic meaning as Canada's national animal and are a symbol of industry as well as an important part of the city's own heritage of symbols.

The collar on the left-hand supporter alludes to the royal crown in the old emblem. The city's floral emblem, the azalea, is featured as the other collar. A Salish spindle whorl hangs from each collar, carved with a representation of a silver salmon honoring the Sto:lo people.

The city's original motto is presented on a scroll above. The Coat of Arms Committee proposed the new motto to set out a goal for the city's people.

---

under fire: "There's a rumor going around PoCo that George's hair stylist doesn't live in town," Ranger said. "But he's listed in the Yellow Pages under hedge trimming."

In the end, the affectionate impulse behind the roast surfaced. "He was the wind under my sails," Mayor Traboulay said. "When you're the mayor of a city, you want a George Laking." And Alderman Mike Thompson summed it up: "You've worked your tail off for Port Coquitlam," he told Laking. "Good times, bad times, we're a helluva lot better off for you being here."

Laking's response was uncharacteristically brief: "They accepted me for what I am. I've had a pretty nice time. I've enjoyed all the b.s. that went on."

His "retirement" has included these duties: chairman of the advisory committee on community policing, chairman of the citizens' committee on the remand centre, chairman of the Canada Day committee, secretary of Elks Lodge #49, secretary-treasurer of Elks Canada, involvement in the Purple Cross Fund (which assists kids with medical problems) . . . and, oh yes, he plays golf five mornings a week with his cronies when the weather's right. In his spare time he reads. The Laking Room at Wilson Centre is a tribute to this human dynamo.

When Ron Freeman, PoCo's city clerk for twenty-four years, retired the year after Laking did, he was succeeded by Susan Rauh. She had worked "just about everywhere" for PoCo, beginning in 1975 as a concession stand operator! She was a cashier, a building inspector and eventually was appointed a secretarial assistant to Ron Freeman. Ron recognized her talents, groomed her for advancement, and Susan took a lot of night school courses. In 1999 the city clerk's duties were expanded, and Susan Rauh's title is now Director of Corporate Services.

The West Coast Express pulls into Port Coquitlam Station.

The decade of the 1990s was a busy time for the clerk and the city. A major facility study of the increasingly overcrowded Terry Fox Senior Secondary School was completed in July 1992. The original idea was to see what would be required for a renovation of the thirty-three-year-old building, but the report's conclusions were that there were too many structural, mechanical and electrical deficiencies to warrant a renovation. Instead, it recommended that a new facility be constructed.

The overcrowding of Terry Fox School was an indication of the city's vibrant—even if slow-arriving—growth. To get a grip on that growth, Port Coquitlam prepared an Official Community Plan in 1993. There's more detail on this blueprint for the city's future in the sidebar.

The city's future is bright, partly because it is in an enviable situation with regard to land holdings. According to Ron Freeman, "Except for land purchased in the last fifteen or twenty years, almost all the land owned by the city down through the years has been land that reverted to the city at tax sales in the Depression days of the late 1920s and early 1930s." Jim Maitland, the city treasurer since 1976, says that since the mid-1980s PoCo has financed projects through the sale of that land and still has a fair amount of it left. "There's a full block on Shaughnessy, half a block on McAllister, a big chunk near the base of Mary Hill Road."

Greg Beaumont, manager of bylaw and legislative services in the clerk's department, says the city does not tend to go out and actively sell the land it owns. Rather, it waits for someone

HISTORICAL FOOTNOTE

In 1998 Port Coquitlam was awarded the Distinguished Budget Presentation Award by the Government Finance Officers Association. The city was cited for its use of the "highest principles of government budgeting." That's the work of Jim Maitland and his staff.

He Goes Beyond

Michael Savvis is well-known in PoCo for his restaurant, Michael's on Wilson, and for his many community involvements—including the sponsorship of the city's annual Greek Days—but his path to the Port Coquitlam of 2000 has occasionally been rocky.

Michael, one of ten children, was born on the Greek island of Rhodes. At thirteen he started working six days a week at a hotel restaurant in Rodos City. "All of us were workaholics," he says. He wanted to be an electrical engineer, took night courses, got his diploma and in October 1972 followed his brother Dimitrios, older by a year and a half, to St. Catharines, Ontario.

His diploma had no force in Canada, and the electrical system was different. To get certification, Michael would have to take four more years of study.

"Well, some friends of my father owned two restaurants in St. Catharines, so I took a job as a bar porter at one of them. I worked there for a year while I was taking English lessons at Niagara College." His schedule was somewhat full: he spent from 8 a.m. to 3 p.m. in school, from 6 p.m. to midnight as the hotel bar porter, and from 2 a.m. to 6 a.m. cleaning the restaurant. He slept in short stretches in between these tasks. "I was making $1.65 an hour. After a year, I had saved $500."

By 1973 he was in Vancouver. "I found a one-room place and shared it with Dimitrios, who had followed me to BC. He got a job as a bartender in a pub in Deep Cove, and I got a weekend job there as a busboy. I would take a bus to the North Shore, then I would hitchhike to Deep Cove and back. Finally, in December I got a full-time job at the Blue Horizon Hotel. I was there nine years, I started as a busboy and I made my way up to be the maitre d' at the Top of the Horizon. Then a bunch of doctors bought the Blue Horizon and I became their food and beverage manager. They ran eight hotels throughout BC and Alberta, and I went to all the grand openings and re-openings for them and set up their food and beverage systems. I was also taking business courses in supervisory management at Douglas College in New Westminster.

"In July 1981 I heard from Dimitrios about a restaurant in Port Coquitlam. It was one floor, well-built, but not up to date. I didn't know Port Coquitlam existed, I thought it was all Coquitlam! The restaurant had been built in 1979 and had had three owners in three years. I had made a couple of fortunate real estate deals, so Dimitrios and I bought the restaurant. There were four mortgages. I more than doubled the business in the first year. We didn't make a lot of money the first few years—1981 to 1983 was very rough, but in 1984 I bought Dimitrios out and took over the mortgages. From 1984 the business took off. I bought more real estate. In 1991 I did a lot of renovations: new skylights, a new roof, I brought in new

to approach it, especially when land prices are low. "But when the market gets hot," says Beaumont, "we may issue a Request for Proposals." He shows a map of the South Shaughnessy area where, in the early 1990s, the city sold a package of land that now holds twenty-six detached family homes.

There's building activity in the non-residential sector, too, and Janet Lee of PoCo's planning department (she's involved in long-range planning) keeps a watchful eye on its quality. She says the city encourages heritage themes in new construction and points to the courthouse, with its suggestion of medieval forms, as an example. The use of brick and wrought-iron railings, heavy cornices and careful "massing" of the development is encouraged for a sense of stability. "Developers tell us what they'd like to build, then we suggest areas and style. They go away and hire architects, then come back with preliminary plans, we make comments and suggestions. They *can* come back two or three times. It does vary." Some recent china for the tables, changed the cuisine to continental. I spent $100,000.

"On Sunday, October 14, 1994, I got a call at my home in Burnaby from one of the staff at the restaurant. He said there was a fire there. It didn't sound too major at the time, but I got in my car and drove over. From a long way away I could see the smoke, and I thought 'I hope that is not the restaurant.' But when I got very near I saw that it was. More than 75 percent of the building had been destroyed, and rules were with that extent of damage the building had to be demolished. It was a very, very bad time for me. And thirty people out of work. Randy Shaw, the fire chief, helped me a lot.

"We were closed for two years. It took that long just to settle everything. So I started again. I changed the name to Michael's. The Royal Bank gave me $2 million. I rebuilt the restaurant; it cost $2.6 million. I added a second floor, but in retrospect I shouldn't have. The last five years have been very hard for me and for my family.

"But no other restaurant in the Lower Mainland has more regular clientele. I go beyond ..." He leaves the thought unfinished.

Michael Savvis goes beyond in everything he does. He is involved in myriad activities in PoCo, with the Chamber of Commerce, the Elks, the Seniors Brunch he instituted, fundraising activities for Eagle Ridge Hospital, and with Greek Days.

"How did Greek Days start? I was asked by the city to do some-

A proud Michael Savvis (second from right, front row) beams as PoCo mayor Len Traboulay cuts the ribbon for the official re-opening of Michael's on Wilson. (Photo courtesy M. Savvis)

thing special for the city's seventy-fifth anniversary in 1988. Mayor Traboulay wanted to do something multicultural. I hosted it for five years. In 1993 we had three thousand people! It was the biggest community event in PoCo! Then, after the fire, I couldn't afford it any more. I brought it back in 1996 to link it with the re-opening of the restaurant, and now the city helps."

He smiles. "Of course, it's not just a Greek Day ... it's a downtown multicultural celebration."

developments that reflect more thoughtful planning: Parklane, Liberty Homes on Citadel Heights, the townhouse development called Harbour Homes and Riverwood. Janet Lee also recommends looking at the north side of the 2200 block of Welcher as a good example. (Incidentally, before she came to Port Coquitlam in 1991, Lee had worked for West Vancouver. She says that, as a planner, she finds the range of issues in PoCo broader and more interesting. "West Vancouver was essentially a bedroom community.")

A man who had overseen much of PoCo's development following its rather fallow years died on October 18, 1993. Jack Campbell was a popular mayor from 1967 to 1971 and again from 1976 to 1979. "He was a very fine man," said his friend and colleague George Laking, "and I think he did a great job for the city. He came in a time when the city was pretty much at a standstill. He brought the city forward ..."

Just nine days after Jack Campbell's departure, eighty-nine-year-old PoCo pioneer Archie

Putting the Wet Stuff on the Hot Stuff

It's appropriate that Randy Shaw, chief of the Port Coquitlam Fire Department, is a firefighter: he's built like a fireplug. A lifetime of playing soccer, football and rugby, and training in martial arts and bodybuilding—not to mention wrestling firehoses and other equipment for twenty-five years—have shaped him solidly. He was born in The Pas, Manitoba, came to BC with his family while he was still an infant, and grew up in Coquitlam, going to Parkland Elementary, Windsor Junior High and Centennial High School. His father was a police officer in Manitoba and became a guard at the BC Penitentiary. Randy was himself briefly a guard at the Pen. Once he joined the Port Coquitlam Fire Department in 1974 (he applied for a job, unaware the department had put an ad in the paper looking for men), he advanced rapidly and was confirmed a lieutenant in 1990, captain in 1991, deputy chief in 1994 and chief two years later.

The fire department has changed almost beyond recognition since Randy joined. Where there were sixteen firefighters in 1974 under Chief Bill Wingrove, there are now sixty-one under Chief Shaw . . . and women are joining. There was one fire hall on McAllister; now there are two (one in each "half" of the city). The department's equipment has advanced in number, in size (and expense!) and in the range of tasks it's required to do. Computers play an important role now. Most importantly, the duties of the firefighters have broadened dramatically. "You need a broader skill base," says Shaw. "It used to be that the main job was 'see the fire, put it

PoCo's firemen gather at the grill for a community cookout.

out.' Now the firefighter has to respond to fire alarms, confined space rescue calls, know how to administer CPR and first aid, perform rope rescue, handle hazardous materials, attend motor vehicle accidents and more. You have to have post-secondary education these days, and training at the Justice Institute."

Skill-maintenance training goes on all the time. One of the more colourful training aids at the main station is a miniature table-top town, complete with railway tracks. The firefighters use it to advance their knowledge of firefighting tactics and communication skills.

Johnson died. He had moved to Port Coquitlam sometime around the 1913 incorporation (he was about nine years old at the time) and recalled attending elementary school in a tent. His first job was delivering the *Coquitlam Star,* and when he grew older he went to work at Essondale. Archie was a faithful member of Trinity United Church, attending services daily. "He'd sit in the balcony," his friend Marj Kingsbury said, "and he kept a record book of how many people were attending church." After he retired he became an avid beekeeper, winning several trophies for his honey. But, says his October 27, 1993, obituary, "in the latter years of his life he switched his allegiance to bowling." Brian Madaski, owner of the Port Coquitlam Bowladrome, says Archie bowled there for twenty years without missing a date. "Archie Johnson was a pleasant fellow," said his obituary notice in the *Tri-City News*, "and beloved of his community."

The department handled 1,703 calls in 1998, of which 268 were for fire, 1,029 for medical and 406 "other." When someone in PoCo calls 911 to report a fire (or any other emergency in which the fire department will play a role) the call is received at the Surrey Dispatch Centre—which happens to be in the Surrey Fire Hall. The dispatcher determines the nature of the emergency and its location and, if it is in PoCo, switches the call to Port Coquitlam. The person taking it punches the address into the computer, which has information on every structure in the city: within seconds the department knows if there are sprinklers in the building, whether chemicals are kept there, in some cases even what the building's layout is. That information is relayed to the firefighters, already en route to the blaze.

Neighbouring municipalities work together through mutual-aid agreements. If there's a fire in Coquitlam that Coquitlam would like Port Coquitlam to respond to, Port Coquitlam's department will take the call, and vice versa. Just before Christmas 1998 there was a house fire on Cedar Road in the bigger city, and PoCo's firefighters were dispatched under the GVRD Mutual Aid program. "We'll help Maple Ridge or Pitt Meadows," says Shaw, "and if the incident requires it, we'll ask Burnaby or Vancouver for assistance."

One unexciting, but essential, duty for the chief is preparing the budget. That's changed a bit since 1974, too. One particular piece of equipment, for example, a truck called a "Quint," bristling with special gear besides the usual firefighting equipment, costs about $600,000.

An extra expense, perhaps unique in Canada for a city this size, is the second fire hall—necessary because of the CPR's holding and sorting yard dividing the town. One clever budget move was made by having Fire Hall #1 put side by side with the municipal works yard: they share a parking lot, gas pumps and vehicle maintenance facility. The department's annual budget is about $5 million, most of it in salaries. "You don't get everything you want," says Shaw, "but you get everything you need. The mayor and council are more than fair."

Randy Shaw, chief of Port Coquitlam's fire department, poses with one of the modern fire trucks.

A final question, Chief: when you were a kid, what did you want to be when you grew up? He grins. "Like most boys, when I was fairly young I wanted to be a fireman. And here I am."

There was welcome news in March 1995: under the Canada/BC Infrastructure Works Program, PoCo got approval for the construction of a new bridge to replace the Bailey bridge that had served since 1982 as a replacement for the original Red Bridge.

Transportation to and from PoCo (and a lot of other places!) got another boost in the fall of 1995 with the inauguration of the West Coast Express Commuter Rail line. The idea for a commuter train service had been simmering for a long time: as early as 1972 planners considered using existing rail corridors to carry commuter trains. It wasn't until 1992, when a citizens advisory committee reviewed transportation improvements for the northeast sector of Greater Vancouver, that ideas began to turn into proposals. In 1993 the committee recommended the development of a commuter rail service between Mission and downtown Vancouver to run along existing CPR or Burlington Northern tracks. The CPR route was

The community gardens are a bright and welcoming spot in the city, a great place for locals who don't have space for plants at home.

Port Coquitlam MLA Mike Farnworth and his dog pose by the Fraser River.

eventually selected and on November 1, 1995, West Coast Express was launched. The Port Coquitlam Station is at the eastern foot of Wilson Avenue. It has 254 parking stalls, six bus bays, twenty-eight passenger drop-off stalls, five bike lockers . . . and a cappuccino kiosk.

Hyde Creek Recreation Centre re-opened at 1379 Laurier Avenue in the summer of 1995, and the north side finally got its own modern and well-equipped facility, complete with a 25-metre indoor pool and water slide, swim and fitness shop, therapeutic massage room, gymnasium, weight room, fitness programs and judo-martial arts activities room. Public transit came to the centre in September 1998, a year in which registration in children's activities tripled. The Centre includes a youth drop-in with a pool table and other attractions.

Fire Hall #1 went into service from its spanking new headquarters on June 26, 1995, though the official opening was October 27. This replaced the old fire hall that had stood for years in the 2300 block of McAllister and which, by the way, had been built by the volunteer firefighters themselves.

Reeve Park opened in 1995, too. An oddity in the park's history: it turns out that the city's old surveys were based on the location of the Coquitlam River. In the mid-1980s city clerk Ron Freeman started sniffing around and discovered that "our maps, property ownership records, and even the city's boundary did not correspond with the true situation . . . since the river's location had changed over the years . . . As a bonus, the work we did resulted in a great deal of land being included within the city boundaries under city ownership. This land is now part of Reeve Park."

The new Port Coquitlam courthouse opened in February 1996 to serve the growing Port Coquitlam, Coquitlam, Port Moody and Maple Ridge area. The courthouse, modelled after ecclesiastical courts of medieval Europe, is architecturally striking. There are twelve court-rooms in the complex. The arrangement under which Port Coquitlam was awarded the courthouse included accepting a remand centre, where people awaiting trial are held. In 2000 the centre was under construction some distance away from the courthouse, in the light industrial area along Kingsway. George Laking, chair of the committee overseeing the centre, said, "I actually wanted it next to the courthouse with a connecting tunnel, the way they have it in Surrey. You save money, it's more secure, you save travel time. But a lot of people got upset with the idea of a remand centre in town. So we had a committee to choose a site, and I was on that one, too, and we picked the Kingsway location." The Regional Justice Centre, its formal name, will accommodate 250 adult male prisoners and could be expanded to a maximum of 300 beds. The average length of stay for remandees will be seventeen days. The $49 million remand centre will contribute to the PoCo economy: it's expected to have a staff of two hundred and an annual operating budget of $15 million. The value of goods and services purchased locally will be $2 million annually, so it will prove a genuine economic benefit to a small, but growing city.

The 1996 mid-census showed PoCo with a population of 46,682. That was an increase of 9,909 in five years. The city's population had more than doubled between 1976 and 1996—representing a robust growth rate of approximately 3.5 percent per year. In the ten years between 1986 and 1996, PoCo's housing stock grew from 9,340 to 15,890 units—an increase of more than 5 percent per year, outpacing population growth. Two-thirds of that increase occurred south of the highway.

The '96 tabulation also provided an ethnic breakdown of the city's population.

MOTHER TONGUE 1996 population

English	36,870	Tagalog (Filipino)	330
Chinese	3,065	Hindi	205
Punjabi	645	Korean	185
German	620	Dutch	180
French	550	Farsi (Iranian)	165
Polish	375	Japanese	120
Italian	355	Vietnamese	40
Spanish	340		

HISTORICAL FOOTNOTE

In 1992 PoCo became the first city in western Canada to use new Global Positioning System technology to draw up base survey maps. Satellites whirled and beeped 19,300 kilometres (12,000 miles) above the earth, beaming down co-ordinates to special equipment set up here and there throughout PoCo, with the result that the city's maps were accurate to a degree never before reached. City engineer Igor Zahynacz says they aim for an accuracy of *two centimetres* (less than an inch)! Using a Laser Range Finder, a city employee beams co-ordinates up to the satellite and is able to pinpoint the location of missing traffic signs, measure dike elevations and so on. Trains of the West Coast Express also use GPS technology.

Port Coquitlam finally got a new Red Bridge in late 1996, replacing the replacement bridge that had spanned the river for fourteen years.

Riverside Senior Secondary School opened in 1997, though three years later it needed an upgrade to prevent leaks.

Greater Vancouver crime statistics for that year show that Port Coquitlam was eighth on the per capita list with 121 crimes committed or attempted per thousand people. (New Westminster was first on the list with 226, while Vancouver, with 197, was third.)

And there was even a breakdown of where PoCo residents worked. Of the 24,165 PoCo people in the labour force, 16.6 percent commuted to Vancouver to work, 13.6 percent commuted to Burnaby, an equal number to Coquitlam, and 13.8 percent worked in PoCo itself. Nearly 32 percent worked elsewhere, and about 10 percent had no fixed workplace.

There's one fixed workplace in PoCo where the work is rewarding fun: Port Coquitlam's Community Garden in Elks Park, adjacent to the 2300 block of Mary Hill Road. This was a joint venture initiated in 1996 by the PoCo Community Garden Society and supported by the city. Community gardens originated in England during World War II, when produce was hard to come by. The idea gained new life in the 1960s in several American cities, where community gardens provided space for people who didn't have ground to cultivate where they lived. The garden at Elks Park provides forty-two garden plots for residents who live in local multi-unit dwellings. And it's a fine place for socializing, too.

There was activity on the school front in 1996. The new Archbishop Carney School for Catholic students from Grades 8 to 12 opened at 1335 Dominion Avenue in the Riverwood area. (Catholic kids from kindergarten to Grade 7 attend Our Lady of the Assumption School on Fraser Street.) Terry Fox Senior Secondary was reorganized that year to a Grades 9 to 12 school. A reaffirmation ceremony took place in September with the Fox family to celebrate this reorganization and to change the name to Terry Fox Secondary.

A few months later, in November 1996, the new Red Bridge was completed. The 80-metre-long (260-foot) bridge improved the flow of traffic between PoCo and the Lougheed. The $6.4 million project—complete with landscaping, parking areas and bicycle paths connecting to the PoCo Trail—included the construction of a 300-metre (980-foot) three-lane approach road from the Lougheed connecting to the west end of the bridge, as well as the construction of an 800-metre (2,625-foot) four-lane approach road from the east end of the bridge to Reeve Street. Environmental improvements included the construction of a spawning channel in the Coquitlam River for coho salmon. One of the political dignitaries at the opening was local MLA Mike Farnworth. Recalling the famous hand-painted sign that went up in 1972 when Dave Barrett was elected premier, Farnworth told the attending crowd: "We'z now got us a new bridge." It had been fourteen years since the wreck of the old bridge.

Another milestone was reached in 1996: With the payment of one outstanding bill, Port Coquitlam became the largest city in BC to be debt free. "Every street, every park belongs to us," said Mayor Traboulay. The *Vancouver Sun* noted the achievement on April 24, 1996:

> In spite of fiscal restraint, Port Coquitlam has embarked on a series of major projects over the past six years that have given it a host of new features. They include a major expansion of city hall, a new firehall, works yard, a bridge, improved parks and a popular aquatic centre, as well as environmental protection for several sensitive

Shaughnessy Street was a construction zone (above) during the summer of 1999 as crews worked to upgrade and beautify the area. Below, the "new" Shaughnessy, looking south from the underpass.

May Day 1999 started off with a downpour, but that didn't stop spectators from coming out to view the parade, which included an array of pioneer vehicles.

areas around the city's perimeter. By relying on internal funds, including revenue from taxes and sale of lands, the city proved it could have its cake and eat it, too.

PoCo did a bit of bragging that year, listing the assets it had built or improved without having to resort to borrowing: the Hyde Creek Park expansion, Fire Hall #1, city hall expansion, Reeve Park, the Terry Fox Library and the city's operations centre.

The next year, Riverside Senior Secondary School opened and PoCo's planning department completed an overall plan for the downtown area.

Len Traboulay received a long service award in '97 from the Union of BC Municipalities, which presented him with a caricature by cartoonist Bob Krieger that hangs in the Traboulay home today.

The city also got some unwelcome publicity in 1997 when the RCMP discovered what they described as the "biggest designer-drug lab in the world"—in Port Coquitlam. The $800,000 facility was custom-built by Nicholas Sand, the man who masterminded the project. It contained enough material to produce 45 million LSD hits and designer drugs worth $6 million. Police also found guns and more than $500,000 in cash and gold bullion. Sand, originally from the US, is now serving a long sentence in an American jail.

Port Coquitlam Rotary Club, a late arrival among the city's service clubs, began in the spring of 1998. The first president was Brent Ranger, Phil Ranger's son. The PoCo chapter recently represented Canada in "Life Education," an international program educating schoolchildren about the negative effects of drugs.

There was heavy rain in 1998, and several Lower Mainland municipalities experienced flooding . . . but not Port Coquitlam! Igor Zahynacz's engineering crews had planned well. Their preparations included "fish-friendly" Archi-medes' screw pumps installed at Reeve Creek, among the first installed in BC. (The pumps work by carrying water—and the fish in it—up to a higher level by using a rotating screw set inside a cylinder. We can thank Archimedes, who lived 2,200 years ago, for that idea!)

And 1998 ended a busy three-year period of adding soccer pitches to the city's recreational facilities. A year-end report listed the new facilities: "Since the spring of 1995, the city added a new grass field at Citadel Middle School, two new grass fields at Reeve Park, one new grass and one new all-weather field at Kwayhquitlum School. Within the next two years we will also be adding two new grass fields at the new Terry Fox School site, one new grass and/or artificial field at Reeve Park and a new grass field for Riverwood Elementary. If you add those up, over a

May Day is a celebration for children, who take part in the parade (above) as well as a pet parade later in the day. Below is the Monkey Dog.

The ambassadors of the Business Improvement Association kept people up-to-date on the Shaughnessy Street beautification project. Back row: Larry Watkins (past executive director) and Tyler Morison. Front row: (l to r) Lucie Misar, Sandy Jagday, Alexis White.

HISTORICAL FOOTNOTE

A touching and impor- tant ceremony took place at the Hawthorne Care Centre on April 9, 1999, when Port Coquitlam resident Arthur Castle, then 101, was appointed a Knight of the Order of the Legion of Honour. Mr. Castle, a vet- eran of World War I, had the medal pinned on him by Michael Dejaegher, consul general for France. April 9, 1999 was the eighty-second anniversary of the Battle of Vimy Ridge, which means Mr. Castle was nineteen when he joined other Canadian soldiers in storm- ing Vimy Ridge and clearing it of German troops—some- thing the British and French had been unable to do. There was a strong contin- gent of Mr. Castle's Royal Canadian Legion comrades on hand for the ceremony.

six-year time frame, the City in cooperation with the School District will have added nine new soccer pitches for public use."

In 1999 the city set to work on a major beautification of Shaughnessy Street, transforming this entrance to the city with broad and attractive sidewalks, new plantings and improved lighting. One of the major forces behind the push for the $1.5 million beautification, contract- ed out to Jack Cewe & Company, was Port Coquitlam's Business Improvement Association. The BIA, originally formed by Irene Barr and others (like Councillor Jon Baillie), has been active since 1995 and now represents more than 230 businesses and property owners in the downtown, from the Lougheed south to Wilson Street and east along Mary Hill. "The concern was that PoCo's downtown was dying," the former executive director Larry Watkins explained. "Home Hardware, for example, had closed and no new businesses were coming in. There was a strong need for *physical* change, just to make the downtown look better."

The BIA brings business owners together to enhance their area through various marketing initiatives. They get a lot of volunteer help, and assistance from the Lions, Kiwanis, Kinsmen, the Heritage and Cultural Society, the Terry Fox Foundation and others. John Sousa, of Batty's Shoes, donates half the association's office rent. One of their initiatives, October's Harvest Festival, is now one of the most popular annual events in PoCo. When Shaughnessy was being disrupted because of the beautification work, the BIA sent out young, uniformed "ambassadors" to help people negotiate the temporary walkways to shops and to keep shop- keepers and shoppers up-to-date on the work's progress. The BIA also initiated a Christmas

A Voice for Heritage

The groundwork for the establishment of PoCo's major source of historical information was laid in 1988 when Ada Con, director of the city's Terry Fox Library, talked to librarian Lois Milne about the history of the city and expressed a concern that there was no group to oversee its preservation and promotion. That conversation led to the establishment of the Port Coquitlam Heritage and Cultural Society. Councillor Ron Talbot was a charter member.

Since that time the Society has been very actively promoting understanding and preservation of the city's past. Members conduct Heritage Walks, showing some of the more historically interesting homes and other buildings in the city. They have organized displays centred around Terry Fox and given historical talks at local schools, senior centres and community organizations. The Society plays a major role in PoCo's annual May Day celebrations, including showing photographs of the event from days long past, and it preserves and displays artifacts from the area's First Nations populations.

A retired Port Coquitlam-born military man, Douglas Smith, who now lives in Fredericksburg, Virginia, USA, regularly sends the Society valuable pictures and anecdotes of his time in early PoCo. In 1999 he was honoured with a lifetime membership. (Smith's grandfather, Robert Wilson, is the man after whom Wilson Avenue is named.)

Virtually every member of city council is a member of the Society, and the two have co-operated in producing a city brochure. Before the Society found a permanent home (largely financed by city hall) it was allowed to use the second floor of the northside fire hall as a repository for its holdings. Many photographs and other materials could not be displayed simply because of lack of space.

On October 16, 1999, the Society— after a decade of lobbying by Lois Milne and others—reached a milestone with the opening of its display centre on Mary Hill

PoCo historian Lois Milne at the New View Society House.

Road, just a few steps south of McAllister. Now PoCo finally has a home for its historic materials. This book benefited enormously from the resources and the enthusiastic support of the Society.

Tree lighting in City Hall Park. One of the association's wishes is for increased residential density and more restaurants near the downtown core. Translation: more customers. And they'd like to see some sort of tourism initiative based on PoCo's railway past.

President of the BIA since its beginning is Sheila Retallick. Before moving here from England, Ms. Retallick worked for the City of London's police force where she helped organize security arrangements for visits by the Queen and other heads of state. Two of the people in the BIA office working at putting its initiatives into practice were Larry Watkins and Dean McMillan. Watkins, a former football player who really looks the part (he was on the Grey Cup-winning Edmonton Eskimos, and he's BIG), stepped down from the BIA in late 1999. He has since been succeeded by Pat Dales. The success of the group has prompted moves for a similar organization on the north side of the Lougheed.

The area's chamber of commerce is bullish, with good reason, on PoCo's prospects: "High-

New homes fill Port Coquitlam's new subdivisions, making up for the years of slow growth in the first half of the twentieth century.

Joggers on the PoCo trail.

impact industries that could generate pollution or waste," it says, "are not encouraged to develop . . . Benefits to investors are: comparatively affordable housing; affordable land for industry; excellent access to major transportation routes; good access to the inner city of Vancouver as well as the Fraser Valley and available truck, rail and water transport facilities." Another benefit to developers is that Port Coquitlam likes to expedite development projects that meet city criteria. "The developers are the risk-takers," says Len Traboulay. "We *want* to help them. The moment they commit, then we make a real effort to accommodate."

Keith Beedie, principal partner in the Beedie Group, which developed Meridian Industrial Park, says Port Coquitlam was definitely the best city the company had ever dealt with. The mix of industries wouldn't be allowed under most zoning ordinances, but Beedie says Bill Brown, PoCo's planner at the time, helped facilitate the development. Tour Meridian today and you'll see it's quiet, attractive . . . and successful. There are more than nine hundred people working in the complex, and Meridian's tenants pay the city more than $1 million annually in taxes. "I want to make money," Beedie says, "but I also want to leave something behind that I can be proud of."

In terms of residential development, PoCo is close to exhausting its total land area. As a result, expansion is occurring upwards, with new apartment blocks and townhomes. Incidentally, this is one of the few cities in Canada in which it is mandatory for developers to install fire sprinklers in new single-family homes. When a developer's representative came before council to argue against the by-law, Councillor Jon Baillie, a former PoCo fire chief, spoke eloquently in favour of it. "I've pulled too many dead people out of buildings to worry about a builder saying prices are too high."

Oddly, for a city of fifty thousand, Port Coquitlam has no hospital within its borders today: the city is served by Royal Columbian in New Westminster, and Eagle Ridge in Port Moody.

A PoCo tradition that happily endures is May Day. The 1999 May Day Parade took more than an hour to pass one point. It seemed as if half the town had gathered to watch the other half march by! And in keeping with the community spirit of the event, a genuine Good Samaritan emerged out of the crowd. The day had started with a fairly heavy rain, and that meant the entertainment stage was going to be soaked. On the spur of the moment a gentleman named Tim McGowan brought in a wagon full of lumber and equipment and in fifteen minutes had erected a shelter for the stage. The show must go on!

A young PoCo resident gets into the spirit of Canada Day.

One of the nice traditions of May Day is the one that has city councillors pour coffee and tea for the invited guests at the annual May Queen selection held at Wilson Centre. The 1999 selection, for the seventy-sixth consecutive May Day, was a pleasant experience, with a parade of young boys and girls flooding into the Centre. All the boys sported brightly coloured bow ties, while all the girls had colourful sashes. A row of thirteen tiny flower girls completed the spectacle. The 1998 Queen, Christine van Beekum, and Ambassador, Sean Bird, presided over the festivities until the selection by draw of the new Queen, Stephanie Briggs, eleven, a Grade 5 student at Leigh Elementary, and her Ambassador, Ryan Keefe, also eleven, a student at Citadel. (Ryan's dad told the writer that his son said it would be great to win because then he wouldn't have to walk in the May Day parade—he'd be riding on a float!)

When the time came, the outgoing ambassador announced his name in a forthright and confident manner, and Mayor Traboulay, grinning, said "Make a note of that name, Sean Bird. He'll be mayor in 2021." Keep this book handy to see if he predicted correctly!

Other PoCo residents receiving recognition in 1999 included Tim Frick, coach of the Canadian women's wheelchair basketball team, who was honoured by Sport BC; Carlos

How School Has Changed!

A June 1999 tour through PoCo's new Terry Fox Secondary School, with Principal Dave Matheson leading the way, was a revelation. True, the traditional elements are all here: the classrooms, the labs, the gym, the school library, the cafeteria, the sports fields, the students' lockers in long, echoing corridors . . . but everything is different.

The student common at Fox—you walk into it when you enter the school—can hold many hundreds of students at a time. The common is spacious and airy, with lots of natural light streaming in through ceiling skylights. The kids meet here, talk and socialize, and shop at the Raven's Nest, a small concession stand operated by marketing students from Grades 11 and 12. You can buy T-shirts, mugs, school supplies and packaged snacks. Clinging to the lofty walls of the common are six huge frames, each designed to hold elements pertinent to the school: in the very first one, for example, will go a slab of the battered gym floor from the original Terry Fox School, where Terry and thousands of other students played.

The new gym (soundproofed) is twice the size of the one in the old school (it can hold 1,200 people and be divided into two equal parts), and there's a smaller second gym fitted with six basketball hoops and wrestling mats. There's a weight room.

There's a wind tunnel in the physics lab, and the school's choirs and bands have their own soundproofed rehearsal halls.

There are computers everywhere. Students can read CD-ROMs in the school library when they're not accessing the Internet. They can learn Mandarin and video editing on the computer. There are also programs in automotive repair, textiles and foods. What used to be called Industrial Arts is now Technical Education: again, some of

The new Terry Fox Secondary School in 2000. (Photo courtesy Tri-City News)

the elements are familiar—woodworking, metalworking—but the kids learn computer-assisted design, too.

Kids who aren't in school because of illness or other personal reasons can access their lessons electronically from home. For eager beavers, extra courses are available through distance education in the "on-line room." There's a learning centre for kids with dyslexia and other learning disabilities. The word that pops into a visitor's mind is *flexibility*.

There are a lot of computers here . . . but not as many as they'd like. "Kids," says Matheson, quoting, "have the right to be raised in the medium of their time." These days, that's computers. They'll come: more than twenty years of teaching have given Dave Matheson the smarts to know how to raise the funds needed. (There's a technical equipment fund from the ministry of education, but it's limited.)

The school has its own Local Area Nejtwork (LAN). TV monitors on view throughout the complex keep students up-to-date on

Rabiei and Adam Moghari, two of Canada's top-ranked bodybuilders and owners of the Port Coquitlam Athletic Club on Kingsway, who received certificates of appreciation from the city in recognition of their achievements (at the nationals in 1998 Moghari took top prize, and Rabiei placed second); and John and Manuela Lucas, who were congratulated and given a certificate of appreciation by city council for their twenty years of service at Europe Bakery on Shaughnessy.

school activities, sports meets, changes in schedule and last-minute announcements. The LAN is programmed for video, and one supposes Fox's techies will enjoy putting some pizzazz into the school's more humdrum announcements.

Older readers will remember the food from their schools' cafeterias and may be envious of what's available now: the kids at Fox chow down at mini-versions of the White Spot, Panagopolous Pizza and Subway.

Even student *lockers* have changed: they're half the size they used to be. These days, it seems, most students carry their books and other stuff around with them in their backpacks.

All these elements, preparing Fox's faculty and students for the twenty-first century, come with a hefty price tag: the building and its contents cost more than $26 million. (Even so, the costs were significantly lower than comparably sized Riverside Secondary on the city's south side. Riverside cost $1,400 a square metre to build; Fox was just $1,100.)

The old school was built to hold 750 students and eventually peaked at 1,450. That explained the thirty-two portables. Construction of the new building started in February 1998 and took fourteen months. There are no portables (yet!) at the new building, which was designed to hold 1,400 students but has, in fact, already taken in 1,640. They're overseen by Principal Dave Matheson and three vice-principals, taught by eighty-seven teachers and counselled by a staff of four, with a support staff of about twenty-five others. There is a Career Centre. This is a big complex. "We've moved the biggest house into this neighbourhood," says Matheson, "and we're the biggest family here."

Sensitivity for the neighbourhood prompted Matheson to organize a getting-to-know-you barbecue session during which local residents were invited to look the school over and learn what to expect from their new neighbour. "I suspect some of them didn't know we were coming when they bought their houses," he says. The school has outreach programs: when it isn't using its two big sports fields and its baseball diamond, lacrosse box, four tennis courts, jogging track and three-on-three basketball courts, they're available for use by the neighbours and other PoCo residents. So is the school's 350-seat Terry Fox Theatre. There are even community washrooms adjacent to the soccer field, open to the public during non-school hours.

Big schools can have outsized problems and be a scary place, especially for a young student who may have just come from a much smaller school. Fitting in can be difficult. "Senior secondary schools don't have to feel big and intimidating," Matheson says. "They can be made to feel small and welcoming." That's done at Fox with lots of interaction and a unique program in which Grade 12 students—the student elite—act as mentors to younger newcomers. Fox's vice-principals are trained in, among other things, conflict resolution. And there are groups with common interests: the school's car-racing club, for example (made up of teachers and students), took an old beater, buffed it up and ran it at Mission Raceway.

Terry Fox Secondary comes with a proud history. A long row of display cases in the new school gleam with trophies and awards for basketball, music, math, public speaking, wrestling and other athletic and academic accomplishments. The school's well-known alumni include Terry Fox himself, BCTV anchorwoman Lynn Colliar, Bret Anderson of the BC Lions, and Olympic athletes like Steve Marshall, Dan Payne and Chris Rinke. "But," says Dave Matheson, "we have academic 'Olympians,' too. They're not heard of as much, but they're doing work just as valuable."

One of the city's livelier events in 1999 was an open house at Riverside Secondary, where students were able to show what they were learning—and showed how they applied that learning, too: for example, the Riverside yearbook *Currents* was assembled by the students, right down to the computerized layout. A historically themed" Jeopardy" game was going on, in which students dressed as famous figures of the past told players whether their answers were correct or not; a ceramics class featured clever artwork, including a laugh-out-loud rep-

There are still farms on PoCo's agricultural land, like this blueberry farm on Prairie Road where locals can pick fresh berries.

HISTORICAL FOOTNOTE

The Trans-Canada Trail uses a portion of the PoCo Trail—from the Pitt River Bridge north and then east to the Coquitlam River at Lincoln—as it goes through this area. The Trans-Canada Trail is a 15,000-kilometre (9,320-mile) recreation trail winding its way through every province and territory in Canada, linking thousands of communities along its route. It is the longest trail of its kind in the world.

resentation of a bored, blasé frog; the big well-equipped woodworking area featured students' work, including a gigantic wooden wristwatch; one computer student had rigged up his system so that non-techies could watch the hard drive at work; automotive students showed off beautifully reconditioned '50s cars; and at one arresting display, a little spice bottle full of metal was wobbling in midair, a demonstration of electromagnetic levitation.

In early 2000 Riverside got a bit of unwelcome news: a few million dollars would need to be spent on the still young school to upgrade its walls to prevent major damage from leaking.

In October 1999, because of concern for the security of its foundations, St. Catherine's Anglican Church was demolished. The congregation continues to meet in Trinity United Church while a new church is built. (This is as good a place as any to include this story: in February 1999 the new priest at St. Catherine's, the Rev. Celia Howard, late for a meeting with Mayor Traboulay, parked in a space she shouldn't have. She left a note under the windshield, explaining she was late for a meeting and adding, "Forgive us our trespasses." When she returned to the car, there was a ticket neatly tucked under the wiper, with an accompanying note reading, "Lead us not into temptation.")

Openings were coming thick and fast as 1999 and the twentieth century drew to a close. The Port Coquitlam Heritage and Cultural Society achieved a goal on October 16, 1999, with the opening of its display centre. Under the tireless leadership of Lois Milne, with the enthusiastic work of members like Nancy Ogilvie, Wendy Sankey, Frances Fridge and Morley Deans, and with the generous support of civic officials like Mayor Len Traboulay, city treasurer Jim Maitland, planning's Greg Moore and others, the display centre finally provides a home for the city's historic materials. Less than a month later, on Saturday, November 6, 1999, while the writer was at the display centre, PoCo's Darrell Penner (who was elected to council later that month) came in with a plaque that had come to light during some demolition work. It was a 1964 award to the U-Buy-Rite store, now vanished, run by the Useki family at 1475 Prairie Road, for its "promotion of all cheese products." When the museum is established and has room to display material of this kind, it will be sure to trigger memories for some PoCo old-timers. A word to the wise: never throw *anything* like this away. Your museum may want it.

On October 23, two ceremonies were combined in one when the official inauguration of the city's downtown beautification coincided with the BIA's 1999 Harvest Festival. PoCo's downtown was a riot of colour and sound . . . and people tried not to notice the beautification project was behind schedule. (An irresistible story: When pavers first went in in front of city hall, the initial design resulted in a few women complaining the heels of their high-heeled shoes were being broken off. Said John Sousa, who runs a shoe repair shop at his Batty's Shoes across the street: "Keep 'em coming!")

The Heritage Society's next-door neighbour, the Port Coquitlam Community Police Station, held its own opening ceremony a few days later on November 2. RCMP Constable Stephane Hamel, credited by Superintendent Rick Hall as being the main push behind the station, MCd the event. The audience learned that some thirty-five volunteers would patrol the city on bikes, keeping an eye peeled for illicit and unsafe activities. Now the city has two community police stations. The other, established in 1995, is at 3312 Coast Meridian Road on the north side. The two stations receive reports on minor thefts and vandalism, lost or found property, and so on. There have been as many as 164 RCMP officers assigned to the Coquitlam area, but in 2000 that was down to 152. More officers are said to be in the offing.

Two youngsters gather eggs at Rooney Farm on Devon Road, with help from their dog.

On November 4 the new Terry Fox Secondary School was officially opened before a crowd of several hundred. The master of ceremonies was Grade 12 student Shanshan Mou, a straight-A student— and a top-notch MC. Fifteen-year-old piper Kyle Maloney led in the dignitaries, who included Port Coquitlam MLA and then minister of investment and employment Mike Farnworth, a graduate of the school; the recently appointed minister of education Gordon Wilson; and members of city council. The sixty-member school choir sang and the school band played while two scarlet-coated RCMP officers flanked the stage. Betty Fox spoke briefly and proudly of her son and her family. "His motto was 'Keep at it until you get it right'," she said and noted that it was particularly warming to know that "Terry lives on in the minds and hearts of so many people." In his brief speech, Farnworth recalled that he had been a Grade 8 and 9 classmate of Terry's. Principal Dave Matheson told the big audience that the original school, which had opened in 1959, had been built for 750 students and ended up holding nearly 1,500. (One result: thirty-two portables!) And he said that when all the new school's students and staff and faculty and their families were considered, something like five thousand people had a direct connection to the facility. Matheson also passed along his review of the school's handsome theatre: "In a word: WOW!"

The view from Citadel Park, looking out over Port Coquitlam.

In the midst of the speeches came a charming episode: nine children from local elementary schools and kindergartens stepped forward, gave their names and their grades and the schools they attended, and announced the year they would graduate from Terry Fox. Each wore a sash imprinted with that year. It was what stage people would call a *coup de théâtre*, a warming and memorable touch.

When the new school opened, the use of the dozen or so acres of land occupied by the old Fox school was undetermined. It's owned by School District #43, not the city, and is valued at about $14 million. The city can't afford to buy it, and it's likely a residential development will end up there, with the possibility some of the land may be devoted to a new elementary school. (Another elementary school has been announced for Citadel Heights.)

On Saturday, November 6, 1999, just two days after the new Fox school opened, it was time for yet another grand occasion: the re-opening of the expanded Port Coquitlam Recreation Centre. The facility also received a new name. It was now the Port Coquitlam Wilson Centre–Recreation Complex. While rain pelted down outside, the by now familiar parade of dignitaries trooped in, preceded by piper Neil MacGillivray. Twelve-year-old Laura Moulds rattled the windows with a fine and rousing "O Canada," and the mayor read a long list of tributes to the people who had made the expanded complex possible. The work had started in the spring of 1998, so this had been some time coming. Stephanie Briggs, the 1999 May Day Queen, and Ambassador Ryan Keefe made the first cut in a big cake provided by the Elks Club, and then the crowd began to explore the big, shiny new sports complex, its enlargement designed by Don Taylor Architects Inc.

Yet another "opening" occurred November 12. An upgrade of the PoCo Trail had started in May, and now it was ready. Three of the original 1970 Trail Blazers were on hand: Phil Ranger, Charles Saunders and Glenn MacDonald. MacDonald even brought along the machete he had used to help clear the trail nearly thirty years before. The $872,000 project was designed to provide improved access and more recreational opportunities for local residents. Benches, rest areas, interpretive signage and other amenities were added to the downtown section of the trail, paralleling the Coquitlam River. "Now," said Mayor Traboulay, "there can be rollerblading, cycling, walking a baby stroller, people can walk to work along here, wheelchairs can be used. This is a unique trail: it goes completely around the city. We are still actively utilizing the trail and now it's even better . . ."—though some seniors aren't as enthusiastic about in-line skaters and cyclists using the trail!

An excellent interpretive sign honouring Harold Routley is beside the McAllister Avenue pedestrian bridge across the Coquitlam. The upgrade emphasized environmental protection by formalizing access points and diverting the trail from environmentally sensitive areas. There are now viewing platforms at Lincoln Avenue, Prairie Avenue and at Peace Park to take advantage of mountain views along the Pitt River. Sharp & Diamond Landscape Architecture and Karo Design Resources were singled out for their excellent work, and thanks were given to people who had donated funds for benches: Richard Northard, Mr. and Mrs. Blair and Erin Murphy.

Funding for the project was shared equally by the federal and provincial governments and the city, with the senior governments' portion coming from the Canada/British Columbia Infrastructure Works Program. An upgrade of the rest of the trail began in 2000.

By 2001 or 2002 the Jewish community of the Burnaby/ Coquitlam/Port Coquitlam/New Westminster area hopes to open a new synagogue, planned for the corner of Prairie Road and Flint, where four older residences were purchased. The $2.5 million structure will be a large one (1,115 square metres or 12,000 square feet), intended for long-term growth. Until it opens, local Jewish families will continue to hold services in private homes or travel to Vancouver. The new synagogue will be "egalitarian," its planners say, welcoming Orthodox, Conservative and Reform worshippers. Some sixty-five families make up the current congregation and, a nice ecumenical touch, they occasionally meet in an Anglican Church in Coquitlam.

Also in the works is a mosque for Islamic worshippers.

The November 20, 1999, civic election saw one new councillor and the departure of a long familiar one. Mayor Traboulay handily defeated Sylvia Osberg, his one challenger for the mayor's chair, by 4,514 votes to 826, and vote tallies for councillors shook out this way:

Looking up from the Pitt River to Mary Hill, where Port Coquitlam began.

Scott Young	3,912
Michael Wright	3,028
Darrell Penner	3,022
Michael Gates	3,014
Ron Talbot	2,906
Jon Baillie	2,857

The DeBoville Slough is actually in Coquitlam, but is a popular place for PoCo locals on a warm sunny day.

HISTORICAL FOOTNOTE

There is a World War II hero in PoCo's midst, though the hero, Vic Coulter, didn't realize it until late April 1999. That's when he got a letter from the War Pensions Agency in England about an adjustment in his pension payments, and discovered he'd been collecting a weekly "bonus" in addition to his War Disablement Pension (he'd been badly wounded in an air engagement) and his Age Allowance. The bonus was a small weekly sum that recognized his "gallant conduct" during World War II. He was serving with the Fleet Air Arm in Egypt during the war, and when he wasn't flying missions, represented British Armed Forces in rugby, cricket and soccer against New Zealand, Australia and South Africa. An exciting description of one of his sorties is told in the book Telegraphist Air Gunner. Vic came to Canada in 1956 and embarked on a long and distinguished career as a teacher in the Coquitlam School District. By 1973 he was supervising principal at Mountain View and was there to his retirement in 1979. Vic's public service is long and dedicated: he was president of the Trinity United Men's Group for sixteen years, served as a director for the BC Rugby Union, and in 1961 became the founder of the Pocomo (Port Coquitlam and Port Moody) Royal Flying Club. Today, at age eighty-two, he lives quietly in PoCo with his wife, Mary.

Darrell Penner was the newcomer, making a good impression with his concern for the environment and his involvement with cleanup and care of the Coquitlam River. John Keryluk, a twenty-five-year veteran of council, second in seniority only to Len Traboulay, garnered 2,378 votes, not quite enough to make the cut this time around. At the December 6, 1999, swearing in of the new council, Mayor Traboulay paid special tribute to Keryluk, saying, in part: "John was first elected in 1973 and devoted twenty-five years of public service as a councillor for Port Coquitlam. He made a tremendous contribution and most of the improvements to our city had John's hand on them."

Provincial court judge Pedro de Couto administered the statutory declarations and oaths of office to the mayor and councillors.

Scott Young, youngest of the six councillors, had double reason to be happy: he had topped all the polls, and he and his wife Wendy added a new child to the family. Nicholas was born December 1.

Mayor Traboulay's inaugural address during that December 6 session of council included some words that give a snapshot of Port Coquitlam today.

> There is a lot on our plate. Traffic congestion, the growing population, the road system, land use, transit and other transportation matters, air quality, economic strategies, the Green Zone, water quality, First Nations, solid waste and other issues that are bound to emerge. How do our citizens of Port

Coquitlam feel about these issues? Are they willing to support environmental initiatives? Are they willing to pay? It is critical that we involve the public in these matters. Their input is vital if we are to maintain and enhance our quality of life.

The need to eliminate traditional lines and barriers needs to be examined. Our citizens deserve it, our employees expect it and, as leaders, we must deliver it. I believe we can achieve success by working together productively. We must form partnerships and be willing to respond to community needs. It is my considered opinion that by increasing public participation we will be able to act on the ideas that come from the people of our community.

The two sections of the Pitt River bridge (foreground) and the CPR bridge in the distance, cross the Pitt River into Port Coquitlam.

And what of the future? "I see the city managing its growth," says the mayor, "not having the high-growth periods we've had in the recent past. I want to see more Port Coquitlam people working here in the city, working, playing, shopping in their own city, using the various trails and playing fields and open fields for sport. At the same time, we have ample recreational facilities, we can have a vibrant city, increasing its commercial and industrial base. In the Dominion Triangle we want industry that will be compatible with the adjacent agricultural land. We've got to get people willing to come in and manufacture things, and providing good quality, sustainable jobs. Like the rest of the Lower Mainland we've tended to attract big-box warehousing. We need more than that. We need companies making things, even shirts, textiles, canneries, agri-business, breweries, distilleries . . . we need jobs for PoCo people.

"When we have companies expressing interest to me in setting up here, I send them to Ernie Levesque, head of planning. He's got a lot to offer them: industrial land is cheaper here, and we fast-track appropriate applications. We like to call it 'one-stop shopping.'

"There's a lot of community pride here: PoCo Pride! We have more festivals, more celebrations, people getting together: May Day, Canada Day, Greek Days, all sorts of activities. And there's a tremendous volunteer base here: there are volunteers at the community police stations, in all sorts of sports, volunteers for May Day and Canada Day activities, volunteers at the Heritage Display Centre.

"This is a terrific place to live."

INDEX